Law, Science, Technology
Edited by Ulfrid Neumann / Klaus Günther / Lorenz Schulz

AF271537

ARCHIV FÜR RECHTS- UND SOZIALPHILOSOPHIE

ARCHIVES FOR PHILOSOPHY OF LAW AND SOCIAL PHILOSOPHY

ARCHIVES DE PHILOSOPHIE DU DROIT ET DE PHILOSOPHIE SOCIALE

ARCHIVO DE FILOSOFÍA JURÍDICA Y SOCIAL

Herausgegeben von der Internationalen Vereinigung
für Rechts- und Sozialphilosophie (IVR)
Redaktion: Dr. Annette Brockmöller, LL. M.

Beiheft 136

Law, Science, Technology

Plenary lectures presented at the 25th World Congress
of the International Association for Philosophy of Law
and Social Philosophy, Frankfurt am Main, 2011

Edited by Ulfrid Neumann / Klaus Günther /
Lorenz Schulz

Franz Steiner Verlag

Nomos

Bibliografische Information der Deutschen Nationalbibliothek:
Die Deutsche Nationalbibliothek verzeichnet diese Publikation in der Deutschen
Nationalbibliografie; detaillierte bibliografische Daten sind im Internet über
<http://dnb.d-nb.de> abrufbar.

© Franz Steiner Verlag, Stuttgart 2013
Druck: Druckhaus Nomos, Sinzheim
Gedruckt auf säurefreiem, alterungsbeständigem Papier.
Printed in Germany.
Franz Steiner Verlag: ISBN 978-3-515-10328-2
Nomos Verlag: ISBN 978-3-8487-0190-2

Contents

Vorwort

Das vorliegende Beiheft enthält nahezu vollständig die Texte der Plenarreferate des XXV. Weltkongresses der Internationalen Vereinigung für Rechts- und Sozialphilosophie (IVR), der vom 15. bis 20. August 2011 zum Generalthema „Recht, Wissenschaft und Technik" an der Goethe-Universität in Frankfurt am Main veranstaltet wurde. In einem weiteren Beiheft werden die Beiträge des Special Workshops „Junge Rechtsphilosophie" (Herausgeber: Carsten Bäcker und Sascha Ziemann) erscheinen.

Wir möchten allen Referentinnen und Referenten des Kongresses noch einmal sehr herzlich für ihre Mitwirkung danken. Herrn Dr. Sascha Ziemann (Frankfurt am Main) gebührt Dank für seine engagierte Mitwirkung bei der Herstellung dieses Bandes.

Frankfurt am Main,
Oktober 2012

Ulfrid Neumann
Klaus Günther
Lorenz Schulz

Foreword

This volume contains almost the entire plenary lectures held during the XXV. World Congress of the International Association for Philosophy of Law and Social Philosophy (IVR) which took place from 15-20 August 2011 at the Goethe University in Frankfurt am Main on the general topic: "Law, Science and Technology". A further volume will contain contributions of the Special Workshop "Junge Rechtsphilosophie" (editors: Carsten Bäcker and Sascha Ziemann).

We would once again like to thank all speakers of the congress very sincere for their contribution. A special thank is also due to Dr. Sascha Ziemann (Frankfurt am Main) for his committed participation in publishing this book.

Frankfurt am Main,
October 2012

Ulfrid Neumann
Klaus Günther
Lorenz Schulz

Robert Alexy

The Existence of Human Rights[*]

Human rights are understood, worldwide, to be the basis of society. This broad agreement is found not only in philosophical circles but also in politics and law. Numerous human rights covenants as well as the incorporation of human rights into a great many constitutions can be read as an expression of the triumphant march of human rights in the period after the Second World War. In a word, their existence seems to be beyond question.

Still, there are doubts about whether the belief in the existence of human rights amounts to anything more than a collective error or illusion. Fundamental criticism, directed to the assumption that human rights exist, is found not only in the dark regions of political, ideological, and religious extremism but also in highly respectable philosophical writings. Alasdair MacIntyre's claim that 'there are no such rights, and belief in them is one with belief in witches and in unicorns'[1] is an example. This – along with the fact, often corroborated in the history of ideas, that widespread consensus is by no means a guarantee of truth – is reason enough to raise the question of the existence of human rights, in short, the existence question.

I. The Theoretical and Practical Significance of the Existence Question

The question of whether human rights exist has far-reaching consequences for legal philosophy, for the theory of constitutional rights, and for politics.

In legal philosophy, the answer to the question of what law is, that is, to the question of the concept and the nature of law, essentially depends on whether human rights exist. Hans Kelsen has adduced an argument against the non-positivistic thesis of a necessary connection between law and morality, namely, the argument that 'an absolute moral order excluding the possibility of the validity of another moral order does not exist'.[2] One might call this the 'argument from relativism'.[3] Human rights are the core of justice. Every violation of human rights is unjust, even if not every injustice is a violation of human rights. The core thesis implies that if human rights do not exist, then additional absolute, universal, or necessary criteria of justice do not exist either. Neither the Radbruch formula,[4] which in its shortest form says that extreme injustice is not law,[5] nor the thesis that law necessarily raises a

[*] I should like to thank Stanley L. Paulson for suggestions and advice on matters of English style.

1   Alasdair MacIntyre, *After Virtue*, 2nd ed. (London: Duckworth, 1985), 69.
2   Hans Kelsen, *Pure Theory of Law*, trans. (from the 2nd German edn.) Max Knight (Berkeley and Los Angeles: University of California Press, 1967), 63.
3   Robert Alexy, *The Argument from Injustice. A Reply to Legal Positivism* (first publ. 1992), trans. Bonnie Litschewski Paulson and Stanley L. Paulson (Oxford: Clarendon Press, 2002), 53–5.
4   Gustav Radbruch, 'Statutory Lawlessness and Supra-Statutory Law' (first publ. 1946), trans. Bonnie Litschewski Paulson and Stanley L. Paulson, *Oxford Journal of Legal Studies*, 26 (2006), 1–11, at 7.
5   Robert Alexy, 'The Dual Nature of Law', *Ratio Juris* 23 (2010), 167–82, at 175.

claim to correctness, essentially a claim to justice,[6] would any longer make sense. Non-positivism would have to yield to positivism.

The consequences of the existence question for the theory of constitutional rights concern the basic understanding of constitutional rights as well as the basic understanding of constitutional review. If human rights did not exist, constitutional rights would amount to nothing more than what has been recorded, written down, in the constitution. In that case, everything might have been different, for constitutional rights would have an exclusively positivistic character. Originalism and textualism would be the only promising candidates for a theory of constitutional interpretation. If, however, it should be the case that human rights exist, then the picture changes fundamentally. Constitutional rights could then be understood as an effort to positivize human rights. This, in turn, would imply that the ideal character of human rights remains present in the interpretation of constitutional rights. The domain of general practical argumentation in constitutional interpretation would have to be extended accordingly. Originalism and textualism would be confronted with a rationalism in law that is based on human rights.

Finally, with respect to politics the main consequence of the existence question concerns the problem of cultural relativism. If human rights did not exist, that would count as a strong argument for strong forms of cultural relativism. By the same token, the existence of human rights would count as a good reason against strong forms of cultural relativism. Should human rights exist, a common basis of law would then exist that, as the concept of a basis implies, might well be compatible with a considerable scope accorded to cultural diversity. A common basis along these lines seems to be indispensible for a global legal order of whatever kind. All of this shows that the question of the existence of human rights has real theoretical and practical significance.

II. The Concept of Human Rights

The answer to the question of whether human rights exist depends on what human rights are. To begin with, human rights are rights. With respect to their structure, rights in general can be divided into, first, claim rights, second, liberties, and, third, immunities as well as powers.[7] Here, only human rights as claim rights shall be of interest. Claim rights are three-place relations of which the first element is the beneficiary or *holder* of the right (*a*), the second is the *addressee* of the right (*b*), and the third is the *subject-matter* of the right (*S*).[8] If *a* has against *b* a right to *S*, *b* has a duty to *a* with respect to *S*, and vice versa.[9] This implies that the concept of a right is intrinsically connected with the concept of the 'ought'.

Human rights, as rights, are characterized by five properties. The first is *universality*. The beneficiary or holder of human rights is every human being *qua* human being. Universality on the side of the addressees is more complex. Some human rights as, for instance, the right to life are addressed to all who can be addressees of duties, that is, to all human beings but also against all states and organisations. Other human

---

6   Ibid., 171.
7   See on this Robert Alexy, *A Theory of Constitutional Rights* (first publ. 1985), trans. Julian Rivers (Oxford: Oxford University Press, 2002), 120–159.
8   Ibid., 120–1.
9   Ibid., 131–2.

rights such as the right to participate in the process of political will-formation, especially the right to vote, are addressed only to the state to which the holder enjoys
citizenship or in which he resides.

The second property of human rights is the *fundamental* character of their subject-matter. Human rights do not protect all conceivable sources and conditions of
well-being but only fundamental capacities, interests, and needs. The question of
which capacities, interests, and needs are fundamental determines the content of
human rights. Nevertheless, this question will not be discussed here. The solution to
the problem of the content of human rights presupposes that they exist, and an answer to the question of existence requires nothing more than the assumption that
human beings have at least some fundamental needs, interests, or capacities such as,
for instance, life, including good health, freedom, and self-determination.

The third property, too, concerns the subject-matter of human rights. This
property is their *abstractness*. The right to good health is an example of an abstract
right. It is easy to agree that all have a right to good health, but on the question of
what that means in a concrete case, protracted controversy is possible. The distinction between human rights as abstract rights and their application in concrete cases
will be of overriding significance for the question of their existence.

The fourth and the fifth properties concern neither the holder nor the addressees nor the subject-matter of human rights but rather their validity. Human rights as
such have only moral validity. For that reason the fourth property of human rights is
their *morality*. A right is morally valid if it can be justified against each and everyone
who is willing to take part in a rational discourse. In this sense, moral validity is universal validity. The universality of the structure of human rights as rights of all
against, in principle, all is thus complemented by a universality of validity. A right
that is valid is a right that exists. This implies the basic thesis of the theory of the existence of human rights presented here. It runs as follows:

> The existence of human rights consists in their justifiability, and in nothing
> else.

To be sure, the moral validity of human rights can be accompanied by positive validity consisting in due enactment and social efficacy. Examples are the International
Covenant on Civil and Political Rights from December 19, 1966, the European
Convention on Human Rights and Fundamental Freedoms from November 4, 1950,
the Charter of Fundamental Rights of the European Union from December 7, 2000
and December 12, 2007, and the Basic Law of the Federal Republic of Germany
from May 23, 1949. But such transformations of human rights into positive law
never count as ultimate solutions. They are attempts to give institutional shape, secured by positive law, to what is valid solely owing to its correctness. For that reason, constitutional rights have to be defined as rights that have been recorded in a
constitution with the intention of transforming human rights into positive law – the
intention, in other words, of positivizing human rights.[10]

This leads to the fifth property of human rights, their *priority*. Human rights *qua*
moral rights cannot be invalidated by rules of positive law. On the contrary, human
rights are standards for the assessment of positive law. This is to say that human
rights conventions and catalogues of constitutional rights as well as decisions of hu-

---

10   Robert Alexy, 'Discourse Theory and Fundamental Rights', in *Arguing Fundamental Rights*, ed.
     Agustín José Menéndez and Erik Oddvar Eriksen (Dordrecht: Springer, 2006), 15–29, at 17.

man rights courts and decisions of constitutional courts can violate human rights. With this, the list of the five properties that distinguish human rights from all other rights is complete. Human rights are, first, universal, second, fundamental, third, abstract, and, fourth, moral rights that, fifth, take priority over all other norms.

For the question of the existence of human rights, the third defining element, the morality of human rights, is of special importance. Rights exist if they are valid. Human rights *qua* moral rights are valid if they are justifiable. Thus, the question of the existence of human rights turns out to be the question of their justifiability.

III. The Justification of Human Rights

1. The Principles Structure of Human Rights

Human Rights are abstract rights. They refer *simpliciter*, for example, to freedom and equality, life and property, and free speech and protection of personality. As abstract rights, human rights inevitably collide with other human rights and with collective goods such as protection of the environment and public safety. Human rights, therefore, stand in need of balancing. Balancing is the central dimension of proportionality analysis. Proportionality analysis presupposes that the rights involved have the structure of principles. This, in turn, implies that human rights have the structure of principles.[11]

The principles structure of human rights has far-reaching consequences for their justifiability. A justification of human rights does not require that an answer be given to all human rights questions. It only requires that sufficient reasons be given for what has to be balanced, that is, for human rights *qua* principles. This reduces the burden of justification considerably. If all questions about the assessment of claims respecting human rights had to be resolved in order to justify human rights, a justification of human rights could never be achieved. It could never be achieved for in many cases balancing leads to 'reasonable disagreement'.[12] This is a central theme in the theory of discretion as a part of the theory of proportionality.[13] Here, a single point is of interest. The restriction of the justification to human rights *qua* principles implies, indeed, considerable flexibility with respect to what, in the justification of human rights, is justified. It allows even for a certain degree of cultural discretion.[14] This is not to say, however, that flexibility or variability is unlimited. The most important limitation stems from a fundamental rule of balancing, namely, that the power of rights increases overproportionally with an increasing intensity of interference.[15] In cases that concern the core of human rights, this has the consequence that only one solution is compatible with human rights. For this reason, flexibility is by no means to be equated with arbitrariness. This suffices to qualify human rights *qua* principles as objects of justification.

---

11   On the concept of principle see Alexy, *A Theory of Constitutional Rights* (note 7, above), 47–8.
12   See John Rawls, *Political Liberalism* (New York: Columbia University Press, 1993), 55.
13   Alexy, *A Theory of Constitutional Rights* (note 7, above), 414–25.
14   Julian Rivers, 'Proportionality, Discretion and the Second Law of Balancing', in *Law, Rights and Discourse*, ed. George Pavlakos (Oxford: Hart, 2007), 167–88, at 178–80.
15   Alexy, *A Theory of Constitutional Rights* (note 7, above), 103; Alexy, 'On Balancing and Subsumption', *Ratio Juris* 16 (2003), 433–49, at 446.

2. Scepticism and Non-scepticism

Theories about the justifiability of human rights, as well as theories about the justifiability of moral norms in general, can be classified in many different ways. The most fundamental distinction is that between those theories that generally deny the possibility of any justification of human rights and those theories claiming that some sort of justification is possible. The first approach may be termed 'scepticism', the second 'non-scepticism'. Scepticism has its roots in forms of emotivism, decisionism, subjectivism, relativism, naturalism, and deconstructivism. Non-scepticism may well include one or more of these sceptical elements, but it insists that there be a possibility of giving reasons for human rights, reasons that lay claim to objectivity, correctness, or truth.

3. Justification and Thesis

Often certain properties are adduced as reasons for having human rights. To be a human being, to have the capacity to suffer, to have intelligence, self-consciousness, the capacity to make choices or plans, and autonomy – these are all examples. The logical form of arguments that turn on the possession of such properties is:

All individuals possessing the property Φ have human rights.

Often this simple form is extended by means of intermediate steps. It is possible, for instance, first, to appeal to autonomy as a reason for being a person, and then, second, to appeal to being a person as a reason for having human dignity, and then, third, to appeal to human dignity as a reason for having human rights. Fundamental here is that the first step remains the decisive step. It is the step from a Φ-property to a normative conclusion, which is arrived at either directly or by means of intermediate steps. This step includes a transition from 'is' to 'ought'. Such a transition is not valid without justification. Why, for instance, is being a human being or having the capacity to suffer a reason for having human rights? This question can be raised even in the case of autonomy. Why should the mere fact that other individuals are able both to judge what is morally right and wrong and to act accordingly be a reason for granting them human rights? To be sure, autonomy plays an important role in the justification of human rights, but the simple transition from the concept of autonomy to the concept of human rights, as performed in a Φ-sentence, is nothing more than an assertion or a thesis that stands, just as with any thesis, in need of justification.

4. Eight Justifications

The attempts to justify human rights differ greatly. Eight approaches shall be distinguished here.

The first is the *religious* approach. A religious justification of human rights draws its support from a very strong foundation. He who believes that human beings are created by God in his own image will have a good reason for attributing dignity to human beings. Dignity is a solid basis for human rights. With this background, the thesis that all individuals who are human beings have human rights is well grounded.

The argument has, however, a decisive weakness. It counts as an argument only for those who believe in God and his creation of man in his own image. The same applies to every other kind of religious arguments.

The second approach is the *biological* or, more precisely, the socio-biological approach. According to this model, morality is a form of altruism. Certain forms of altruistic behaviour, such as, in particular, caring for one's own children and helping relatives but also reciprocal altruism generating mutual help, are said to promote the genetic pool of individuals, whereas mutual indifference or even aggression does not have this effect in those contexts.[16] Now it has to be granted that the tendency to maximize one's reproductive success may in some cases lead to respect and help vis-à-vis some persons, but it is a pattern of behaviour – to use Günther Patzig's words – 'often accompanied by indifference and even hostility towards outsiders'.[17] This, however, is incompatible with the universal character of human rights.

The third approach is the *intuitionistic* approach. The intuitionistic model claims that human rights are justified because their existence or validity is evident. Evidence, however, does not count as a reason if it is possible not to share the evidence without thereby rendering oneself vulnerable to any reproach other than that one does not conceive the evidence as evident. If intuitionism is not embedded in arguments, it is nothing more than emotivism. If, however, it is embedded in arguments, it is no longer intuitionism.

According to the fourth approach, the *consensual* approach, human rights are justified if they find universal agreement. If, however, this consensus consists in nothing other than the fact of a mere congruence of beliefs, then consensualism is tantamount to a form of collective intuitionism. To be sure, an universal consensus on human rights, especially if it is achieved as the result of a discourse, ought not to be dismissed. Still, such a consensus does not exist, and if it did, it would always be in danger of dissolution. For these reasons, the argument of consensus, if not connected with the idea of rational argumentation or discourse, cannot provide a satisfactory justification of human rights. If, however, this argument is connected with rational argumentation, it is no longer a purely consensual approach, referring exclusively to the facticity of a congruence of beliefs.

The fifth approach is the *instrumental* one. A justification of human rights is instrumental if it is argued that the acceptance of human rights is indispensable for the maximization of individual or collective utility. This approach appears in elementary forms as well as in highly sophisticated models. An example for an elementary version is the argument: 'If you do not want to be killed, you must respect other's right to life.' If it is possible for individuals or collectives to increase their utility by violating the human rights of others, the elementary argument breaks down. History shows that this possibility cannot be ruled out. Highly sophisticated models have been developed in the theory of rational choice, for instance, by James Buchanan and David Gauthier. These theories, however, must either work with provisos that exclude unacceptable outcomes, as Gauthier does when he says that '[r]ights provide the starting point for, and not the outcome of, agreement',[18] or their proponents

---

16   Richard Dawkins, *The Selfish Gene* (first publ. 1976), (Oxford: Oxford University Press, 2006), 93–108, 166–88.

17   Günther Patzig, 'Can Moral Norms be Rationally Justified?', *Angewandte Chemie. International Edition* 41 (2002), 3353–58, at 3355.

18   David Gauthier, *Morals by Agreement* (Oxford: Clarendon Press, 1986), 222.

must be willing to accept outcomes that, to put it in Buchanan's words, 'may be something similar to the slave contract, in which the "weak" agree to produce goods for the "strong" in exchange for being allowed to retain something over and above bare subsistence, which they may be unable to secure in the anarchistic setting'.[19] Buchanan's model is a purely instrumental model, but the possibility of a slave contract shows that it is not compatible with human rights. Gauthier's model may be compatible, but this is entirely owing to reasons addressing elements that can be justified only within a non-instrumental approach. None of this means that the instrumental approach is of no value with respect to the justification of human rights. In so far as it can provide reasons for respecting human rights,[20] it should be incorporated into a more comprehensive model. The more comprehensive model, however, must be governed by principles that purely instrumental reasoning cannot generate.

The sixth approach is the *cultural* one. It claims that the public conviction that human rights exist represents an achievement in the history of human culture. Gustav Radbruch presents a combination of an cultural argument with a consensual argument when – with an eye to 'principles of law … that are weightier than any legal enactment' – he says: 'To be sure, their details remain open to question, but the work of centuries has in fact established a solid core of them, and they have come to enjoy such far-reaching consensus in the so-called declarations of human and civil rights that only the dogmatic sceptic could still entertain doubts about some of them'.[21] The cultural model, similar to the instrumental model, is useful but not sufficient. Human rights are not the result of the history of all cultures. The mere fact that 'the work of centuries' has established human rights in one or more cultures is not enough to justify their universal validity, which is a part of their concept.

The defects in the six approaches considered thus far are greater than their strengths. For this reason, the justification of human rights proposed here is based not on these first six approaches, but on a seventh and an eighth approach. The seventh approach is explicative, the eighth existential. A justification of human rights is *explicative* if it consists in making explicit what is necessarily implicit in human practice. A justification that makes explicit what is necessarily implicit in human practice follows the lines of Kant`s transcendental philosophy. If the practice is the practice of asserting, asking, and arguing, the justification obtains a discourse-theoretic character. This is the version of the explicative argument that I should like to defend here.

The discursive practice, that is, the practice of asserting, asking, and arguing, or, as Robert Brandom calls it, the practice 'of giving and asking for reasons',[22] presupposes rules of discourse that express the ideas of freedom and equality. This implicit normative content can be made explicit by means of statements that explicitly negate it.[23] Examples of such statements are:

> If my reasons do not convince you, you are dismissed

and

---

19   James M. Buchanan, *The Limits of Liberty* (Chicago: University of Chicago Press, 1975), 60.
20   See Robert Alexy, 'Discourse Theory and Human Rights', *Ratio Juris* 9 (1996), 209–35, at 219–20.
21   Gustav Radbruch, 'Five Minutes of Legal Philosophy' (first publ. 1945), trans. Bonnie Litschewski Paulson and Stanley L. Paulson, *Oxford Journal of Legal Studies*, 26 (2006), 13–5, at 14–5.
22   Robert Brandom, *Articulating Reasons* (Cambridge, Mass.: Harvard University Press, 2000), 11.
23   For a more elaborated account, see Alexy, 'Discourse Theory and Human Rights' (note 20, above), 216.

> For me, the reason R, to which I am appealing in support of my assertion,
> is not a good reason; but in light of your low intelligence, you ought to ac-
> cept it as a good reason for this assertion.

The absurdity of these two utterances points to the necessity of the implicit rules
against which they offend. In the first example, this rule is the postulate of discursive
freedom, in the second, the postulate of discursive equality. The ideas of freedom
and equality, however, are the basis of human rights. To recognize another individual as free and equal is to recognize him as autonomous. To recognize him as
autonomous is to recognize him as a person. To recognize him as a person is to attribute dignity to him. Attributing dignity to someone is to recognize his human
rights. With this, one might well think, a justification of human rights has been
achieved.

This impression, however, is mistaken. The explicative argument provides, to be
sure, a necessary part of the justification of human rights, but it is not by itself sufficient. For this reason, the explicative argument has to be supplemented by a further
argument, the eighth. This is the *existential* argument.

The necessity of connecting the explicative argument with the existential one
stems from two defects in the explicative argument. The question of whether human
rights can be justified, that is, the question of their existence, depends then on
whether the existential argument can handle the defects found in the explicative argument.

The first defect concerns the necessity of the rules of discourse *qua* rules of discourse. The necessity of the rules of discourse *qua* rules of discourse is limited in two
respects. In the first respect a relatively small problem arises, but in the second, a
very considerable problem. The first respect concerns the possibility of circumvent-
ing the necessity of the rules of discourse completely, namely, by avoiding any participation in the practice of asserting, asking, and arguing. The price one pays for this
is, however, high. Never to assert anything, never to ask a question, never to offer
any reason, is to forbear from participating in what belongs essentially to the most
general form of life of human beings[24] *qua* 'discursive creatures', as Brandom puts
it.[25] To be sure, none of this completely rules out the option of doing forever without any assertion, any question, or any argument. But it comes close to such an exclusion.[26]

Far more serious than the problems stemming from the possibility of circum-
venting the rules of discourse completely by avoiding any participation in the prac-

---

24 On the concept of the most general form of life, see Alexy, 'Discourse Theory and Human
    Rights'(note 20, above), 217–8; Alexy, 'A Discourse-Theoretical Conception of Practical Reason',
    Ratio Juris 5 (1992), 231–51, at 241–2.

25 Brandom, *Articulating Reasons* (note 22, above), 26.

26 It might be objected that this argument turns on an 'is'/'ought' fallacy. That the most general form
    of life of human beings includes the practice of asserting, asking, and arguing can be considered,
    from the point of view of an observer, a matter of fact. The postulates of freedom and equality are,
    by contrast, norms, and norms cannot be derived from facts. This objection misses, however, the
    point of the explicative argument. The explicative argument is an argument that explores the per-
    spective of a participant in the practice of discourse. The 'is'/'ought' objection would arise only if
    the explicative argument were an argument made from the external perspective of an observer. This,
    however, is not the case. The explicative argument brings to light norms that are valid in a practice
    in which the party offering the explication is already a participant. If one wishes to speak of a transi-
    tion in this case, it is a transition not from an 'is' to an 'ought' but from an implicit 'ought' to an ex-
    plicit 'ought'.

tice of asserting, asking, and arguing is the problem stemming from the possibility of abandoning discourse not completely or generally but only partially. It is possible that one may have discussions solely in one's own community and to lapse into propaganda, force, and terror directed to outsiders. The price paid for is much lower than the price for completely abandoning any form of discourse. This defect of the explicative argument can only be repaired by means of the existential argument.

Thus far, only the defects of the explicative argument that concern the rules of discourse *qua* rules of discourse have been considered. Human rights, however, are essentially rules that concern not only discourse but also real social life, that is, the realm of action. The necessity of treating the other as free and equal in discourse does not imply the necessity of accepting him as free and equal in social life. It is, for instance, possible to engage in discussion with slaves.

This problem as well as the problem of abandoning discourse partially stems from the difference between capabilities on the one hand and interests on the other. The explicative argument can only establish the discursive capabilities. Having discursive capabilities, however, does not imply an interest in making use of them. This might be called the 'interest problem'. The interest problem concerns the dimension of discourse as well as the dimension of action. The interest in making use of discursive capabilities solely in the sphere of discourse might be called a 'weak interest in correctness'. By contrast, the interest in making use of discursive capabilities not only in the sphere of argument but also in the realm of action can be characterized as a 'strong interest in correctness'. The strong interest in correctness is a matter of taking seriously the discursive capabilities in real life. This, again, includes the interest in solving social conflicts by means of discursively generated and discursively controlled rules.[27] One who wishes to solve social conflicts through discursively generated and discursively controlled rules recognizes as free and equal the other individuals, and this is to take seriously their human rights. In this way, the interest in correctness makes it possible to arrive at the object of our justification – to arrive, in other words, at human rights.

It might be objected, however, that this is no justification at all. It has lost its character as a justification, so the objection runs, once the premise concerning interests is introduced. And this objection is not without merit. It must, however, be qualified. As with any interest, the interest in correctness is connected with decisions. These decisions concern the fundamental question of whether we want to see ourselves as discursive, reasonable creatures. This is a decision about who we are. With this decision one 'choose[s] oneself' as Kierkegaard puts it.[28] This decision is an existential decision. Still, to talk here about justification or substantiation seems to be warranted, for this decision is not based on groundless or arbitrary preferences, drawn, so to speak, from nowhere. Rather, the decision has the character of an endorsement of something that has been proven, by means of explication, to be a capability necessarily connected with human beings – or, to put it another way, a necessary possibility. As an endorsement of a necessary possibility, the existential argument is intrinsically connected with the explicative argument. One might call this connection the 'explicative-existential justification'.

---

27   On this issue, see Alexy, 'Discourse Theory and Human Rights' (note 20, above), 223–4.
28   Søren Kierkegaard, *Either/Or,* Part II (first publ. 1843), trans. Howard V. Hong and Edna H. Hong (Princeton: Princeton University Press, 1987), 258.

The explicative argument exhibits the discursive nature of human beings. This discursive nature might be characterized as the ideal dimension of the individual. It is, to use Kierkegaard's words again, 'his ideal self, which he cannot acquire anywhere but within himself'.[29] For this reason, the existential argument concerns not only the endorsement of a necessary possibility of some kind or other. It concerns, over and above this, the endorsement of a possibility or capability that defines, *qua* ideal dimension, the higher dimension of our self, or, to put it in Kant's terms, its 'highest vocation'.[30]

This endorsement of the ideal dimensions that the individual finds within himself connects objective with subjective elements. The objective dimension consists of two elements, first, the necessary discursive capabilities and, second, their ideal character. The subjective dimension consists of the existential decision that transforms these ideal possibilities into reality. This means that human rights can only be justified by a connection of objective and subjective elements. This connection can be characterized as a dialectic of the objective and the subjective.

Against this position, a final objection might be raised. The objection would have us believe that a justification can only be either objective or subjective, and not, so to speak, 'half-objective', and that any contamination with subjective elements eliminates objectivity altogether. The reply to this is that objectivity connected with subjectivity is, to be sure, less than pure objectivity, but it is also more than pure subjectivity. For this reason, one can qualify the explicative-existential argument as a genuine justification of human rights, even though it is not a purely objective justification. Owing to its objective elements this objective-subjective justification provides, however, good reasons for human rights, and this, in turn, suffices to justify them. This justification establishes their validity *qua* moral rights, which is to say that human rights exist.

---

29   Ibid., 259.
30   Immanuel Kant, *Critique of Practical Reason* (first publ. 1788), trans. Mary J. Gregor, in Kant, *Practical Philosophy* (Cambridge: Cambridge University Press 1996), 137–271, at 210. See Robert Alexy, 'Normativity, Metaphysics and Decision', in *New Essays on the Normativity of Law*, ed. Stefano Bertea and George Pavlakos (Oxford: Hart, 2011), 219–28, at 227–8.

Samantha Besson[*]

The Egalitarian Dimension of Human Rights

Abstract: Recently, some authors have tried to link international human rights to equality and equal status in particular, and hence to fill a gap that was left open by human rights theorists and equality specialists alike. Neglect for that connection is attributable both to the lack of interest for international law and politics beyond domestic boundaries that has long plagued theories of egalitarianism, but also to the resilience of foundationalist and especially monist approaches to the justification of human rights. Even though the egalitarian dimension of international human rights has now been uncovered, more work is needed on what that normative ideal means in the human rights context and from the perspective of human rights theory, and in particular on how it may be combined with a universal justification of human rights. My argument in the chapter is three-pronged. A first section of the chapter presents a conception of equal moral status and uncovers its intimate relationship to political equality. There, I delineate the notion of equal moral status from that of dignity and argue that while the latter plays a meaningful role *qua* requirement of respectful treatment, it should not be confused with the former and only plays a limited role in the human rights context. In the second section, I argue that human rights are grounded in interests and that political equality works as threshold in the recognition of the importance of certain interests *qua* human rights. In turn, the egalitarian dimension of human rights explains how human rights are both moral and legal rights, on the one hand, and both domestic and international legal rights, on the other. The third section of the argument is dedicated to exploring the implications of the egalitarian dimension of human rights for some vexed issues in international human rights law, such as the relationship between human rights, non-discrimination rights and the equality principle in international law. The tensions between ideal and non-ideal political theory, on the one hand, and between international and domestic equality, on the other, that often obscure the connections between those different themes are unpacked and made the most of in the course of the argument.

[*] Professor of Public International Law and European Law, University of Fribourg and 2011–12 Fellow of the Wissenschaftskolleg zu Berlin. Special thanks are due to Ulfrid Neumann, Klaus Günther, Lorenz Schulz and Sascha Ziemann, but also to Robert Alexy, Tom Campbell, Rainer Forst, Stefan Gosepath, Stephan Kirste and other participants in the IVR 25th World Congress in Frankfurt am Main on 15 August 2011 at which I was invited to present this chapter as a plenary lecture. Many thanks also to Eva Erman and Sofia Näsström for inviting me to present a draft of this chapter in the workshop *Political Equality in Transnational Democracy* at Stockholm University on 2–3 June 2011, and to them as well as to Jim Bohman and Rainer Schmalz-Bruns for comments on that occasion. Over the years, I have benefited from lively discussions with my doctoral students Eleonor Kleber and Alain Zysset, and would like to thank them. Last but not least, many thanks to Eleonor Kleber for her help with the editing and formatting of the chapter.

'A remarkable feature of the robust and nuanced contemporary philosophical literature on egalitarianism is its lack of engagement with the theory and practice of human rights. This disconnect is puzzling because the modern human rights movement is arguably the most salient and powerful manifestation of a commitment to equality in our time. Perhaps philosophers writing on equality have not articulated the implications of their work for human rights because they have operated within the strictures of a problematic, but largely unquestioned, assumption: that it is possible to develop a political philosophy for the individual state, considered in isolation. [...] The lack of engagement between the egalitarianism literature and the human rights literature is mutual. For the most part, international lawyers and others professionally concerned with human rights, to the extent that they have examined the theoretical grounding of human rights at all, have not utilized the rich philosophical literature on egalitarianism.'

(Buchanan, A., 'Equality and Human Rights', (2005) 4 *Politics, Philosophy and Economics* 69–90, 69–70)

Introduction

Curiously, the gap between international human rights[1] and equality has long been left open. Of course, the relationship between domestic human rights and equality, and especially political equality, has been explored in depth by political and legal theorists, especially from the German tradition.[2] The implications of that relation-

---

1   I am concentrating on international human rights in this chapter and not only on domestic human rights. However, that distinction is not one of content or structure (Besson, S., 'Human Rights and Democracy in a Global Context – Decoupling and Recoupling', (2011) 4:1 *Ethics and Global Politics* 19–50; Gardbaum, S., 'Human Rights as International Constitutional Rights', (2008) 19:4 *European Journal of International Law* 749–68), but one of function and hence of locus of legalization and legitimation (Besson, 'Decoupling and Recoupling', *supra* note 1). As a matter of fact, international and domestic human rights are in a relationship of mutual reinforcement, relationship that may precisely be explained by reference to political equality and democratic law-making. See also Besson, 'Decoupling and Recoupling', *supra* note 1; Benhabib, S., *Dignity in Adversity. Human Rights in Troubled Times*, Cambridge: Polity Press, 2011, 16 and 126.

2   See e.g. in the Habermasian and co-original tradition, Gosepath, S., *Gleiche Gerechtigkeit: Grundlagen eines liberalen Egalitarianismus*, Frankfurt am Main: Suhrkamp, 2004; Menke, Ch. and Pollmann, A., *Philosophie der Menschenrechte. Zur Einführung*, Hamburg: Junius Verlag, 2007; Forst, R., 'The Justification of Human Rights and the Basic Right to Justification. A Reflexive Approach', (2010) 120:4 *Ethics* 711–40; Habermas, J., 'The Concept of Human Dignity and the Realistic Utopia of Human Rights', (2010) 41:4 *Metaphilosophy* 465–80. Again, there is a noticeable difference between the state of development of German and Anglo-American human rights theories in this respect, a difference I have elaborated on elsewhere: see Besson, S., 'Human Rights – Ethical, Political ... or Legal? First Steps in a Legal Theory of Human Rights', in Childress, D. (ed.), *The Role of Ethics in International Law*, Cambridge: Cambridge University Press, 2011, 211–45. See, however, Dworkin, R., *Justice for*

ship once either human rights or equality, or both, are internationalized remain to be assessed, however.

This disconnect between international human rights and equality is actually evident in the work of human rights theorists and equality scholars alike.[3]

Among egalitarian theorists, on the one hand, neglect for human rights is attributable to the lack of interest for international law and for politics beyond domestic boundaries.[4] This may largely be explained by the apparent, albeit largely unreflected upon, incompatibility between the defence of a universal equal moral status that fits the universality of international human rights, on the one hand, and a robust approach to equality of welfare or resources or to equality of outcome or opportunity of the kind that requires a well-organized political and social community and does not fit the universality of international human rights that well, on the other.[5]

Human rights theorists, on the other hand, have been just as guilty of neglecting the egalitarian dimension of human rights. This is due in part to the resilience of foundationalist, but also to monist approaches to the justification of human rights; those approaches either exclude any reference to other values, including equality, or concentrate on one of them exclusively. Another explanation lies in the lack of reference to the institutional and political practice, history and function of human rights in many traditional human rights theories; those theorists look at international and domestic human rights law merely as a way to implement a moral reality, but without any impact on that moral reality in return.[6] This kind of separation between the morality and the legality of human rights has a price, however: it severs links to the collective and political role of human rights and to their egalitarian dimension in particular. This is even more surprising as equality and non-discrimination are not only preeminent traits of international and domestic human rights law and practice, but

Hedgehogs, Harvard: Belknap, 2011; Buchanan, A., 'The Egalitarianism of Human Rights', (2010) 120:4 *Ethics* 679–710; Christiano, T., *The Constitution of Equality*, Oxford: Oxford University Press, 2008; Buchanan, A., 'Equality and Human Rights', (2005) 4 *Politics, Philosophy and Economics* 69–90.

3   See the egalitarian challenge raised against current human rights theories by Buchanan, 'Equality', *supra* note 2, Buchanan, A., 'Moral Status and Human Enhancement', (2009) 37:4 *Philosophy and Public Affairs* 346–81 and Buchanan, 'Egalitarianism', *supra* note 2. See for a short reply, Griffin, J., 'Human Rights: Questions of Aim and Approach', (2010) 120:4 *Ethics* 741–60.

4   See e.g. Gosepath, *Gleiche Gerechtigkeit*, *supra* note 2, and Gosepath, S., 'Equality', in Zalta, E. N. (ed.), *Stanford Encyclopedia of Philosophy (2007 Edition)*, available at: >http://plato.stanford.edu/entries/equality<; Scheffler, S., 'What is Egalitarianism?', (2003) 31 *Philosophy and Public Affairs* 5–39; Pojman, L., 'On Equal Human Worth: A Critique of Contemporary Egalitarianism', in Pojman, L.P. and Westmoreland, R. (eds), *Equality: Selected Readings*, Oxford: Oxford University Press, 1997, 282–298; Arneson, R., 'Equality and Equal Opportnity for Welfare', (1989) 56 *Philosophical Studies* 77–93; Roemer, J., 'Equality of Resources Implies Equality of Welfare', (1986) 101 *The Quarterly Journal of Economics* 751–84; Cohen, G.A., 'On the Currency of Egalitarian Justice', (1989) 99 *Ethics* 906–44; Dworkin, R., 'What is Equality? Part 1: Equality of Welfare', (1981) 10 *Philosophy and Public Affairs* 185–246 and Dworkin, R., 'What is Equality? Part 2: Equality of Resources', (1981) 10 *Philosophy and Public Affairs* 283–345. See, however, Dworkin, R., *Is Democracy Possible Here?*, Princeton: Princeton University Press, 2006 and Dworkin, *Justice*, *supra* note 2, who now has an account of (international) human rights and their relationship to his domestic 'political rights' and their criterion of 'equal concern and respect'. Note that this may be a lesser problem in the German discussions of equality: see e.g. Gosepath, *Gleiche Gerechtigkeit*, *supra* note 2; Menke/Pollmann, *Philosophie der Menschenrechte*, *supra* note 2, section IV.

5   See e.g. Gosepath, 'Equality', *supra* note 4, section 4.

6   See for those two critiques, Buchanan, 'Egalitarianism', *supra* note 2; Besson, 'Human Rights', *supra* note 2. Contra: Griffin, 'Human Rights', *supra* note 3; Tasioulas, J., 'Are Human Rights Essentially Triggers for Intervention?', (2009) 4:6 *Philosophical Compass* 938–50, and Tasioulas, J., 'Taking Rights out of Human Rights', (2010) 120:4 *Ethics* 647–78.

often source of intriguing legal complexities in that context. A final explanation may be that all contemporary human rights theories are struggling with the parochialism objection and the difficulties it raises for their claim about the universality of human rights. The fact that most egalitarians defend robust theories of equality of some kind would actually make the case against human rights parochialism even more powerful if those theories were somehow to be more deeply connected to human rights.

Recently, however, some human rights theorists have tried to link international human rights more closely to equality, and hence to fill the gap between them.[7] Even though the egalitarian dimension of international human rights has now been slowly uncovered, more work is still needed on what that normative ideal means in the human rights context. Often, indeed, human rights theorists gesture at equality as being related to human rights, for instance in the latter's justification, without, however, explaining what kind of equality is at stake and the exact nature of its justificatory relationship to human rights.[8] That is the project this chapter takes up, albeit modestly and from the perspective primarily of human rights theory. The concept of equality and its justifications being one of the most complex fundamental questions in contemporary moral and political philosophy, its relationship to human rights is bound to constitute an even more complex issue. As a result, any attempt at clarifying that relationship has to thread cautiously.[9]

Importantly, from a methodological perspective, the tensions between ideal and non-ideal theory that often obscure the connections between those different themes will be unpacked and made the most of in the course of the argument. Human rights theory ought to provide a critical reconstruction of human rights practice,[10] both international and domestic. This implies, and this is the topic of this chapter, accounting for the egalitarian dimension of human rights one observes in human rights practice and in the history of human rights since the 18th Century.[11]

My argument unravels in three consecutive stages. A first section of the chapter presents a conception of equal moral status and its relationship to political equality,

---

7   See Buchanan, 'Equality', *supra* note 2, Buchanan, 'Moral Status', *supra* note 3 and Buchanan, 'Egalitarianism', *supra* note 2; Gérard, P., *L'esprit des droits. Philosophie des droits de l'homme*, Brussels: St Louis, 2007, 184 ff. See also Dworkin, *Democracy*, *supra* note 4 and Dworkin, *Justice*, *supra* note 2, 327 ff. on political and human rights. See, more generally, in the Habermasian and co-original tradition, Gosepath, *Gleiche Gerechtigkeit*, *supra* note 2; Menke/Pollmann, *Philosophie der Menschenrechte*, *supra* note 2; Forst, 'Justification of Human Rights', *supra* note 2; Habermas, 'Concept of Human Dignity', *supra* note 2.

8   Thus, Tasioulas, J., 'Justice, Equality and Rights', in Crisp, R. (ed.), *The Oxford Handbook of the History of Ethics*, (2012) forthcoming, discusses the justifications of equality and human rights as two 'broad contemporary philosophical concerns with equality and rights' and hence with justice but without, however, linking them or their respective justifications in any way except by mentioning equal rights as the entitlements stemming from equality and by considering that human rights 'have become the most influential way of giving substance to the basic equality of human beings'. He does venture the idea that human rights could be what basic moral equality consists in, but does not associate this idea to any author in particular and does not pursue the idea any further.

9   For instance, this chapter's focus on equality in the notion and justification of human rights is not meant to exclude their other ties to justice and other principles of justice. On this question, see e.g. Tasioulas, 'Justice, Equality', *supra* note 8.

10   See also Raz, J., 'Human Rights without Foundations', in Besson, S. and Tasioulas, J. (eds), *The Philosophy of International Law*, Oxford: Oxford University Press, 2010, 321–37 and Raz, J., 'On Respect, Authority, and Neutrality: A Response', (2010) 120:2 *Ethics* 279–301; Beitz, C.R., *The Idea of Human Rights*, Oxford: Oxford University Press, 2009; Besson, 'Human Rights', *supra* note 2.

11   See also Buchanan, 'Egalitarianism', *supra* note 2.

on the one hand, and a delineation from dignity, on the other. In the second section, I argue that human rights are grounded in interests, but that political equality works as threshold in the recognition of the importance of certain interests *qua* human rights. In turn, this explains how human rights are both moral and legal rights, on the one hand, and both domestic and international legal rights, on the other. The third section of the argument is dedicated to exploring the implications of the egalitarian dimension of human rights for some vexed issues in international human rights law, such as the relationship between human rights, non-discrimination rights and the equality principle in international law.

1. Equality

The first task in the elucidation of the relationship between human rights and equality is clarifying the concept of equality that is at stake in the human rights context. This requires, first of all, an analysis of the most basic notion of equality: that of equal moral status. In a third step, the discussion moves to a more robust notion of equality: that of political equality. I argue that the latter is an elaborate form of equal moral status in the political context, explain how one can move from equal moral status to political equality and elaborate on the relationship between the two.[12] In a second step, however, I argue that dignity is not a required passage in the reasoning.

a. From Equal Moral Status …

Basic moral equality is usually referred to as equal moral status or basic equal status. It is useful to distinguish between the concept of equal moral status, on the one hand, and its justification, on the other.

The concept of equal moral status, first of all, is best explained by dissociating the notion of moral status from that of equal moral status. In a nutshell, *moral status* pertains to the way in which a being is subject to moral evaluation, how it ought to be treated, whether it has rights, and what kind of rights it has.[13] Moral status goes further therefore than mere moral considerability: the latter is a standing that may be shared with many other sentient animals and even with things, whereas moral status only belongs to human beings.[14] When it is *equal*, moral status refers to the idea that 'all people are of equal worth and that there are some claims people are entitled to make on one another simply by virtue of their status as persons'[15].

---

12   Parts a and c of this section are revised versions of Besson, S., 'International Human Rights and Political Equality. Some Implications for Global Democracy', in Erman, E., and Näsström, S. (eds), *Equality in Transnational and Global Democracy*, London: Palgrave Macmillan, 2012, forthcoming.

13   On moral status, see Nussbaum, M., *Frontiers of Justice: Disability, Nationality, Species Membership*, Cambridge Mass.: Belknap, 2006; McMahan, J., *The Ethics of Killing: Problems at the Margin of Life*, Oxford: Oxford University Press, 2002. See also Buchanan, 'Moral Status', *supra* note 3, more generally. Note that it is an understanding of status that pre-exists the position the individual occupies in the political group.

14   Of course, that difference does not preclude applying human rights theory *mutatis mutandis* to animal rights: see Buchanan, A., 'Do we Need a Philosophical Theory of Human Rights?', (2012) forthcoming; Buchanan, 'Moral Status', *supra* note 3, 358 ff.

15   See e.g. Scheffler, 'What is', *supra* note 4, 22.

There are two core ideas in this understanding of equal moral status: the idea that all persons should be regarded as having the same moral worth (i) and the idea that this equal moral status is relational and the basis for mutual moral claims (ii). Those two aspects of equal moral status are indissociable.[16]

First of all, the idea of equal moral worth of all persons pertains to the intrinsic and non-instrumental value of personhood. According to that idea, no person may be deemed inferior morally to another: all those who have the characteristics that are sufficient for being a person and hence the capacity for rational and moral agency have the same moral status.[17] Equal moral status is of course compatible with important inequalities on other counts such as health, beauty, luck, etc. It is important to stress that what matters here is personhood and not human nature.[18] The former captures what ought to be protected morally in human beings *qua* moral agents, and it escapes the naturalistic fallacy and many other misconceptions that come with the notion of human nature.[19]

The second core idea in equal moral status pertains to its inherently relational dimension.[20] One is at once a person valuable in herself and a person equal to others, i. e. a person whose status and moral worth is defined by one's moral relations to others. The relational or, as Elizabeth Anderson calls it, the social nature of equal moral status explains why the latter amounts to more than mere autonomy or rational capacity that is covered by the first core idea.[21] The denial of equal status amounts to a judgement of exclusion and inferiority *to others* where this kind of judgement is 'thought to disqualify one from participation as an equal in important social practices or roles'.[22]

As a result, equal moral status does more than simply entitle persons to mutual claims. It is actually defined by reference to those mutual claims. This is why it is often deemed as consisting in those mutual moral entitlements.[23] The mutual entitlements inherent in equal moral status are usually described as mutual basic moral

---

16   See also Rosen, M., *Dignity: Its History and Meaning*, Harvard: Harvard University Press, 2012, 26 about a similar articulation between autonomy or moral worth, on the one hand, and respect or treatment, on the other, in Kant's moral philosophy.

17   Buchanan, 'Moral Status', *supra* note 3, 347. There are ways to palliate the inherent limitations of this rational and moral agency dimension of equal moral status and its consequences for the personal scope of human rights that may no longer look general enough, in particular with respect to the mentally impaired, the children or the elderly. See, however, Feinberg, J., 'The Nature and Value of Rights', (1970) *Journal of Value Inquiry* 243–57, about the idea of rights in trust and ways of accommodating the increase or decrease of moral agency and competence in a human rights account. Moreover, dignity implies duties to respect that are independent from human rights and may be invoked in this context (e.g. Rosen, *Dignity*, *supra* note 16).

18   See Buchanan, 'Moral Status', *supra* note 3. This is particularly important as one often reads explanations of non-discrimination rights and principles that refer to natural inequalities and not to inequalities of (social) status. See Anderson, E., *The Imperative of Integration*, Princeton: Princeton University Press, 2010, on racialization and the socially constructed nature of racism.

19   See Buchanan, 'Moral Status', *supra* note 3, 348–9: this is also why human rights are better described as persons' rights. That term avoids naturalistic conclusions and confusing debates about human nature.

20   See Anderson, E., 'What is the point of equality?', (1999) 109:2 *Ethics* 287–337, 289 and 313.

21   See Anderson, 'Point of Equality', *supra* note 20, 288–9. See also Anderson, *Imperative of Integration*, *supra* note 18 on non-discrimination law and integration.

22   See Buchanan, 'Egalitarianism', *supra* note 2, 708–10.

23   See Buchanan, 'Moral Status', *supra* note 3, 378–9; Buchanan, A., *Beyond Humanity?*, Oxford: Oxford University Press, 2011, 233. See also Waldron, J., 'Dignity, Rank and Rights', 2009 Tanner Lectures at UC Berkeley', (2009) *New York University Public Law and Legal Theory Working Papers* 151, on dignity referring both to a status and to the corresponding entitlement that it be respected.

rights.[24] Those basic moral rights are equal rights.[25] They are also universal moral rights. As we will see, human rights are among those basic moral rights that constitute one's equal moral status, although they do not exhaust them. Those mutual moral entitlements include indeed other basic moral rights than human rights: rights that may bind other individuals and not institutions like human rights, on the one hand, and rights that do not need to be institutionalized and legalized unlike human rights, on the other.[26]

What those basic moral rights or entitlements amount to are rights or entitlements to equal treatment or respect in a broad sense. Of course, it is one of the interesting features of equal moral status that it amounts both to a normative status, on the one hand, and to the entitlements stemming from that status and actually constituting that status in return, on the other.[27] This seeming circularity will become more patent when explaining how human rights are grounded in interests but only those that can give rise to mutual entitlements that are themselves constitutive of equal moral status, with that status itself amounting to those mutual entitlements in return. This dialectical relationship actually explains why human rights cannot be said to be 'grounded' in political equality, even though the latter can be a 'ground' for the recognition of more human rights[28] and human rights a 'ground' for the recognition of equal political status.

Secondly, the next question is the justification of persons' equal moral status. Curiously given its pivotal role in morality, but maybe because of that pivotal or even liminal role, the concept of equal moral status remains a largely unquestioned notion in much of contemporary moral theory.[29] So, the problem with the justification of equal moral status is not so much that moral philosophers are divided but that they rarely provide a justification of the equal moral status of persons.[30] Some authors, like Jeremy Waldron, actually see this lack of justification as a shortcoming of current moral theory on basic moral equality.[31] Others like Bernard Williams saw that absence of justification as a virtue of the idea of equality.[32]

Schematically, one may distinguish between two kinds of justification of basic moral equality: a Christian one that refers to God and that is mostly based on

24   See Buchanan, *Beyond Humanity?*, *supra* note 23, 233.
25   This is compatible with people having other moral rights that are different from one another as long as they are neither basic moral rights nor human rights. See Buchanan, 'Moral Status', *supra* note 3, 378–9.
26   As I will argue later on, while equal moral status constitutes the threshold in the recognition of universal moral rights based on fundamental interests, it is political equality that constitutes the threshold in the recognition of human rights.
27   See also Rosen, *Dignity*, *supra* note 16, 25 ff about a similar articulation between autonomy and respect in Kant's moral philosophy. See also Waldron, 'Dignity', *supra* note 23, on dignity being both something to describe and something normative to evaluate and to require.
28   See for a similar argument albeit on dignity: Waldron, 'Dignity', *supra* note 23, on dignity as a 'ground' for the recognition of human rights, and not a 'foundation' or 'grounding' of human rights.
29   See also Tasioulas, 'Justice, Equality', *supra* note 8; Gosepath, 'Equality', *supra* note 4, section 2.3.
30   See Tasioulas, 'Justice, Equality', *supra* note 8, for a more detailed discussion.
31   See Waldron, J., *God, Locke, and Equality: Christian Foundations in Locke's Political Thought*, Cambridge: Cambridge University Press, 2002, reviewed by Fabre, C., 'Review: *God, Locke and Equality: Christian Foundations in Locke's Political Thought* by Jeremy Waldron', (2003) 66:3 *Modern Law Review* 470–73. See also Tasioulas, 'Justice, Equality', *supra* note 8; Buchanan, 'Equality', *supra* note 2, Buchanan, 'Moral Status', *supra* note 3, and Buchanan, 'Egalitarianism', *supra* note 2.
32   Williams, B., 'The Idea of Equality', in Hawthorn, G. (ed.), *In the Beginning was the Deed: Realism and Moralism in Political Argument*, Princeton: Princeton University Press, 2005, 97–114.

Locke[33] and a non-religious one that refers to shared rational nature and that is mostly based on Kant.[34]

The difficulty with the former is its religious and hence non-inclusive and teleo-logical nature.[35] But the latter also suffers from important shortcomings. One of them is its metaphysical, and non-naturalistic or empirical inclination.[36] A way of re-butting this objection may actually be found in the second core idea to equal moral status, however: its relational or social nature. The social nature of basic moral equal-ity implies making a certain number of empirical assumptions about people and their relationship in society.[37] It provides a third way of justifying equal moral status and the one used in this chapter. This feature of equal moral status and its justification is actually something that will prove crucial in the context of the justification of human rights and their defence against the parochialism critique.

Contrary to what has been the case for a long time in theories of equality, and following Anderson,[38] it is important therefore to understand equality by reference to equal moral status. This avoids focusing too narrowly on a specific form of equal-ity, such as distributive equality, for instance, and its various kinds depending on the respect to which distributive equality is granted (the 'equality of what' question). The recognition of equality in that primary form does not yet imply, in other words, more robust notions of equality such as distributive equality which have to be justi-fied and defended separately once basic moral equality has been defined and justi-fied. This explains also in turn why equal moral status is compatible with a wide range of differences and their social recognition in the form of material inequali-ties.[39]

b. ... Without Dignity ...

Dignity is sometimes used as another way of referring to equal moral status, or at least to the way in which equal moral status has been used so far in this chapter. This is especially the case in the human rights context.[40] Besides being an extremely inde-terminate and historically complex concept,[41] often used as placeholder in morality,[42]

---

33 See e.g. Waldron, *God, Locke and Equality*, *supra* note 31, Ch. 3.
34 See e.g. Habermas, 'Concept of Human Dignity', *supra* note 2.
35 See Fabre, 'Review', *supra* note 31; Buchanan, 'Moral Status', *supra* note 3, for a critique of the reli-gious justification of moral equal status.
36 See Tasioulas, 'Justice, Equality', *supra* note 8; and Williams, 'Idea of Equality', *supra* note 32, 102 for this critique.
37 See e.g. Buchanan, 'Equality', *supra* note 2, 77–8. See also Wingert, L., 'Was ist und was heisst "un-verfügbar"? Philosophische Überlegungen zu einer nicht nur ethischen Frage', in Forst, R. et al. (eds), *Sozialphilosophie und Kritik*, Frankfurt am Main: Suhrkamp, 2009, 384–408. See also Margalit, A., 'Human Dignity between Kitsch and Deification', (2011) manuscript on file with author, for a similar third way between kitsch and deification (including Kantianism) in the context of dignity. See even Waldron, 'Dignity', *supra* note 23, in relation to dignity *qua* legal concept.
38 See e.g. Anderson, 'Point of Equality', *supra* note 20, 313 who opposes her relational theory of equality to distributive theories of equality; Buchanan, 'Egalitarianism', *supra* note 2, 688.
39 See Waldron, *God, Locke and Equality*, *supra* note 31, Ch. 3; Buchanan, 'Egalitarianism', *supra* note 2, 685.
40 See e.g. Waldron, 'Dignity', *supra* note 23; Habermas, 'Concept of Human Dignity', *supra* note 2; Forst, 'Justification of Human Rights', *supra* note 2; Habermas, J., *Zur Verfassung Europas. Ein Essay*, Berlin: Suhrkamp, 2011; Tasioulas, 'Justice, Equality', *supra* note 8.
41 See e.g. Rosen, *Dignity*, *supra* note 16, 48: 'The concept of dignity has developed into an amalgam of humanist, liberal, Christian, socialist and Kantian ideas.'

it is not clear that dignity does some work in the human rights context that equal moral status cannot do.[43]

To start with, authors use dignity to refer to what is unique in human beings and shared by all of them: their personhood and capacity for rational and moral agency.[44] This is, however, the very idea captured by the concept of equal moral status.[45] In this sense, the way dignity is used by a majority of authors, i. e. dignity *qua* status or rank albeit equalized to all human beings,[46] does not add anything to the proposed model of equal moral status and human rights. Another important element about dignity as it is used in the human rights context is its socio-comparative dimension.[47] Here again, however, the fact that authors usually refer to 'equal dignity'[48] to refer to that socio-comparative or relational dimension shows how the question of equality cannot be escaped by gesturing to dignity or, alternatively, to inviolability[49]. There are in any case grounds, in the intellectual history of the concept of dignity, for concern about how egalitarian dignity really was for those endorsing dignity as a ground for human rights.[50] Confirmation of the redundancy of equal dignity with equal moral status *qua* equal universal moral rights may actually be found in Art. 1 of the Universal Declaration of Human Rights (UDHR) that refers to human beings being 'equal in dignity *and* rights' (emphasis added).

Of course, there are other invocations of dignity in the human rights context that are not redundant with the notion of equal moral status. One of them is the reference to dignity as the ultimate value of human beings and hence as the foundation of human rights. Another is the reference to a human right to dignity itself. The latter is easy to disparage as there cannot be rights to values and dignity is a value. Of

---

42   For famous philosophical critiques, see e.g. Pinker, S., 'The Stupidity of Dignity', *The New Republic*, 28 May 2008. See also Ladwig, B., 'Menschenwürde als Grund der Menschenrechte', (2010) 1:1 *Zeitschrift für Politische Theorie* 51–69, 65 on dignity as status-indicator and not as a status-justificator.

43   On this redundancy between dignity and status, see also Waldron, 'Dignity', *supra* note 23, by reference to Dworkin on the use of redundant terminology. Both concepts have a lot in common: they are both threshold concepts and are concepts one may use to ground human rights, or as goods or interests one has a human right to.

44   Albeit maybe with a theological twist as most moral philosophers and human rights theorists currently referring to dignity in this context seem to be religious or seem to think that religious justifications of human rights are acceptable: see e.g. McCrudden, C., 'Dignity and Judicial Interpretation of Human Rights', (2008) 19:4 *European Journal of International Law* 655–724, 673; Waldron, 'Dignity', *supra* note 23; Habermas, 'Concept of Human Dignity', *supra* note 2; Bielefeldt, H., *Auslaufmodell Menschenwürde? Warum sie in Frage steht und warum wir sie verteidigen müssen*, Freiburg: Herder, 2011. See also Rosen, *Dignity, supra* note 16, 3 on dignity in faith-based ethical discourse.

45   This becomes clear when one looks at Habermas, 'Concept of Human Dignity', *supra* note 2, 468–9 and 472 as much of his argument can actually be read as one of equal moral status.

46   See e.g. Waldron, 'Dignity', *supra* note 23; Margalit, 'Human Dignity', *supra* note 37; Hennette-Vauchez, S., 'A human *dignitas* ? Remnants of the Ancient Legal Concept in Contemporary Dignity Jurisprudence', (2011) 9:1 *International Constitutional Law Review* 32–57.

47   See e.g. Buchanan, 'Egalitarianism', *supra* note 2, 690–1, 702.

48   See e.g. Gosepath, 'Equality', *supra* note 4, 27; Waldron, 'Dignity', *supra* note 23, 20; Habermas, 'Concept of Human Dignity', *supra* note 2; Forst, 'Justification of Human Rights', *supra* note 2; Tasioulas, 'Justice, Equality', *supra* note 8. The egalitarian use of dignity may also be exemplified in Waldron, 'Dignity', *supra* note 23, 57 when he refers to political equality and equality before the law.

49   By contrast to those authors, I argue that the idea of inviolability amounts to something else than dignity. It is an idea that may be accounted for by reference to equal moral worth and the egalitarian dimension of human rights. In practice, this understanding is often captured by the notion of fundamental or minimal core of human rights. See below section 2.

50   See e.g. Rosen, *Dignity, supra* note 16, 47 ff. on the clearly inegalitarian agenda of the Catholic *milieux* endorsing dignity as foundation for the international human rights project.

course, human rights can be of value, but that is a different question. The former reference to dignity is more widespread, especially in the legal discourse,[51] and more difficult to circumvent. There is no need to get into a discussion of the relative merits of status-based and interest-based accounts of moral rights here, as the chapter endorses an interest-based account of human rights that ties them, however, to equal moral status and sees human rights as constitutive of equal moral status as a result and not as one of its consequences. I will argue that this prevents them from being founded only in moral status, and hence either in equal moral status or in dignity as a matter of fact.

In a nutshell, however, and in place of a full argument,[52] what makes it the case that human rights should be grounded in interests, and not in status, is the latter's pluralism at every time and place, the dynamism of the rights that protect them across time and place, and their non-speciesist quality.[53] First of all, unlike status, interests can be multifarious and this accommodates moral pluralism better. Secondly, interests need not be protected similarly against standard threats and this explains how, despite the interests remaining the same, the content of human rights can change. Finally, interests are compatible with many different kinds of moral statuses and in particular with the moral status of non-human animals, thus leaving the door open for an interest-based account of non-human animal rights and not connecting human rights tightly to human nature as a result.

If this counter-argument against dignity *qua* foundation of human rights and as a placeholder for equal moral status holds morally, one still needs to explain why dignity[54] is omnipresent within major international and domestic legal guarantees of human rights adopted post-1945.[55] There are historical explanations for this, how-

---

51   It is allegedly the one used in the German Constitutional Court's case-law, although dignity is also used with other meanings such as something there is a human right to, an interpretive principle of all other human rights, a 'limit on the limits' to other human rights, etc. (see e.g. BVerfGE 45, 187 [227]; 39, 1 [59]; 115, 118). See the discussion in Rosen, *Dignity*, *supra* note 16, 77 ff., 114 ff.; Bielefeldt, *Auslaufmodell Menschenwürde?*, *supra* note 44; Möllers, C., 'Democracy and Dignity in German Constitutional Law', (2009) 42 *Israel Law Review* 416–39, 423–4; Baer, S., 'Menschenwürde zwischen Recht, Prinzip und Referenz. Die Bedeutung der Enttabuisierung', (2005) *Deutsche Zeitschrift für Philosophie* 571–88.

52   There is, of course, a kind of circularity in dignity accounts that define it by reference to human rights without a distinct understanding of human rights (e.g. McCrudden, 'Dignity', *supra* note 44, who disparages certain understandings of dignity because they cannot justify human rights, but without giving a full account of human rights and hence begging the question about dignity; see also Ladwig, 'Menschenwürde', *supra* note 42, 62), or in human right accounts that define them by reference to dignity without a distinct understanding of dignity (e.g. Feinberg, 'Nature', *supra* note 17; Kateb, G., *Human Dignity*, Cambridge, Mass.: Harvard Belknap, 2011). On that circularity, see e.g. Waldron, 'Dignity', *supra* note 23; Rosen, *Dignity*, *supra* note 16, 54 ff., 57. The best way, and the one chosen here, is to start from human rights practice and its specificities (e.g. mutual perfection, systematicity, correlativity, universality, equality, etc.) and then see how dignity fits or not.

53   See Buchanan, A., 'Moral Progress and Human Rights', in Holder, C. and Reidy, D. (eds), *Human Rights: The Hard Questions*, Amsterdam: Springer, 2012, forthcoming.

54   Note that I am concerned here with both the moral and legal concepts of dignity as they are used by domestic and international lawyers indistinctively. See also Waldron, 'Dignity', *supra* note 23. For the same argument in the human rights context, see section 2 below.

55   See e.g. Art. 1 German Basic Law and Art. 1 UDHR, but also all Preambles to the UN human rights conventions post-1945. See for a brilliant exposition of dignity in domestic and international human rights law, McCrudden, 'Dignity', *supra* note 44. Of course, there are also counter-arguments in international and domestic human rights practice, as not all constitutional traditions know of dignity. Further, some that did have now abandoned it: see e.g. the decision by the Canadian Supreme Court of 27 June 2008, R. *c.* Kapp, [2008] 2 R.C.S. 483, 2008 CSC 41.

ever. One of them, of course, is the political coming together after the Second World War of two extremely powerful traditions that had very little in common morally: Christian theology and Kantian philosophy.[56] However, historical compromises do not necessarily make for good moral interpretations of law, and historical understandings do not necessarily stick therefore in judicial interpretations of the text of legal norms.[57] They may, but then it would have to be on the basis of a full legal and moral argument and not merely an historical one. And originalism is not one of the methods of interpretation of international law that is favoured by the international law of treaties; this applies even more to international human rights law.

True, there is a resurgence of interest for dignity these days, both legally and morally. Explanations are easy to find, however. Legal reasons may lie in the development of comparative constitutional law, and the German constitutional influence in that context,[58] but also within EU fundamental rights law and international human rights law. Morally, one may find reasons in the return of the religious,[59] as well as in the coming under threat of Kantian moral philosophy within moral philosophy in general. Furthermore, as Michael Rosen argues, the historical alliance between Christian personalism and Kantian rationalism seems to have imploded. More particularly, the controversies in which dignity is increasingly invoked, in particular in the bioethics realm and debates surrounding technology, show the limits of the former when nature becomes increasingly rationalized. At the same time, of course, those debates ensure that the fascination for dignity can endure. And this may not necessarily be a regrettable state of affairs given the role such essentially contestable concepts play in a democratic legal order.[60] Besides, if dignity works as a moral placeholder and status-indicator, to borrow Bernd Ladwig's terms,[61] then its resilience may be good news for the protection of equal moral status and human rights.

56 See Rosen, *Dignity*, *supra* note 16, 53, 80 ff and 90 ff. See also Moyn, S., 'Personalism, Community and the Origins of Human Rights', in Hoffmann, S.L. (ed.), *Human Rights in the Twentieth Century*, Cambridge: Cambridge University Press, 2011, 85–106, on the religious background to the adoption of international human rights law treaties post-1945. See, more generally, Morsink, J., *The Universal Declaration of Human Rights: Origins, Drafting and Intent*, Philadelphia: University of Pennsylvania Press, 1999; Glendon, M.A., *A World Made New, Eleanor Roosevelt and the Universal Declaration of Human Rights*, New York: Random House, 2001. For a slightly different take on the religious background of the first interpreters of the German Basic Law as opposed to its drafters, see Möllers, 'Democracy and Dignity', *supra* note 51; Goos, C., *Innere Freiheit. Eine Rekonstruktion des grundgesetzlichen Würdebegriffs*, Bonn: Bonn University Press, 2011; Rosen, *Dignity*, *supra* note 16, 102.
57 See Möllers, 'Democracy and Dignity', *supra* note 51, for a similar argument about why one should actually refer to Kantian moral philosophy when interpreting Art. 1 of the German Basic Law. See also Rosen, *Dignity*, *supra* note 16, 1 ff. on why we should refer to *imago dei* or Pico's notion of dignity and not others.
58 German constitutional law was very influential, for instance, when drafting the Japanese Constitution or the South African one.
59 See on the choice between kitsch and deification of dignity, e.g. Margalit, 'Human Dignity', *supra* note 37. Of course, some may argue that the redundancy is not entirely useless given the religiously loaded or, at least, sacred and hence religion-compatible nature of the concept of dignity (see e.g. Joas, H., *Die Sakralität der Person. Eine neue Geneaologie der Menschenrechte*, Berlin: Suhrkamp, 2011; Habermas, J., *Die Zukunft der menschlichen Natur Auf dem Weg zu einer liberalen Eugenik?*, Frankfurt am Main: Suhrkamp, 2001; Dworkin, R., *Life's Dominion*, New York: Vintage Books, 1994) and its benefits in inter-religious dialogue: see e.g. Bielefeldt, *Auslaufmodell Menschenwürde?*, *supra* note 44.
60 See e.g. Waldron, J., *Law and Disagreement*, New York: Oxford University Press, 1999; Besson, S., *The Morality of Conflict. Reasonable Disagreement and the Law*, Oxford: Hart Publishing, 2005. For a similar idea in the dignity concept, see also Möllers, 'Democracy and Dignity', *supra* note 51.
61 See Ladwig, 'Menschenwürde', *supra* note 42, 65. On dignity as trigger for the recognition of political-moral status, see also Habermas, *Zur Verfassung*, *supra* note 40, 26.

All this is not to say, of course, that dignity does not have a moral existence of its own besides equal moral status, but merely that it is redundant to equal moral status in its relationship to human rights. Among the other moral meanings and roles dignity has, and that may matter outside of human rights, one should mention the most important one. It is the third understanding of dignity besides equal moral status, on the one hand, and moral value, on the other: dignity as a way to be treated, i. e. the idea of being treated with dignity or dignified respect (as opposed to respect for dignity).[62] It usually takes the shape of a duty to dignified treatment, as opposed to a right. Some authors also explain this understanding of dignity by reference to self-respect and a self-referential moral duty.[63] This understanding of dignity is actually one that is present in certain parts of anti-discrimination law that cannot be explained by reference to the entitlements of equal moral status, such as the prohibition of harassment for instance. It may even explain, according to some authors, some resolutely non-egalitarian streaks in parts of anti-discrimination law.[64] Curiously, this self-referring understanding of someone's dignity is sometimes used as a moral justification for the restriction of that very person's other human rights.[65] Finally, one may also find traces of this understanding of dignity *qua* dignified respect in international humanitarian law.[66]

c. ... To Political Equality

Equal moral status holds an intermediary ground between moral considerability, on the one hand, and more specific or robust notions of equality, on the other. Based on the equal moral or basic status of individuals, however, one may want to justify more robust egalitarian and especially distributive ideals such as equality of resources or equality of welfare, or such as equality of opportunities or equality of outcomes. Scope precludes entering into a highly contested debate over those different robust forms of equality, and distributive equality in particular.[67] What I would like to do, however, is focus on one of them in particular without excluding the others nor attempting to link it to the others, and that is public or political equality. Political equality is indeed the kind of robust equality that matters in a legal order and, accordingly, in the context of human rights law.

---

62   See Rosen, *Dignity*, *supra* note 16, 58, 114 ff. and 125 ff. on this third understanding of dignity. See also Hennette-Vauchez, 'A human *dignitas* ?', *supra* note 46.
63   See e.g. Schaber, P., 'Menschenwürde und Selbsbetrachtung: Ein Vorschlag zum Verständnis der Menschenwürde', (2004) 63 *Studia Philosophica* 93–106; Hennette-Vauchez, 'A human *dignitas* ?', *supra* note 46.
64   See Hennette-Vauchez, 'A human *dignitas* ?', *supra* note 46; Rosen, *Dignity*, *supra* note 16, 63 ss.
65   See e.g. the dwarf case: UN Human Rights Committee, *Manuel Wackenheim v. France*, Communication No. 854/1999, 15 July 2002, UN Doc CCPR/C/75/D/854/1999,. See also the controversial use of dignity in justifying restrictions to Art. 8 ECHR in ECtHR, *SH and others v. Austria*, Application No. 57813/00, 3 November 2011, par. 113. Many thanks to Roger Brownsword for drawing my attention to these self-referential dignity-based forms of human rights restrictions that are not based on the rights of others, but on the dignity of the right-holders themselves and therefore come very close to the Dworkinian "Sarah-lovers"-critique of double-counting of preferences.
66   See Rosen, *Dignity*, *supra* note 16, 58 ff.
67   See e.g. Gosepath, 'Equality', *supra* note 4; Scheffler, 'What is', *supra* note 4; Pojman, 'Equal Human Worth', *supra* note 4; Arneson, 'Equality', *supra* note 4; Roemer, 'Equality of Resources', *supra* note 4; Cohen, 'Currency', *supra* note 4; Dworkin, 'What is Equality', Part 1 and 2, *supra* note 4.

Before discussing political equality itself, it is important to explain how one can get to political equality from equal moral status and elaborate on the relationship between the two. That passage and relationship are actually reflected, I will argue, in the recognition of universal moral rights as human rights (moral and legal), and the passage from the ones to the others.

First of all, from equal moral status to political equality. The relational or social nature of equal moral status alluded to before implies that, to borrow Allen Buchanan's words, 'the proper acknowledgement of a person's moral status requires some sort of fundamental public recognition of equality'.[68] Equality is distinctly public or political as result.[69] In a nutshell, public or political equality implies that people can see that they are being treated as equals by others and this takes the form of its recognition by the law and institutions.[70]

The inherently political dimension of equality implies reconciling the moral universality of equality with both the relativity and contingency of political life. With respect to the relativity of politics, first of all, political equality depends on the existence of a political community, but corresponding political communities are not (yet) universal. Here it is important to emphasize the normative nature of political equality and the fact that is used both to refer to a state of affairs and to how it should be. As to the contingency of politics and its implications for political equality, secondly, the tension may be alleviated by reference to the conditions or circumstances of political equality. If it is true that the public recognition of equal moral status requires public institutions and processes and hence a political community, the existence of the latter depends on other elements. Those further conditions of existence of a political community and hence of political equality are, on the one hand, the common subjecthood to decisions and laws, and the interdependence of stakes and the rough equality of those stakes among the members of the future community, on the other.[71] If those conditions are given, the equal moral status of the members in that community implies their political equality.

What this means is that there are pre-political circumstances in which individuals merely benefit from a social form of equal moral status.[72] It also means that not all individuals may claim political equality in a given political community on grounds of their equal moral status; their political equality will follow their full membership in the community, i. e. their being subjected to the community's decisions and law, and their sharing interdependent and roughly equal stakes with others. This is particularly interesting in the context of post-national political communities, such as the European Union (EU) or other international communities of states.

Secondly, political equality. Once the political conditions are such that political equality may be required on the grounds of equal moral status, the next question to arise is how political equality can be vindicated.

---

68   See Buchanan, 'Moral Status', *supra* note 3, 379; Anderson, 'Point of Equality', *supra* note 20, 288–9. See also Habermas, 'Concept of Human Dignity', *supra* note 2, 472.
69   See Anderson, 'Point of Equality', *supra* note 20, 288–9. See also Williams, 'Idea of Equality', *supra* note 32.
70   See Christiano, T., 'Democratic Legitimacy and International Institutions', in Besson, S., and Tasioulas, J. (eds), *The Philosophy of International Law*, Oxford: Oxford University Press 2010, 119–37, 121.
71   See Christiano, *Constitution of Equality*, *supra* note 2, 2; Christiano, 'Democratic', *supra* note 70, 121–2.
72   See also Erman, E., 'Should All Political Contexts be Democratic? Contours of a Two-Faced Theory of Legitimacy', in Erman, E., and Näsström, S. (eds), *Political Equality and Global Democracy*, London: Palgrave Macmillan, 2012, forthcoming.

The political dimension of equal moral status together with its rights-based nature lead to a further process: the struggle for equal participation rights is based on the idea of equal moral status.[73] And this in turn implies struggling for the establishment of a democratic regime that includes all those subjected to a decision into the decision-making process. Democracy is indeed the way 'of publicly realizing equality when persons who have diverse interests need to establish rules and institutions for the common world in which they live'[74] and this in spite of persistent and widespread reasonable disagreement.[75] Democracy enlivens and enables political equality. The idea of equal political status or membership may also be referred to as democratic membership therefore.[76] Of course, democracy implies more than political equality. Scope precludes discussing it extensively, but democracy *qua* political regime also requires egalitarian deliberation and decision-making procedures. There may be political communities as a result where there is political equality but where other elements necessary to democracy are missing.[77] One may think of the EU, for instance.

In conclusion, when the political circumstances are given and when individuals are not only subjected to the same decisions and laws, but also share interdependent and roughly equal stakes, equal moral status implies political equality. In turn, as a person's equal moral status implies mutual moral rights and duties, political equality gives rise to equal participation rights and is therefore best served by a democratic regime where individuals are recognized those equal participation rights. Of course, one may object to the parochial dimension of democratic equality. It is here that the proposed minimalist approach to political equality *qua* principle of transnational justice becomes most interesting. Its institutional and political dimension and its need for contextual specification enable it to escape over-specification and parochialism.[78]

2. Equality and Human Rights

The next step in the argument is dedicated to clarifying how equality fits into the concept of human rights.[79] This is what one may refer to as the egalitarian dimension of human rights.

---

73   See Buchanan, 'Moral Status', *supra* note 3, 380 by reference to Waldron, *God, Locke and Equality*, *supra* note 31,, Ch. 3 and the liberal political tradition. See also Anderson, 'Point of Equality', *supra* note 20, 317–8.

74   See Christiano, 'Democratic', *supra* note 70, 121–2.

75   On the connection between equality and democracy, see also Anderson, 'Point of Equality', *supra* note 20, 289.

76   See Christiano, *Constitution of Equality*, *supra* note 2, 2; Christiano, 'Democratic', *supra* note 70, 121–2.

77   See Erman, 'Political Contexts', *supra* note 72, for a more complete distinction between political equality and democracy.

78   For such a minimalist and non-parochialist approach to equal status as a component of international human rights, see e.g. Buchanan, 'Egalitarianism', *supra* note 2; and Buchanan, 'Equality', *supra* note 2, 78–80. See also Buchanan, A., 'Human Rights and the Legitimacy of the International Order', (2008) 14 *Legal Theory* 39–70 for an institutional proposal.

79   This section is a revised version of a section of previously published work: see Besson, 'Decoupling and Recoupling', *supra* note 1.

a. The Morality and the Legality of Human Rights

To start with, the relationship between human rights and equal moral status, and political equality more specifically, explain the inherently moral-political but also legal
nature of human rights.

i. The Morality of Human Rights

Human rights are a sub-set of universal moral rights (i) that protect fundamental and
general human interests (ii) against the intervention, or in some cases non-
intervention of (national, regional or international) public institutions (iii). Those
three elements will be presented in turn.

First of all, a human right exists *qua* moral *right* when an interest is a sufficient
ground or reason to hold someone else (the duty-bearer) under a (categorical and
exclusionary) duty to respect that interest against certain standard threats vis-à-vis
the right-holder.[80] For a right to be recognized, a sufficient interest must be established and weighed against other interests and other considerations with which it
might conflict in a particular social context.[81] Once the abstract right is recognized,
specific duties will be determined in each concrete case by reference to the specific
circumstances and potential duty-bearers. Rights are, on this account, intermediaries
between interests and duties.[82]

Turning to the second element in the definition, *human* rights are universal
moral rights of a special intensity that belong to all human beings by virtue of their
humanity. Human rights are universal moral rights because the interests they protect
belong to all human beings. *Qua* general moral rights, they protect fundamental human interests that human beings have by virtue of their humanity and not of a given
status or circumstance (unlike special rights). Human rights are universal and general
rights that protect fundamental interests. Those interests constitute part of a person's well-being in an objective sense; they are the objective interests that, when
guaranteed, make for a decent or minimally good individual life.

Of course, there has to be a threshold of importance at which a given interest is
regarded as sufficiently fundamental to give rise to duties and hence to a right. True,
the fundamental nature of the protected interests has to be determined by reference
to a context and time rather than established once and for all.[83] More specifically,
however, what makes it the case, that a given individual interest is regarded as sufficiently fundamental or important to generate a duty and that, in other words, the
threshold of importance and point of passage from a general and fundamental interest to a human right is reached, may be found in the normative status of each individual *qua* equal member of the moral-political community, i. e. their political equal-

---

80   Raz, J., 'On the Nature of Rights', (1984) 93 *Mind* 194–214, 195.
81   Ibid., 200, 209.
82   Ibid., 208.
83   See on the ahistorical and synchronic universality of human rights: Tasioulas, J., 'Human Rights,
      Universality and the Values of Personhood: Retracing Griffin's Steps', (2002) 10 *European Journal of
      Philosophy* 79–100; Tasioulas, J., 'The Moral Reality of Human Rights', in Pogge, T. (ed.), *Freedom
      from Poverty as a Human Right: Who Owes What to the Very Poor*, Oxford: Oxford University Press,
      2007, 75–101, 76–7. See also Raz, J., 'Human Rights in the New World Order', (2010) 1:1 *Transna-
      tional Legal Theory* 31–47. Contra: Griffin, J., 'First Steps in an Account of Human Rights', (2001) 9:3
      European Journal of Philosophy 306–27.

ity or equal political status.[84] Only those interests that are recognized as socio-comparatively important by members of the community can be recognized as sufficiently fundamental to give rise to duties and hence as human rights. A person's interests merit equal respect in virtue of her status as member of the community and of her mutual relations to other members in the community. The recognition of human rights is done mutually and not simply vertically and top-down, and as a result human rights are not externally promulgated but mutually granted by members of a given political community.[85] This is particularly important as it allows for the mutual assessment of the standard threats on certain interests that deserve protection, on the one hand, and of the burdens and costs of the recognition of the corresponding rights and duties, on the other.

As a matter of fact, human rights are not merely a consequence of individuals' equal political status, but also a way of actually earning that equal status and consolidating it. Without human rights, political equality would remain an abstract guarantee; through mutual human rights, individuals become actors of their own equality and members of their political community.[86] Human rights are power-mediators, in other words:[87] they enable political equality. Borrowing Arendt's words: 'we are not born equal; we become equal as members of a group on the strength of our decision to guarantee ourselves mutually equal rights.'[88] Human rights protect those interests tied to equal political membership and whose disrespect would be tantamount to treating them as outsiders.[89] Of course, some human rights, such as civic and political rights, are more closely tied to actual political membership, while others such as the right to life, for instance, are closer to basic demands of humanity and hence to access to political membership. Even the latter rights, however, constrain what equal membership can mean if it is to be legitimate and the kind of interests it must protect. By submitting individuals to genocide, torture and other extreme forms of cruel treatment, a community excludes them and no longer treats them as equal members, thus violating the threshold of recognition of human rights: political equality.[90] This is in line with the republican idea of the political community *qua* locus of rights.[91]

Although there may seem to be a contradiction in arguing both that human rights require political equality as a constitutive threshold and, in the previous sec-

---

84   See Forst, 'Justification of Human Rights', *supra* note 2; Forst, R., 'The Basic Right to Justification: Toward a Constructivist Conception of Human Rights', (1999) 6:1 *Constellations* 35–60, 48; Christiano, *Constitution of Equality*, *supra* note 2, 138, 156.

85   See Cohen, J., 'Minimalism about Human Rights: The Most We Can Hope For?', (2004) 12:2 *The Journal of Political Philosophy* 190–213, 197–8; Forst, 'Justification of Human Rights', *supra* note 2; Baynes, K., 'Towards a Political Conception of Human Rights', (2009) 35:4 *Philosophy and Social Criticism* 371–90, 382.

86   See Cohen, 'Minimalism', *supra* note 85, 197–8; Cohen, J.L., 'Rethinking Human Rights, Democracy and Sovereignty in the Age of Globalization', (2008) 36:4 *Political Theory* 578–606, 585–6.

87   For the original idea of mediating duties, see Shue, H., 'Mediating Duties', (1988) 98 *Ethics* 687–704, 703. See also Reus-Smit, C., 'On Rights and Institutions', in Beitz, C. and Goodin, R. (eds), *Global Basic Rights*, Oxford: Oxford University Press, 2009, 25–48. On liberal rights and the exercize of power in general, see Christiano, *Constitution of Equality*, *supra* note 2, 134.

88   Arendt, H., 'The Decline of the Nation-State and the End of the Rights of Man', in *The Origins of Totalitarianism*, London: Penguin, 1951, 147–82; reprinted in Goodale, M. (ed.), *Human Rights: An Anthropological Reader*, Oxford: Blackwell, 2009, 32–57, 147–82.

89   The following argument is a specific development of Cohen, 'Minimalism', *supra* note 85, 197–8's argument.

90   As a result, it is not possible to distinguish, among human rights, between those that are connected to political equality and to democracy and those that are not.

91   See Cohen, 'Rethinking', *supra* note 86, 604 fn. 47.

tion, that political equality amounts to the mutual entitlements that are human rights, the contradiction is only apparent. Like basic moral rights and equal moral status, human rights and political equality are synchronic and mutually reinforcing: *à la fois* the moral entitlements that are constitutive of a status and the status made of those entitlements. Again, this explains why, if human rights are constitutive of equal moral-political status, they are not themselves grounded in that status. All this does not prevent, of course, human rights from being in conflict with more robust forms of equality, such as equality of welfare or even equality of opportunity for welfare, or vice-versa.[92]

In short, the proposed account of the nature of human rights follows a modified interest-based theory: it is modified or complemented by reference to considerations of equal moral-political status in a given community.[93] Considerations of political equality are not simply considered as objective interests, but are distinct from them, albeit articulated with those interests in the process of grounding human rights. Nor would political equality be a sufficient ground for human rights without objective interests in a decent or minimally good individual life; there are cases in which a person's political or public equality is threatened without this affecting its decent or minimally good life. The relationship between human rights and political equality bridges the sterile opposition between the individual and the group, on the one hand, and the good and the right, on the other.[94] Under a purely status-based or a purely interest-based model, the manichean opposition between the individual and the group, and between his private and public autonomy would lead to unjustifiable conclusions that are tempered in the proposed account.[95]

Evidence of the egalitarian threshold of human rights may actually be found in the relational and socio-comparative nature of human rights. This comes out in many of the facets of human rights in practice. One may think of their systematic nature, for instance.[96] Human rights belong to everyone equally and mutually so, and, accordingly, their systematicity is a testimony to their relational nature. Another confirmation may be found in the non-inherently individualistic nature of human rights that protect basic individual interests deemed comparatively important within the political community. Of course, some human rights protect individual interests

---

92   On this question, see section 3 below.
93   The role of equal moral-political status as a threshold is echoed in Buchanan, 'Egalitarianism', *supra* note 2, 707's idea of 'articulating' equal status with human rights but it is more specific than his idea of inclusion 'at the deepest level in one's grounding of human rights'.
94   The proposed account comes very close to Forst, 'Justification of Human Rights', *supra* note 2; Forst, 'Basic Right', *supra* note 84, 48–50; and Forst, R., *Das Recht auf Rechtfertigung. Elemente einer konstruktivistischen Theorie der Gerechtigkeit*, Frankfurt am Main: Suhrkamp, 2007. My account differs ultimately as Forst's is based on a reflexive *right* to political justification, whereas the present account is based on political equality and its mediation through human rights (see also Christiano, *Constitution of Equality*, *supra* note 2, 156). Both accounts, of course, rely on Habermas' idea of co-originality between democratic sovereignty and human rights (Habermas, J., *Faktizität und Geltung. Beiträge zur Diskurstheorie des Rechts und des demokratischen Rechtsstaats*, Frankfurt am Main: Suhrkamp, 1998, Ch. III), although they provide different variations of that idea, notably by referring to an external right or value as foundation for their co-originality. See Brettschneider, C., *Democratic Rights – The Substance of Self-government*, Princeton: Princeton University Press, 2007, 29–38 for a similar interpretation of Habermas' co-originality.
95   See Tasioulas' critique of Griffin, *On Human Rights*: Tasioulas, 'Taking Rights', *supra* note 6.
96   See e.g. Waldron, J., 'Taking Group Rights Carefully', in Huscroft, G. and Rishworth, P. (eds), *Litigating Rights: Perspectives from Domestic and International Law*, Oxford: Hart, 2002, 203–220, on the difficulties of group rights in this respect.

in collective goods or individual interests whose social importance is part of the reason to protect them as rights.[97] Those rights reflect the very egalitarian dimension of all human rights, albeit maybe more strongly than others. One may think of anti-discrimination rights, in particular. All other human rights, however, also have a socio-comparative dimension through their egalitarian threshold. Finally, the egalitarian dimension of human rights may also be echoed in the idea of a fundamental or inviolable core of a human right as a limit on human rights' restrictions.[98] That dimension corresponds to the notion of inviolability as it captures what is inviolable in every individual right whatever the justifications. Contrary to the standard inviolability approaches,[99] each human right is grounded exclusively in an interest and not in a status, but in one that is deemed socio-comparatively fundamental and constitutive of one's political equality. What is inviolable is not the interest, as a result, but the fact that everyone without exclusion ought to benefit from its protection and hence from the right to have rights that protect it:[100] the discriminatory exclusion from the protection of the rights of certain people (usually due to their belonging to a sub-group that is vulnerable and structurally disadvantaged), as opposed to their mere restriction is what is precluded by inviolability.[101]

The relationship between human rights and political equality explains how closely tied human rights are to democracy.[102] If democracy is required by political equality and human rights and political equality are mutually constitutive, democracy is a requirement of human rights and implies human rights in return. Of course, one may object to the parochial dimension of a human rights account based on democratic equality. The parochialism objection is that international human rights law embodies a 'parochial' set of values or ordering of the same values that it unjustifiably imposes, through its quasi-universal or universal scope, on people and societies who do not share it. The proposed minimalist approach to political equality *qua* principle of transnational justice can escape this objection, however. Its institutional and po-

---

97   See e.g. Waldron, 'Taking Group Rights', *supra* note 96; Tasioulas, 'Human Rights', *supra* note 6.
98   It corresponds arguably to the German or Swiss notion of *Kerngehalt* and the idea of the inviolability of the fundamental core of every human right, including against democratic restrictions (e.g. popular constitutional initiatives in Switzerland; see e.g. Swiss Federal Council, *Rapport additionnel du Conseil fédéral au rapport du 5 mars 2010 sur la relation entre droit international et droit interne*, 31 March 2011, FF 2011 3401–47).
99   See e.g. Kamm, F., *Intricate Ethics: Rights, Responsibilities and Permissible Harm*, Oxford: Oxford University Press, 2007, 254; Kamm, F., 'Rights', in Coleman, J. and Shapiro, S. (eds), *The Oxford Handbook of Jurisprudence and Philosophy of Law*, Oxford: Oxford University Press, 2002, 476–513; Nagel, T., 'La valeur de l'inviolabilité', (1994) 99:2 *Revue de métaphysique et de morale* 149–66; Tasioulas, 'Justice, Equality', *supra* note 8. See also Wingert, 'Was ist', *supra* note 37.
100   See also Ladwig, 'Menschenwürde', *supra* note 42, 64 albeit in the dignity context.
101   This may actually explain, for instance, why direct forms of discrimination on prohibited grounds such as gender or race may not be justified in many legal orders. See Besson, S., 'Never Shall the Twain Meet? Gender Discrimination under EU and ECHR Law, (2008) 8.3 *Human Rights Law Review* 647–682.
102   See Christiano, *Constitution of Equality*, *supra* note 2; Gosepath, *Gleiche Gerechtigkeit*, *supra* note 2, 322 and 345. The proposed account differs from Gosepath's, however, in two important ways: first of all, it is meant as an account of vertical recoupling between *international* human rights and *domestic* democracy (see Besson, 'Decoupling and Recoupling', *supra* note 1) and, secondly, it understands human rights as *moral-political and inherently legal* and hence does not see a difference between moral human rights directly related to equal moral status and political democracy only indirectly related to equal moral status. See also Menke/Pollmann, *Philosophie der Menschenrechte*, *supra* note 2, 178 for this critique.

litical dimension and its need for contextual specification enable it to escape over-specification and parochialism.

This brings me to the third element in the definition of human rights: human rights are entitlements against *public institutions* (national, regional or international). Human rights are rights individuals have against the political community, i. e. against themselves collectively. They generate duties on the part of public authorities not only to protect equal individual interests, but also individuals' political status *qua* equal political actors. Public institutions are necessary for collective endeavour and political self-determination, but may also endanger them. Human rights enable the functioning of those institutions in exchange for political equality and protection from abuse of political power. This is why one can say that human rights both are protected by public institutions and provide protection against them; they exist because of collective endeavour in order both to favour and constrain it. Of course, other individuals may violate the interests protected by human rights and ought to be prevented from doing so by public institutions and in particular through legal means.[103] This ought to be the case whether those individuals' actions and omissions may be attributed to public authorities or not *qua de jure* or *de facto* organs. However, public institutions remain the primary addressees of human rights claims and hence their primary duty-bearers.[104]

Of course, there may be many overlapping political communities (e.g. international organizations (IOs), regional organizations and states) at stake and the present argument is not limited to the national polity and to the state – although we will see later how it excludes a world state. Nor is the argument limited to formal citizens[105] only or at least to those citizens who are also nationals; membership ought to include at varying degrees all those normatively subjected to the activities of political authorities and who are therefore subjects to the laws or decisions of the community.[106] This includes asylum seekers, economic migrants, stateless persons and so on. As we will see, human rights work as political irritants and mechanisms of gradual inclusion that lead to the extension of the political franchise and in some cases of citizenship itself to new subjects in the community. Nor, finally, does the argument

---

103   See Shue, H., *Basic Rights: Subsistence, Affluence and US Foreign Policy*, 2nd edn, Princeton: Princeton University Press, 1996, on the different types of negative and positive duties corresponding to a human right, including duties to protect and hence to prevent other agents from violating them.

104   This normative argument actually corresponds to the state of international human rights law that only directly binds states and/or international organizations to date and no other subjects (e.g. individuals and groups of individuals). The universality of human rights obligations does not imply the generality of the duty-bearers of the corresponding duties, i.e. a personal scope that reaches beyond institutional agents whether domestic or international (contra: O'Neill, O., 'The Dark Side of Human Rights', (2005) 81:2 *International Affairs* 427–39; Lafont, C. 'Accountability and Global Governance: Challenging the State-centric Conception of Human Rights', (2010) 3:3 *Ethics and Global Politics* 193–215, 203). See also Besson, 'Decoupling and Recoupling', *supra* note 1 on this question.

105   I am using 'citizenship' to mean democratic membership. Of course, one may be a citizen of a non-democratic state or a non-democratic post-national political community more generally, but this will not be my concern here.

106   Scope precludes not only addressing the question of the boundaries of democracy in this article, but also providing a full defence of the all-subjected principle endorsed here. See for a discussion of the all-affected or the all-subjected principles, e.g. Goodin, R., 'Enfranchising All Affected Interests, and Its Alternatives', (2007) 35 *Philosophy and Public Affairs* 40–68; Näsström, S., 'The Challenge of the All-Affected Principle', (2011) 59 *Political Studies* 116–34. See on the boundaries of democracy debate, Abizadeh, A., 'Closed Borders, Human Rights and Democratic Legitimation' in Hollenbach, D. (ed.), *Driven from Home: Human Rights and the New Realities of Forced Migration*, Washington DC: Georgetown University Press, 2010, 147–66.

imply that human rights apply within national borders only; if national political authorities subject the fundamental interests of individuals to norms and decisions outside its borders, those individuals deserve equal protection both in the decision-making process and the application of those decisions. This includes individuals and groups subjected to law-making and decision-making abroad.[107]

The institutional nature of human rights' duty-bearers is the main ground for the distinction between universal moral rights and human rights that are a subset of universal moral rights. Human rights are the universal moral rights of the individual members of a given political community. This explains their mutual relation to political equality. Universal moral rights also have an egalitarian dimension, of course, but it is one that pertains to the basic equal moral status of all persons as it was discussed in the previous section. As discussed, their equal moral status gives rise to mutual entitlements that one may refer to as universal moral rights. Those rights may be held against individuals and do not require institutions for the protection. This also explains, as we will see, the difference between human rights and universal moral rights regarding legalization.

ii. The Legality of Human Rights

It follows from the moral-political nature of human rights that the law is an important dimension of their recognition and existence. It is time to understand exactly how this is the case and to unpack the inherently legal dimension of human rights.

Just as moral rights are moral propositions and sources of moral duties, legal rights are legal propositions and sources of legal duties. They are moral interests recognized by the law as sufficiently important to generate moral duties.[108] The same may be said of legal human rights: legal human rights are fundamental and general moral interests recognized by the law as sufficiently important to generate moral duties.

Generally speaking, moral rights can exist independently from legal rights, but legal rights recognize, modify or create moral rights by recognizing moral interests as sufficiently important to generate moral duties.[109] Of course, there may be ways of protecting moral interests or even independent moral rights legally without recognizing them as legal 'rights'. Conversely, some legal rights may not actually protect pre-existing moral rights or create moral rights, thus only bearing the name of 'rights' and generating legal duties at the most.[110] The same cannot be said of human rights more specifically, however. True, universal moral interests and rights may be legally protected without being recognized as legal 'rights'. But, as we will see, human rights

---

107   See also Besson, S., 'The Extra-territoriality of the European Convention on Human Rights', (2012) 25:4 *Leiden Journal of International Law* forthcoming.

108   Raz, J., 'Legal Rights', (1984) 4:1 *Oxford Journal of Legal Studies* 1–21, 12. For a recent restatement of his theory of moral and legal rights and their relationship, see Raz, 'New World Order', *supra* note 83.

109   Legal recognition of human rights can therefore be taken to mean, depending on the context, both the legal recognition of an interest *qua* human right and the legal recognition of a preexisting human right.

110   Note that this duty is the primary moral duty to protect the interest that founds the legal human right, and not the secondary moral duty to obey the legal norm 'human right': see Besson, S., 'The Democratic Authority of International Human Rights', in Follesdal, A. (ed.), The Legitimacy of Human Rights, Cambridge: Cambridge University Press, 2012, forthcoming.

can only exist as moral rights *qua* legal rights. Conversely, one may imagine legal norms referred to as human rights that do not correspond to moral human rights. In such a case, the legal norms named 'human rights' would only give rise to legal duties and not to moral (rights-based) duties. Legal human rights, however, can only be regarded as rights *stricto sensu* when their corresponding duties are not only legal, but also moral.

Two additional remarks on the relationship between moral and legal rights and the relationship between moral and legal human rights are in order. The differences between rights and human rights, on the one hand, and between their respective moral and legal dimensions, on the other, can be quite important given the moral-political nature of human rights and what this implies in turn for their inherently moral and legal nature.[111]

Not all moral rights are legally recognized as legal rights, on the one hand. There are many examples of moral rights which have not been recognized as legal rights. Nor should all moral rights be recognized and protected legally. Respect for them should be a matter of individual conscience in priority.

The same cannot be said about human rights, however. True, not all universal moral rights have been or are recognized as legal human rights. Some are even expressly recognized as universal moral rights by the law even though they are not made into legal rights or modulated by the law.[112] A distinct question is whether they ought to be legalized and hence protected by law. Again, respect for universal moral rights ought to be voluntary in priority, and this independently from any institutional involvement. However, the universal moral rights that will become human rights create moral duties for institutions,[113] and hence for the law as well, to recognize and protect human rights.[114] Based on the moral-political account of human rights presented previously, the law provides the best and maybe the only way of mutually recognizing the socio-comparative importance of those interests in a political community of equals.[115] It enables the weighing of those interests against each other and the drawing of the political equality threshold or comparative line. Further, the law provides the only institutional framework in which the necessary pre-human rights recognition assessment of the abstract feasibility of human rights can take place, and in particular the abstract assessment of a feasible identification and egalitarian allocation of human rights duties and duty-bearers.

---

111 Contra Wellman, C.H., *The Moral Dimensions of Human Rights*, Oxford: Oxford University Press, 2011; Tasioulas, 'Taking Rights', *supra* note 6; Griffin, J., *On Human Rights*, Oxford: Oxford University Press, 2008, I argue that human rights are necessarily legal and not only moral.
112 One may think here of the moral rights mentioned by the 9th Amendment of the US Constitution.
113 Of course, as alluded to in section 1, mutual moral entitlements stemming from equal moral status also include other basic moral rights than human rights (which are a specific subset of universal moral rights), rights that may bind other individuals and not institutions like human rights, on the one hand, and rights that do not as a result need to be legalized unlike human rights, on the other.
114 See Raz, 'New World Order', *supra* note 83.
115 See e.g. Cohen, 'Rethinking', *supra* note 86, 599–600; Forst, 'Justification of Human Rights', *supra* note 2; Forst, 'Basic Right', *supra* note 84, 48–50. See even Pogge, T., 'Human Rights and Human Responsibilities', in De Greiff, P. and Cronin, C. (eds), *Global Justice and Transnational Politics*, Cambridge Mass.:The MIT Press, 2002, 151–196; reprinted with revisions in Kuper, A. (ed.), *Global Responsibilities: Who Must Deliver on Human Rights?*, New York: Routledge, 2005, 3–35, 3, fn. 26 who concedes this point in the case of civil and political rights. It seems, however, that the egalitarian dimension of human rights and hence their inherently legal nature would apply even more to the case of social and economic rights than to others.

In short, the law makes universal moral rights into human rights, just as politics turn equal moral status into political equality. As a result, in the moral-political account of human rights propounded here, the legal recognition of a fundamental human interest, in conditions of political equality, is part of the creation of a moral-political human right. In other words, while being independently justified morally and having a universal and general scope, human rights *qua* subset of universal moral rights are also of an inherently legal nature. To quote Jürgen Habermas, 'they are conceptually oriented towards positive enactment by legislative bodies.[116] Thus, while legal rights *stricto sensu* are necessarily moral in nature (*qua* rights), human rights (*qua* rights) are also necessarily legal and they are as a result both moral and legal rights.

Nor, on the other hand, do legal rights necessarily always pre-exist as independent moral rights. Most do and are legally recognized moral rights,[117] but others are legally created or legally specified moral rights.[118] In some cases, law and politics may affect a person's interests, thus in a sense enhancing the moral interest and/or its moral-political significance which are necessary for that interest to be recognized as a source of duties and hence as a right. One may think of zoning rights in the context of land planning, for instance, or of government bond-holders' rights.[119]

The same cannot be said about legal human rights, however: all of them necessarily also pre-exist as independent universal moral rights that are constitutive of equal moral status. However, the law can specify and weigh moral human interests when recognizing them as legal human rights. One may imagine certain political interests whose moral-political significance may stem from the very moral-political circumstances of life in a polity. As a result, the law does not create universal moral rights, but it can modulate them when recognizing them. Furthermore, the inherently moral-political nature of human rights and the role the law plays in recognizing given interests as sufficiently important in a group as to generate duties and hence human rights, make it the case that the law turns pre-existing universal moral rights into human rights and hence actually makes them human rights. As a result, human rights cannot pre-exist their legalization as independent moral human rights, but only as independent universal moral rights.

---

116 Habermas, J., 'Die Legitimation durch Menschenrechte', in *Die postnationale Konstellation. Politische Essays*, Frankfurt am Main: Suhrkamp, 1998, 170–92, 183. See also Habermas, *Faktizität*, *supra* note 94, 310–12; Habermas, 'Concept of Human Dignity', *supra* note 2, 470; Habermas, *Zur Verfassung*, *supra* note 40, 22 who now distinguishes between the *moral content* and the *legal form* of human rights, even though he talks of legal 'creation' (*Erzeugung*) in the corresponding footnote 19.

117 The legalization of preexisting moral rights is rarely a mere translation; it usually specifies and somehow changes the moral rights. See Meckled-Garcia, S. and Cali, B., 'Lost in Translation: The Human Rights Ideal and International Human Rights Law', in Cali, B. and Meckled-Garcia, S. (eds), *The Legalization of Human Rights, Multidisciplinary perspectives on human rights and human rights law*, London: Routledge, 2006, 11–31; and Cali, B. and Meckled-Garcia, S., 'Introduction: Human Rights Legalized – Defining, Interpreting and Implementing an Ideal', in Cali, B. and Meckled-Garcia, S. (eds), *The Legalization of Human Rights, Multidisciplinary Perspectives on Human Rights and Human Rights Law*, London: Routledge, 2006, 1–8.

118 See Raz, 'Legal Rights', *supra* note 108, 16–17. See also Raz, 'New World Order', *supra* note 83.

119 Both examples are given by Raz, 'Legal Rights', *supra* note 108, 16–17; and Raz, 'New World Order', *supra* note 83.

b. The Domestic and International Legality of Human Rights

The next question pertains to the political community that ought to be recognizing the existence of human rights legally, and hence whose members' political equality is in the making, and hence to the level of legalization of those rights.[120]

1. The Right to Have Rights

Per se, the legalization of human rights, i. e. the legal recognition and modulation of universal moral rights qua human rights, could take place either at the domestic or at the international level: through national or international legalization. Given what was said about the interdependence between human rights, political equality and democracy, however, the political process through which their legalization takes place ought to be democratic and include all those whose rights are affected and whose equality is at stake. As a result, using international law as main instrument to recognize fundamental and general human interests as sufficiently important to generate state duties at the domestic level is difficult. Not only does international law-making include many other states and subjects than those affected by the laws and decisions of the polity bound by human rights, but the conditions of political equality and the democratic quality of its processes are not yet secured at the international level.[121]

To solve this riddle and succeed in recoupling human rights and democracy across levels of governance, it is important to distinguish between two categories of rights: rights that pertain to the access to membership in a political community (rights to membership) and those that pertain to actual membership in the political community (membership rights). Interestingly, this distinction corresponds to two competing readings of Hannah Arendt's 1949 idea of the 'right to have rights' depending on whether one understands them as being moral or legal rights, first, and as being domestic or international rights, second.[122]

Starting with the former category, rights to equal political membership contribute to the constitution of an equal political status, as opposed to the second category of rights that protect that very equal political status. Rights to membership prohibit, for instance, submitting individuals to genocide, torture and other extreme forms of

---

120 The argument presented in this section is a summary of a lengthier argument developed in Besson, 'Human Rights', supra note 2. See also Besson, 'Decoupling and Recoupling', supra note 1.

121 See e.g. Christiano, 'Democratic', supra note 70, on the lack of representativity and the assymetry of international law-making processes from a democratic theory's perspective. See also Cohen, 'Rethinking', supra note 86, 599–600; Besson, 'Democratic Authority, supra note 110.

122 Arendt, 'Decline', supra note 88, 177–8. For her first essay on the topic, see Arendt, H., '"The Rights of Man": What Are They?', (1949) 3:1 Modern Review 24–37. For Arendt's views on human rights, see e.g. Benhabib, S., '"The right to have rights": Hannah Arendt on the contradictions of the nation-state', in The Rights of Others: Aliens, Residents, and Citizens, Cambridge: Cambridge University Press, 2004, 49–70; Gosepath, 'Hannah Arendts Kritik der Menschenrechte und ihr ,Recht, Rechte zu haben,' in Heinrich-Böll-Stiftung (ed), Hannah Arendt: Verborgene Tradition – Unzeitgemäße Aktualität?, Berlin: Akademie Verlag, 2007, 253–62; Cohen, J., 'Sovereignty and Rights: Thinking with and beyond Hannah Arendt', in Heinrich-Böll-Stiftung (ed.), Hannah Arendt: Verborgene Tradition – Unzeitgemäße Aktualität?, Berlin: Akademie Verlag, 2007, 291–309; Menke, Ch., 'The Aporias of Human Rights and the One Human Right: Regarding the Coherence of Hannah Arendt's Argument', (2007) 74:1 Social Research 739–62; Besson, S., 'The Right to Have Rights – From Human Rights to Citizens' Rights and Back', in Goldoni, M. and McCorkindale, C. (eds), Arendt and the Law, Oxford: Hart Publishing, 2012, 335–55.

cruel treatment, through which a community excludes individuals and does not treat them as equal members.[123] They also include rights to asylum (Art. 14 UDHR) and the customary right to *non-refoulement*.

Moral and legal rights to membership of this kind cannot be guaranteed exclusively from within a given political community since they work as constraints on democratic sovereignty and self-determination. This is why they are usually protected from the outside and through international human rights law.[124] Of course, to be democratically legitimate, they have to be recognized legally through inclusive and deliberative processes. This may prove difficult in the current circumstances of international law, but processes of that kind are incrementally developed in international law-making. Importantly, the legalization of international human rights is a two-way street that is not limited to a top-down reception but is also bottom-up and comes closer to a virtuous circle of legitimation. The recognition and existence of those rights *qua* international human rights that constrain domestic polities ought therefore to be based on democratic practises recognized domestically. And only those polities that respect international human rights are deemed legitimate in specifying the content of those rights and hence in contributing to the recognition and existence of those rights *qua* international human rights that will constrain themselves in return. This is what Buchanan refers to as the mutual legitimation of domestic and international law, and it applies very well to international human rights law.[125]

In short, rights to membership correspond to a first and main reading of Arendt's right to have rights: those universal moral rights, and potentially also international legal rights to membership, are rights that guarantee the ulterior benefit of human rights within each political community.[126] Those universal moral rights to have human rights are constitutive of one's equal moral status and amount, in political circumstances where the conditions of political equality are given, to a right to equal political membership and participation.

The second group of rights that guarantee membership in the political community, i. e. most human rights, can at least be regarded as legally protected universal moral rights and most of the time as legal rights as well. However, unless they refer to and correspond to existing domestic (moral-political and legal) human rights, they cannot (yet) be regarded as human rights for lack of an international moral-political community.[127]

Qua legal rights, those international human rights norms guarantee rights to individuals under a given state's jurisdiction, on the one hand, and to other states (or arguably IOs) (international human rights are usually guaranteed *erga omnes*), on the

---

123 See Cohen, 'Rethinking', *supra* note 86, 587.

124 See also Dworkin, *Justice, supra* note 2, 335–9 for a similar account of the difference between international human rights law and domestic human rights law.

125 On the bootstrapping between international human rights law-making and their democratic reception and interpretation at domestic level, see Buchanan, A., *Justice, Legitimacy, and Self-Determination: Moral Foundations for International Law*, Oxford: Oxford University Press, 2004, 187–189; Buchanan, 'Egalitarianism', *supra* note 2.

126 See e.g. Cohen, 'Rethinking', *supra* note 86; Benhabib, "'The right to have rights'", *supra* note 122, 56–61.

127 There is, in other words, a form of political parochialism or legal contingency of human rights that conditions their recognition as international legal human rights, well before parochialism arises as a problem for the scope of legitimacy of an existing legal human right. See also Raz, 'New World Order', *supra* note 83.

other, to have those rights guaranteed as 'human rights' within a given domestic community. They correspond to states' (and/or arguably IOs) duties to secure and ensure respect for those rights as 'human rights' within their own jurisdiction.[128] In that sense, international human rights duties are second-order duties for states (and/or arguably IOs) to generate first-order human rights duties for themselves under domestic law, i. e. international duties to have domestic duties. What those international human rights norms do, in other words, is protect legally the universal moral right to have rights discussed as a first kind of human rights, i. e. the right to equal membership in a moral-political community with all the other human rights this status implies.

Unlike most readings of Arendt's right to have rights,[129] this reading understands rights in the second category, i. e. membership rights, as universal moral rights which may also be protected as international legal rights. Their underlying nature as universal moral rights actually explains their *erga omnes* effects. They are not human rights themselves but are rights to have human rights, the latter being at once moral and legal rights and not only positive legal rights.

In sum, there are two groups of rights among the rights usually referred to as international human rights: the first group (rights to membership) to be legalized at the international level, while rights belonging to the second group (membership rights) have to be legalized in domestic law in a given political community before they can be recognized as human rights under international law. In the meantime, international law's human rights norms that protect rights in the latter category guarantee rights to have human rights protected under domestic law.

ii. From International Human Rights to Domestic Human Rights and Back

Interestingly, the normative considerations presented before about the locus of legitimation and legalization of human rights are reflected in contemporary processes of legalization of human rights under domestic and international law. They fit and justify, in other words, our current international human rights law and practice. The latter are indeed usually drafted in abstract and minimal terms, thus calling for domestic reception and specification.[130]

As a matter of fact, it is through the relationship of mutual reinforcement between citizens' rights and human rights and the productive tension between external guarantees and internal ones that human rights law has consolidated at both domestic and international levels.[131] International human rights generate duties of inclusion

---

128   See O'Neill, 'Dark Side', *supra* note 104, 433 on the distinction between first-order human rights duties at domestic level and second-order human rights duties generated by international human rights law.

129   See e.g. Benhabib, '"The right to have rights"', *supra* note 122; Gosepath, 'Hannah Arendts Kritik', *supra* note 122.

130   See Besson, 'Decoupling and Recoupling', *supra* note 1; Dworkin, *Justice*, *supra* note 2, 337–8.

131   See Besson, 'Decoupling and Recoupling', *supra* note 1; Habermas, 'Concept of Human Dignity', *supra* note 2, 478; Benhabib, S., 'Claiming Rights across Borders: International Human Rights and Democratic Sovereignty', (2009) 103:4 *American Political Science Review* 691–704; Benhabib, *Dignity in Adversity*, *supra* note 1, 16 and 126; Habermas, *Zur Verfassung*, *supra* note 40, 31–2, 36–8. Interestingly, neither Habermas, *Zur Verfassung*, *supra* note 40, nor Benhabib, *Dignity in Adversity*, *supra* note 1, whose accounts of human rights use Arendt's 'right to have rights', do distinguish between the

on domestic authorities and the democratic concretizations of citizens' rights, and the latter feed into international human rights guarantees in return. This constant interaction between human rights and citizens' rights is reminiscent of Arendt's universal right to have particular rights and the to-ing and fro-ing between the universal and the particular highlighted in the previous sections. Human rights are specified as citizens' rights but citizens' rights progressively consolidate into human rights in return.

This virtuous circle can actually be exemplified by the sources of international human rights law. International human rights law is indeed deemed to belong to general international law and finds its sources in general principles of international law, but arguably also in customary international law. Both sets of sources derive international norms from domestic ones and this jurisgenerative process is actually epitomized by the sources of international human rights law.[132] The mutual relationship between human rights and citizens' rights can also be confirmed by recent human rights practice, whether it is of a customary, conventional or even judicial nature. Citizens' rights contribute to the development of the corresponding international human rights' judicial or quasi-judicial interpretations. This is clearly the case in the European Court of Human Rights' case-law where common ground is a constant concern and is sought after when interpreting the European Convention on Human Rights (ECHR).[133]

Besides its explanatory force in light of current human rights practice, the proposed approach to international human rights has the further benefit of fitting the structure of the international legal order more generally. It puts international human rights law back into its political context. State sovereignty and political self-determination constitute indeed one of the pillars of the international order, a pillar which is complemented and not replaced or, strictly speaking, even restricted by the second pillar of international human rights law.[134] Through those two pillars and its dualistic structure, the international legal order protects the very interdependence between democracy and human rights alluded to before and hence keeps the tension between the individual and the group at the core of international law-making. International law guarantees the basic conditions for political equality and self-determination by protecting peoples through state sovereignty, on the one hand, and by protecting individuals through human rights, on the other.[135]

---

moral/legal nature, on the one hand, and the domestic/international legal nature, on the other; they conflate both issues.

132   See Besson, S., 'General Principles in International Law – Whose Principles ?', in Besson, S. and Pichonnaz, P. (eds), *Les principes en droit européen – Principles in European Law*, Zürich: Schulthess, 2011, 21–68, on general principles of international law as sources of international human rights law. See also Simma, B. and Alston, P., 'The Sources of Human Rights Law: Custom, *Jus Cogens* and General Principles', (1988–89) 12 *Australian Yearbook of International Law* 82–108; Flauss, J.F., 'La protection des droits de l'homme et les sources du droit international', in Société Française pour le Droit International, *La protection des droits de l'homme et l'évolution du droit international*, Colloque de Strasbourg, Paris: Pédone, 1998, 11–79.

133   See Besson, S., 'The *Erga Omnes* Effect of ECtHR's Judgements – What's in a Name?', in Besson, S. (ed.), *The European Court of Human Rights after Protocol 14 – First Assessment and Perspectives*, Collection Forum de droit européen, Zurich: Schulthess, 2011, 125–175.

134   See for a similar argument, Macklem, P., 'What is International Human Rights Law? Three Applications of a Distributive Account', (2007) 52 *McGill Law Journal* 575–604, 577; Cohen, 'Rethinking', *supra* note 86, 595–7.

135   See for a more detailed argument on the relationship between state sovereignty and international human rights, Besson, S., 'Sovereignty, International Law and Democracy: A Reply to Waldron',

3. Equality and International Human Rights Law

According to Buchanan, once the relationship between international human rights and equality has been established in a human rights account, the latter still needs to be tested in the light of the strong or robust non-discrimination rights enclosed in international human rights guarantees.[136] This section takes up the challenge and shows how the proposed model illuminates the current international human rights practice in the field of equality and non-discrimination. It also argues that it sheds light onto the relationship between international non-discrimination rights and other human rights, on the one hand, and that between the international non-discrimination principle and human rights, on the other.

Interestingly, indeed, equality and non-discrimination have been central to international human rights law ever since 1945.[137] Its pivotal role has taken many forms. One may mention, for instance, international human rights treaties combatting discrimination (e. g. the International Convention on the Elimination of All Forms of Racial Discrimination [CERD] and the International Convention on the Elimination of All Forms of Discrimination against Women [CEDAW]), but also international non-discrimination rights in human rights treaties (e.g. Art. 23 of the Charter of Fundamental Rights of the European Union) and international non-discrimination principles in human rights treaties (e. g. Art. 14 ECHR, Protocol 12 ECHR and Art. 26 of the International Covenant on Civil and Political Rights [ICCPR]). Whereas the second category of norms protects the self-standing individual right not to be discriminated against on certain suspect grounds without objective reasons, the third one gives domestic authorities the duty to respect human rights in a non-discriminatory way in practice. Anti-discrimination treaties, finally, usually comprise both individual non-discrimination rights of various types and a non-discrimination principle (e.g. Art. 5 CERD).

Curiously, despite the complexity of the different types and layers of rights and principles pertaining to equality and non-discrimination in international and domestic human rights law, human rights theorists have so far neglected to unpack those relationships.[138] Non-discrimination law is often assumed to be grounded in equality[139], and the principle of equality taken to justify (international human) rights to

---

(2011) 22 *European Journal of International Law* 373–87; Besson, S., 'Sovereignty', in Wolfrum, R. et al. (eds), *Max Planck Encyclopedia of Public International Law*, Oxford: Oxford University Press, 2012, online edition, [www.mpepil.com].

136 See Buchanan, 'Egalitarianism', *supra* note 2, 687–90, 709. This also implies *a contrario* that current international human rights law and, within it, international anti-discrimination law may be explained without reference to dignity, as I argued in the first section of the chapter.

137 See e.g. McCrudden, C., 'Human Rights and European Equality Law', in Meenan, H. (ed.), *Equality Law in an Enlarged European Union*, Cambridge: Cambridge University Press, 2007, 73–114; Bayefsky, A., 'The Principle of Equality or Non-discrimination in International Law', (1989) 10 *Human Rights Law Journal* 1–34.

138 For a few exceptions, however, albeit coming from the non-discrimination law side: Reibetanz Moreau, S., 'What is Discrimination?', (2010) 38:2 *Philosophy and Public Affairs* 143–79; Hellman, D., *When Is Discrimination Wrong?*, Cambridge, Mass.: Harvard University Press, 2008; McCrudden, 'European Equality Law', *supra* note 137; Holmes, E., 'Non-discrimination Rights without Equality', (2005) 68:2 *Modern Law Review* 175–94.

139 This is the case of the major international and European human rights treaties who guarantee the principles of equality and non-discrimination interchangeably in the same clauses. The same may be observed in the decisions and conclusions of the corresponding human rights monitoring bodies. See e.g. Besson, 'Never Shall', *supra* note 101; Besson, S., 'Evolutions in Anti-Discrimination Law within the ECHR and the ESC Systems', (2012) 60 *American Journal of Comparative Law* 147–80. In-

non-discrimination[140]. Very little more is usually added, however, to disentangle or connect those egalitarian norms in international human rights law. What explains the distinctiveness of non-discrimination rights and principles cannot, however, merely consist in the equal moral status underlying each human right and its egalitarian grounding. Their relationship to equal moral status has to be more specific than that or, at least, more central to the non-discrimination rights or principles if one is to be able to distinguish them from other human rights.

In what follows, I will take non-discrimination rights and principles in turn and show how this could play out. As I will argue, however, this need not imply that they ought to be related to a more robust form of equality than equal moral status. They may, of course, but this then branches into a different debate.

a. International Non-discrimination Rights and Human Rights

The scope of this paper precludes surveying the characteristic features of all forms of domestic, regional and international non-discrimination legislation.[141] Notably, however, some entail individual rights, while some do not.[142]

Non-discrimination rights are self-standing individual rights not to be discriminated, i. e. treated unfavourably either through equal treatment in different situations or different treatment in comparable situations on certain suspect grounds and without objective reasons. What is specific about non-discrimination rights is their collective dimension. They protect individuals against inequalities of status that are socially generated by reference to their membership in a structurally disadvantaged group.

In a nutshell, there are three understandings of group or collective rights one may encounter depending on the criterion used to qualify them as collective.[143] The

---

terestingly, when it is no longer a principle that is at stake, but an individual right, as there cannot be an individual right to a value such as equality, those decisions and conclusions mention a right to non-discrimination and not to equality.

140　In this sense, this consists in the same dual usage of equality *qua* value that grounds human rights and *qua* something one has a human right to (it is the case in EU law e.g.: ECJ, Case 149/77, *Gabrielle Defrenne v Société Anonyme Belge de Navigation Aérienne Sabena* [1978] ECR 1365; Charter of Fundamental Rights of the European Union, OJ 2010/C 83/02, 30 March 2010, Preamble and Art. 20 ff.; Directive 2006/54/EC of the European Parliament and of the Council of 5 July 2006 on the implementation of the principle of equal opportunities and equal treatment of men and women in matters of employment and occupation (recast), OJ 2006/L 204/23, 26 July 2006, Preamble, par. 2 and Art. 4 ff; Council Directive 2004/113/EC of 13 December 2004 implementing the principle of equal treatment between men and women in the access to and supply of goods and services, OJ 2004/L 337/37, 21 December 2004, Preamble, par. 4 and Art. 1), as the one observed in the context of dignity –the latter is both used as a grounding principle of human rights and as something one has a right to (see e.g. Waldron, J., 'Dignity and Rank', (2007) 48 *Archives européennes de sociologie* 201–37, on this dual usage of dignity).

141　See e.g. Moeckli, D. et al. (eds), *International Human Rights Law*, Oxford: Oxford University Press, 2010, Ch. 9; Fredman, S., *Discrimination Law*, 2nd edn, Oxford 2011; De Schutter, O., *International Human Rights Law*, New York: Cambridge University Press, 2010, Ch. 7.

142　Using individual rights and not mere norms or principles in this context may be explained by reference to the duty-bearers and the kind of entitlements and reciprocal duties one is addressing. See Altman, A., 'Discrimination', in Zalta, E. N. (ed.), *Stanford Encyclopedia of Philosophy*, available at: >http://plato.stanford.edu/archives/spr2011/entries/discrimination<.

143　See Besson, S., 'Gruppen, Rechte und Konflikte – Kommentar zu Martha Nussbaum', in Holderegger, A., Imbach, R., Weichlein, S. and Zurbuchen, S. (eds.), *Hat der Humanismus eine Zukunft? Heraus-*

first one understands group rights by reference to the *exercize* of the right. The right and the interest protected are individual but the right is exercized collectively, such as the right to self-government. There the interest of the group is the sum of individual interests in the group. The second understanding of group rights refers to the *kind of interest* protected by the right or to the kind of value it has. The right is individual but the interest protected or its value is collective. One may mention the right to be elected, the right to due process or minority rights such as the rights that belong to women, children, ethnic or religious groups. Finally, a third understanding of group rights is based on the *right-holder* and beneficiary of the interest it protects. Two sub-groups may be distinguished: both the interest and the right may be collective,[144] although it may also be the case that the interest is individual but the right is collective because the individual interest pertains to a collective good.[145] Importantly, the collective interest in the first sub-group is not merely the sum of individual interests in the group.[146] As examples, one may mention cultural rights, the right to self-determination or the right to security. Of all three, it is the third kind of group rights that is most commonly referred to *qua* group rights *stricto sensu*. The third meaning is also the most controversial one. Of course, the third meaning is usually combined with the first and second understandings. But it need not be the case. And the first and second understandings may not imply group rights *stricto sensu*.

Non-discrimination rights are individual rights, but they belong to the second group of collective rights: the rights are individual but the interests protected are collective as the inequalities at stake affect individuals with heightened vulnerability to the standard threats protected by human rights due to their belonging to a structurally disadvantaged group. Those individual rights are needed to protect the equal moral status of each individual within the larger group when his or her belonging to a sub-group is a source of social inequalities.[147] The key difference to other human rights, however, is that the absence of unequal treatment constitutes the actual objective interest protected by non-discrimination rights. Equal moral status does not merely play a role as a threshold of recognition of the importance of the protected interests, but actually becomes the interest to protect as well. The groups whose members are protected through non-discrimination rights may vary from society to society and from period to period depending on which social dimension is used by others to treat individuals as inferiors at each point in time and place. This explains why grounds of discrimination used by non-discrimination rights are usually part of an open list so as to be able to adapt across time and place.[148]

Of course, the *prima facie* inegalitarian nature of those group-specific non-discrimination rights has been criticized.[149] Recognizing unequal rights to correct social inequalities seems indeed to fly in the face of the principle of equal moral status

---

forderungen-Antworten im Fragment, Basel: Schwabe Verlag and Academic Press, Fribourg, 2011, 200–14; Buchanan, *Justice, supra* note 125, 409–13.

144 See e.g. Waldron, 'Taking Group Rights', *supra* note 96.

145 See e.g. Raz, J., *The Morality of Freedom*, Clarendon: Oxford 1986, 247–55.

146 Contra: Miller, D., 'Group Rights, Human Rights, and Citizenship', (2002) 10 *European Journal of Philosophy* 178–95, 184–85.

147 See Altman, 'Discrimination', *supra* note 142. See also Nickel, J., *Making Sense of Human Rights,* 2nd edn., Oxford: Blackwell Publishing, 2007, 155 on what he refers to as 'minority rights'.

148 See Lippert-Rasmussen, K., 'The Badness of Discrimination', (2006) 9 *Ethical Theory and Moral Practice* 167–85.

149 For a discussion, see Besson, 'Gruppen', *supra* note 143; Waldron, 'Taking Group Rights', *supra* note 96.

qua threshold of importance of all protected interests and human rights. This has even generated conflicts between individual rights of members and non-members of the protected groups, on the one hand, and non-discrimination rights, on the other. One may argue, however, that depending on the society and the kind of group inequalities it is faced with, non-discrimination rights are necessary to the protection of other human rights. It is difficult to see indeed how the egalitarian dimension of other human rights could be respected were those social inequalities to subsist. In that respect, non-discrimination rights reinforce the protection of the equal moral status of every person by other individual human rights. This enhanced egalitarian dimension of non-discrimination rights has numerous consequences for their regime *qua* human rights. One may mention, for instance, the specific restriction and justification regimes that apply to them, and the ways conflicts of non-discrimination rights are resolved in particular.

Finally, it is important to note that some individual rights that often go by name as non-discrimination rights are in fact 'dignity rights'. They may be explained by reference to the third understanding of dignity discussed in the first section of the chapter. One may think here of the right not to be object to harassment in particular. That right is often included into non-discrimination rights' catalogues, but does not require a differentiated treatment and cannot therefore be analysed in a non-discrimination law and rights framework.[150]

b. International Non-Discrimination Principle and Human Rights

There is a second concretization of equal moral status in international human rights law that is also referred to as the principle of non-discrimination. It differs from the general principle of equal treatment as it prohibits, in the context of the enjoyment of human rights, treating equally or differently individuals situated in different or equal circumstances when that treatment takes place on prohibited grounds and without an objective and proportionate justification.

Again, the idea is to protect individuals belonging to vulnerable or structurally disadvantaged groups against exclusion and to promote their integration. The non-discrimination principle protects equal moral status by making sure no discrimination arises in the context of the implementation of human rights. The groups whose members are protected through non-discrimination clauses of that kind may vary from society to society and from period to period depending on which social dimension is used by others to treat individuals as inferiors at each point in time and place. This explains why those grounds of discrimination are usually part of an open list so as to be able to adapt across time and place.[151]

The role of the principle of non-discrimination is to reinforce the protection of equal moral status by each human right and to complement self-standing non-discrimination rights. It gives domestic authorities the duty to respect other human rights in a non-discriminatory way in practice. The fact that it amounts to an additional layer of protection of equal moral status, distinct from human rights, clearly results from its location in international human rights treaties. It is usually protected through a general equality or non-discrimination clause at the end of the enumera-

---

150 See also Besson, 'Evolutions', *supra* note 139.
151 See Lippert-Rasmussen, 'Badness', *supra* note 148.

tion of various human rights.[152] Moreover, it is usually not formulated as an individual human right like all others, but as a principle for that very same reason.

Note that the non-discrimination principle should not be confused with other more general uses of equality, and in particular with the principle of equality before and in the law that is one of the founding principles of any legal order. Equality before the law is indeed one of the dimensions of political equality and political emanations of equal moral status and of the right to have rights in political circumstances as a result.

c. International Human Rights and Other Forms of Robust Equality

Finally, there are other legal means than non-discrimination rights and the non-discrimination principle to combat social inequalities. One may use more robust versions of the principle of equality to do so, and in particular the principle of distributive equality. Various legal instruments have been devised to promote the equality of resources or welfare, and the equality of outcome or opportunity.

Those various forms of robust equality often trickle into the application of non-discrimination rights and principles that are then interpreted and used so as to promote those forms of equality. There is no necessary connection between the two, however.

First of all, non-discrimination rights and principles aim at protecting individuals against treating them as inferiors, and not so much against other forms of unequal treatment.[153] There are two further dimensions one may emphasize to distinguish non-discrimination rights and principles from those robust understandings of equality: non-discrimination rights and principles usually prohibit certain intents (and correlated actions or omissions) and not necessarily a given state of affairs, on the one hand, and non-discrimination rights and principles do not usually require more than a heuristic comparator, on the other.[154]

Secondly, those robust forms of equality are also distinct from international human rights in general. They may actually be in conflict with international human rights law and its basic egalitarian dimension. It suffices to think here of affirmative action programmes promoting equality of outcome. This is why one cannot assume that human rights and robust equality are inherently connected beyond equal moral status. Nor can one simply assume that human rights are instrumental to robust equality or vice-versa. Of course, non-discrimination rights may contribute in practice to securing equality of opportunity, but this is not necessarily always the case. The common basic egalitarian dimension of both human rights and the conflicting equality-based measures may help resolve the conflict in some cases, moreover.

Identifying the egalitarian dimension of human rights by reference to equal moral status and not to those more robust forms of equality is essential to rebut the equality-based parochialism critique of international human rights. Clearly, the egalitarian dimension of human rights is bound to raise concerns of that kind. And I

---

152 See e.g. Art. 2 UDHR; Art. 14 ECHR and Art. 1 P12 ECHR; Art. 26 ICCPR.
153 See Buchanan, 'Egalitarianism', *supra* note 2, 687–90, 709.
154 On this difference, see Dworkin, R., *Taking Rights Seriously*, Cambridge M.A: Harvard University Press, 1977, 370. For others in the field of non-discrimination theory, see Moreau, 'What is Discrimination', *supra* note 138; Hellman, *Discrimination*, *supra* note 138; Holmes, 'Non-discrimination', *supra* note 138.

have alluded to this before in the context of political equality and the relationship between human rights and democracy. Here, one should stress that the distinction between equal moral status and more robust forms of equality actually fits the practice and law on international human rights. Except in Europe,[155] international human rights and non-discrimination rights and principles have not been interpreted to imply some of the most robust egalitarian goals. States Parties are allowed to do so and promote them through their implementation of international human rights and non-discrimination rights and principles, but there are generally no positive duties to promote equality of opportunities or outcome, e. g. through affirmation action programmes or other special measures.[156]

Note that those robust versions of equality should not be confused with one kind of international human rights: social and economic rights. Those rights' content and protected interests have been recognized as human rights by reference to equal political membership and so as to make sure the material conditions for that membership are respected. Those rights are the mere confirmation of the egalitarian dimension of all human rights across the board and they contribute, as a consequence, to combatting material and social inequalities. They do not as such justify or require measures to promote and protect robust forms of equality.

Conclusion

A remarkable feature of the contemporary philosophical literature on international human rights is its lack of in-depth engagement with the principle of equality. The reverse is also true as egalitarian scholars rarely dwell on the relationship between equality and international human rights. Following other authors who have recently threaded the same path, this chapter had as its aim to uncover the egalitarian dimension of human rights and draw some of its implications for international human rights and non-discrimination law. The chapter's argument unravelled in three steps.

A first section of the chapter presented a conception of equal moral status and its relationship to political equality. It claimed that the basic moral equality or equal moral status of persons may be defended separately from more robust forms of equality, such as distributive equality in particular. Equal moral status comprises two indissociable elements: the idea that all persons should be regarded as having the same moral worth and the idea that this equal moral status is relational and the basis for mutual moral claims of which some are basic universal moral rights. When the political circumstances are given and when individuals are not only subjected to the same decisions and laws, but also share interdependent and roughly equal stakes, I argued that equal moral status implies political equality. In turn, just as a person's equal moral status implies corresponding mutual moral rights and duties, political equality gives rise to corresponding equal participation rights. Political equality is

---

155 See e.g. on EU anti-discrimination law or the European Social Charter, Bell, M., *Racism and Equality in the European Union*, New York: Oxford University Press, 2008; Bell, M., 'Combating Discrimination through Collective Complaints under the European Social Charter', in De Schutter, O. (ed), *The European Social Charter. A Social Constitution for Europe*, Bruxelles: Bruylant, 2010, 39–48; Besson, 'Evolutions', *supra* note 139.

156 For an exception, however, see e.g. CERD, General recommendation No. 32, *The meaning and scope of special measures in the International Convention on the Elimination of All Forms Racial Discrimination*, 24 September 2009, UN Doc CERD/C/GC/32; and Art. 2 and 4 ICERD.

therefore best served by a democratic regime where individuals are recognized and can practice those equal participation rights effectively. In the first section, I also argued that dignity works at the most as placeholder and indicator of equal moral status and is therefore redundant in the human rights context. More specifically, I explained how it cannot be used to ground human rights.

In the second section, I explained how human rights *tout court* are related to political equality and how human rights theory can explain that connection while, at the same time, salvaging their universal justification against the parochialism critique. I argued that human rights are a sub-set of universal moral rights that protect fundamental and general human interests against the intervention of (national, regional or international) public institutions. I focused on the ties between political equality and human rights to explain how human rights are a subset of universal moral rights that bind political entities and have a moral-political nature. Human rights are based on objective interests that are recognized as sufficiently fundamental to give rise to duties. The threshold of importance of those interests lies in political equality: members of the polity grant each other those rights mutually and become political equals by doing so. The grounding of human rights in objective interests but by reference to political equality explains in turn why human rights and democracy are closely related.

The second section then turned to the implications of the egalitarian dimension of human rights for international human rights and especially international human rights law. The proposed egalitarian account of human rights confirms, I argued, the inherent legality of human rights as the law provides the best and maybe the only way of mutually recognizing the social-comparative importance of those interests in a political community of equals. Democratic law actually enables the weighing of those interests against each other and the drawing of the political equality threshold or comparative line. Given the moral-political and inherently legal nature of human rights and given their ties to political equality and democracy, the legalization of human rights ought to take place within democratic settings. As international law-making processes may not (yet) be deemed sufficiently democratic, the locus of legalization and hence of legitimation of human rights remains domestic, or at the most regional. This raises a puzzle for the role and justification of international human rights law. That puzzle may be solved, I argued, by reference to Arendt's right to have rights and by distinguishing between two types of universal moral rights: rights to political membership and rights of membership. The former are universal moral rights and can be guaranteed in international law as legal rights, but may not be regarded as human rights *stricto sensu*. The latter, by contrast, are universal moral rights and legal rights that become human rights on the basis of their domestic guarantees and the way in which those guarantees are then fuelled back into international law guarantees. Indeed, international human rights generate duties of inclusion on domestic authorities and the democratic concretizations of citizens' rights, and the latter feed into international human rights guarantees in return. This finds a confirmation, I argued, in the international and domestic human rights law practice where the sources and the legitimacy of those norms are closely intertwined.

A third and final section of the argument was dedicated to exploring the implications of the egalitarian dimension of human rights for the relationship between human rights, non-discrimination rights and the equality principle in international law. It explained how to distinguish the egalitarian dimension of all human rights from specific international non-discrimination rights, from the non-discrimination principle that apply to human rights enforcement within all major international human rights treaties and, finally, from more robust international non-discrimination norms based on distributive equality. This third section showed how the proposed egalitarian reading of human rights not only fits our international human rights law practice, but also that it explains how international human rights relate to the non-discrimination rights, principles and norms that international human rights law includes.

Olivier Jouanjan

A Philological Turn in the Science of Law:
History and Metaphysics in Savigny's Work[1]

In 1815, Fr. C. von Savigny founded, together with two of his colleagues from the University of Berlin, the *Journal for historical legal science*. The name of the journal alone is enough to give us a clear indication of Savigny's scientific agenda. It was not a journal for the *history of law*, but a journal *for historical legal science*[2]. Thus, the project's main object was not history. The object was not a reform of legal history; its aim was essentially a reform of the science of law, via a *historisation* of this science, a historisation that deeply affects it on a methodological level.

Though this interest for the history of law is evidently considerable for Savigny, it is nevertheless secondary; it is the consequence of a wider project aiming at the establishment of a philosophical or theoretical foundation of the science of law and its object.

Hence the distance between Savigny's program and the one that made its appearance as soon as the middle of the 18th century, aiming at the modernization of historical science; its main laboratory was the University of Goettingen, and its main agent among the legal scholars was Gustav Hugo (1764–1844). In his *Historik*, Droysen (1808–1884) described the University of Goettingen at the turn of the century as an environment where a "monumental historical activity" was taking place, where "Gatterer, Spittler, Michaelis, Heyne, Pütter, all the way to Hugo, that is theologists, legal philosophers and public law scholars, all took action in the same direction"[3]. This orientation of the Goettingen school consisted of an effort to "go beyond a historiography that contends itself with simply recording major political events", to try to offer causal explanations to scientific data; it was fundamentally a "pragmatic, non speculative movement"[4]. As a causalist and thus mechanical movement, it was basically still mainly influenced by the Enlightenment.

Even though Hugo was an innovator of the history of law, he is not *per se* the founder of the "Historical School of Law", especially if the latter is understood as the specific direction that Savigny, and, after him, Puchta gave to legal thinking. Savigny undoubtedly appreciated and valued the impressive erudition of the Goettingen professor, and tried, as early as 1806, to enlist him as one of the supporters of the new science, whose basic principles had already taken form and shape

---

1   For the translation, I want to thank warmly Vasiliki Vouleli, Strasbourg/Freiburg im Breisgau.
2   See J. Rückert, "Geschichtlich, praktisch, deutsch. Die 'Zeitschrift für geschichtliche Rechtswissenschaft' (1815–1850), das 'Archiv für die civilistische Praxis' (1818–1867) und die 'Zeitschrift für deutsches Recht und deutsche Rechtswissenschaft' (1839–1861)", in M. Stolleis (ed.), *Juristische Zeitschriften. Die neuen Medien des 18.–20. Jahrhunderts*, Frankfurt a.M., Klostermann, 1999, p. 125 *sq.*
3   Quoted in M. Behnen, "Statistik, Politik, und Staatengeschichte von Spittler bis Heeren", in H. Boockmann / H. Wellenreuther (eds.), *Geschichtswissenschaft in Göttingen*, Göttingen, Vandenhoeck & Ruprecht, 1987, p. 76–77.
4   R. Vierhaus, "Göttingen und die Anfänge der modernen Geschichtswissenschaft", in H. Boockmann / H. Wellenreuther (eds.), *Geschichtswissenschaft in Göttingen*, *op. cit.*, p. 11.

in Savigny's mind[5]. However, when it came to the question of the meaning and the place of history in legal studies, the difference of opinion between the two men couldn't have been greater. As Joachim Rueckert rightly points out, the link that Savigny was trying to establish between the "historical" and the "scientific" was perfectly obscure to Hugo[6]. What was incomprehensible or inconceivable to him was the meaning of the adverb that Savigny employed to insist on the scope of his own project, when he spoke of a science of law that would be "truly" or "genuinely" historical. What was perfectly strange to Hugo was this revolution of thought that was taking place, at the end of the 18th and the beginning of the 19th century, not only directly against Kant – especially in Herder's new philosophy of history – but also, following in Kant's footsteps, in the german idealism, in Hegel's philosophical history and, in particular, in Schelling's history of the subject. These new approaches gave a new ontological significance to history[7].

For reasons that we cannot possibly elucidate in a few pages, if one wants to understand and interpret the sense of historical thinking of *this* Historical School of Law[8], one must take special interest in the first German romanticism, mainly expressed through the Schlegel brothers' journal *Athenaeum,* as well as in the work of Schelling, who was in his youth, in Jena, close to the circle of the first romantics[9].

*

When Schelling delivered his famous *"Lessons on the method of academic studies"* at the University of Jena in the summer of 1802, he emphasized the new cult of history that was being established in German thought and science: "The study of science and art in light of their historical development has become some sort of religion: the philosopher recognizes, in their history, the as yet unveiled inventions of the universal spirit – so to speak, the greatest science and genius are expressed in this

---

5   See Savigny's recension of the 3rd edition of Hugo's *Lehrbuch der Geschichte des Römischen Rechts* in *Allgemeine Literatur-Zeitung* (1806) (reprinted in Savigny, *Vermischte Schriften*, vol. 5, Berlin, Veit, 1850, pp. 1 *sq.*).

6   J. Rückert, "Savigny et la méthode juridique", in *L'esprit de l'école historique du droit, Annales de la Faculté de Droit de Strasbourg*, nouvelle série, n° 7, 2004, p. 85; "Geschichtlich, praktisch, deutsch ...", *op. cit.*, p. 119.

7   See: G. Hugo, "Rezension zu 'Zeitschrift für geschichtliche Rechtswissenschaft', Band 1", *Göttingische Gelehrte Anzeigen*, 1816, pp. 1145 *sq.*

8   "This" historical school: during the 1820's–1830's arises another historical school, the "Germanist" one. The domination of roman law has to be contested. The german spirit has his particular way that cannot be included in the roman law. The reception of roman law in the 16th century was a violence done by an educated elite against the very german people. The most important testimony of the harshness of this opposition remains the book that the Germanist Georg Beseler wrote especially against Puchta, the disciple of Savigny: *Volksrecht und Juristenrecht*, Leipzig, Weidmann, 1843.

9   Concerning his relationship to the romantics, it should be here briefly noted that Savigny went to Jena, heart of the so-called "first romantics", as he just finished his studies. At the time he was a passionate reader of the *Athenaeum*. He married later one of the Brentano sisters, Kunigunde. Clemens von Brentano and Achim von Arnim were some of his best friends. The brothers Grimm were his students in Marburg and Jakob Grimm became later a loyal friend, even if some tensions appeared between him and Savigny. About his intellectual link to German Idealism, see: Rückert, *Idealismus, Jurisprudenz und Politik bei Friedrich Carl von Savigny*, Ebelsbach, Gremer, 1984; Jouanjan, *Une histoire de la pensée juridique en Allemagne,* Paris, PUF, 2005. About the relationship of the most important disciple of Savigny, Georg Friedrich Puchta, with Schelling, see: H.-P. Haferkamp, *Georg Friedrich Puchta und die "Begriffsjurisprudenz"*, Frankfurt a.M., Klostermann, 2004, especially p. 315 *sq.*

knowledge".[10] Thus, the ultimate science is philology: "Its object is the historical construction of works of art and science, whose history (*Geschichte*) it must understand and expose in living intuition (*lebendige Anschauung*)[11]." Philology becomes in a way the science of all sciences, since even the natural sciences find in it a model, a prototype – at last if we consider philology in its true sense, as an internal history reaching for the living intuition of its object, and not in the way it was seen by the archaic knowledge practiced until then in the shape of an external and mechanical history: "Nature is a book composed of fragments and rhapsodies of different eras. Each mineral is a true philological problem. Geology is still waiting for a Wolf[12] that will deconstruct the earth as Wolf did with the works of Homer, in order to expose its composition[13]". Geologists would soon speak of the "archives of the earth" the same way historians speak of the archives of humanity.

Savigny's ambition was no different. The object of his science of law, whose conception he'd been meditating since his youth, was precisely the object of a philological science of law in Schelling's sense: the historical construction of law and of legal science, whose history one must understand and expose in the form of a *living intuition*[14]. The *historisation* of legal thinking that he aimed to accomplish by doing that was nothing but an effort to raise the dated *Jurisprudenz* to the level of a true legal science; form the viewpoint of this philological paradigm, historisation necessarily means scientification. If we look at it this way, the parallel is striking: in the same way that Wolf, following his master Heyne, had imposed the expression "science of antiquity" (*Altertumswissenschaft*) in order to designate a renewed philology, Savigny would impose the term "Legal science" (*Rechtswissenschaft*) to qualify the *Jurisprudenz* such as the latter was renewed through the efforts of the historical school[15].

If the project of the *Altertumswissenschaft* can be caracterised, as by Wolf, as a "questioning of the archaic humanism, stuck in the simple critique of text and language, as a transformation of philology from a simple study of language into a sci-

---

10   F.W.J. Schelling, *Vorlesungen über die Methode des akademischen Studiums*, *SW* I, 5, p. 226. *SW* = F.W.J. Schelling, *Sämtliche Werke*, ed. by K.F.A. Schelling, Stuttgart, Cotta, 1856–1861, I: Erste Abtheilung, vol. 1–10; II: Zweite Abtheilung, vol. 1–4.

11   *Ibid.*, p. 45. *SW* I, 5, p. 246.

12   Friedrich August Wolf (1759–1824) was the most famous philologist in Germany at the beginning of the 19th century. His masterpiece remains his *Prolegomena ad Homerum* (1795). Savigny knew the main works of Wolf, not only the work about Homer (letter to Friedrich Creuzer, 1807 July the 14th, in Stoll, *Friedrich Karl v. Savigny. Ein Bild seines Lebens mit einer Sammlung seiner Briefe*, vol. 1, Berlin, C. Heymann, 1927, p. 304) but also (letter to Creuzer, 1808 January the 29th, *ibid.*, p. 313) the fundamental essay, in which Wolf intended to renew the old philology as a "science of Antiquity" ("Darstellung der Altertumswissenschaft nach Begriff, Umfang, Zweck und Werth", in Wolf/Buttmann [eds.], *Museum der Altertumswissenschaft*, vol. 1, Berlin, Reimer, 1807). In 1810, Wolf and Savigny became colleagues at the new founded University of Berlin.

13   *Ibid.*, p. 46. *SW* I, 5, p. 247.

14   These two terms, "intuition" (*Anschauung*) and "living" (*lebendig*), are also key-words in Savigny (*lebendige Anschauung, lebendigste Anschauung, Anschaulichkeit und Lebendigkeit*, etc.). See: D. Nörr, „Savignys Anschauung und Kants Urteilskraft", N. Horn (dir.), *Europäisches Rechtsdenken in Geschichte und Gegenwart. Festschrift für Helmut Coing zum 70. Geburtstag*, vol. 1, München, Beck, 1982, pp. 615 *sq*.

15   The expression "science of law" (*Rechtswissenschaft*) is not an "invention of the historical school of law", as Paul Koschaker says (*Europa und das römische Recht*, 3rd ed., München, Berlin, C.H. Beck, 1958, p. 210). *Iuris scientia* was already occasionally used in the Antiquity, probably under the influence of the Stoa which contested the aristotelian sepration between *prudentia* and *scientia*. In the second half ot the 18th century, this expression can be found in Blackstone or Kant for instance. However, it is true that Savigny has popularized the word *Rechtswissenschaft* among the german lawyers of the 19th century. See: J. Schröder, *Wissenschaftstheorie und Lehre der "praktischen Jurisprudenz" auf deutschen Universitäten an der Wende zum 19. Jahrhundert*, Frankfurt a.M., Klostermann, 1979.

ence that conceives the whole and its implications without drowning in erudite details", if its purpose is "the apprehension of Antiquity as a living totality, as *Gesamtleben,* as an organism that evolves according to its own laws of life, whose spirit one must penetrate, something that can only be achieved through a comprehensive approach aiming to coincide with the object of one's studies", which, in its turn, would have to pass by the "representation of language as essentially historical[16]", one cannot possibly ignore the resemblance between this project and Savigny's one for an essentially historical science of law. The knowledge of the latter would have to pass by a renewal of legal hermeneutics, not without a certain affinity with the establishment, at that time, of a general theory of hermeneutics by theologist Friedrich Schleiermacher[17]. Though criticized in some of its aspects, Wolf's approach, as well as his *Prolegomena,* was approved by Goethe, by Wilhelm von Humboldt, even by the Schlegel brothers, that is by some of the most significant intellectual forces of that time[18]. And these are precisely the sources of young Savigny's intellectual training[19].

One can just as easily see to what extent Savigny's project corresponded to what Ernst Behler considers as a turn in Fr. Schlegel's esthetic thinking: aiming to constitute a theory of poetry based on its history, a history that is unbalanced due to the significance of the Greek literature paradigm[20]. In Savigny's work, too, the aim is to construct a legal theory on the basis of its history, a history that is also unbalanced, due this time to the specific significance of the Roman law paradigm.

Because law *is* history, legal science *must be* historical. History of law is consequently not to be considered as an auxiliary science (*Hilfswissenschaft*), external to, and distinct from the true legal science, but as the science that constitutes legal science itself. Savigny clearly stated that as early as 1802, in his course on methodology in Marburg: "The *Jurisprudenz* is an historical science[21]." It is also, and to the same extent, a "philosophical science", the two aspects being necessarily linked and legal science being "perfected" or "accomplished" (*vollendet*) by this liaison. That was, as Savigny said back in 1802, "a new vision for science" that must be subjected to "proper scientific treatment". Desiring to associate Hugo, the great master, to this

---

16 J. Quillien, *G. de Humboldt et la Grèce. Modèle et histoire*, P.U. Lille, 1983, p. 17.

17 About these links: J. Rückert, "Savignys Hermeneutik – Kernstück einer Jurisprudenz ohne Pathologie", in Jan Schröder (ed.), *Theorie der Interpretation vom Humanismus bis zur Romantik – Rechtswissenschaft, Philosophie, Theologie*, Stuttgart, Franz Steiner, 2001. Schleiermacher's *Hermeneutik*, his lectures on this topic, has been translated in french: F.D.E. Schleiermacher, *Herméneutique*, Paris, Cerf, 1987. Such as Wolf and Savigny, Schleiermacher belongs to the first group of professors who came to the University of Berlin right at the beginning in 1810.

18 See: G. Gusdorf, *Les origines de l'herméneutique*, Paris, Payot, 1988, p. 107. Wolf had a close relationship to Goethe. Eckermann relates how Goethe gave a dinner in honour of Wolf on April 1824 the 19th (*Conversations avec Eckermann*, french translation, Paris, Gallimard, 1988, p. 114). About the relationships between Humboldt and Wolf, see: Quillien, *op. cit.*, pp. 15 *sq*. A friendly correspondence started since 1793 (W. v.Humboldt, *Briefe*, München, Carl Hanser, 1952, pp. 73, 81, 89) and took a particular intensity as the foundation of the University of Berlin was being prepared (*ibid.*, pp. 304, 305, 309, 310). Friedrich Schlegel submitted the manuscript of his *Geschichte der Poesie der Griechen und Römer* to Wolf (E. Behler, *op. cit.*, p. 81) and wrote in 1796 an essay on *Homeric Poesie* that largely deals with the Wolf's interpretation. In his text "The Essence of the Critique", Schlegel eulogizes Wolf's work (in P. Lacoue-Labarthe et J.-L. Nancy, *L'absolu littéraire*, Paris, Seuil, 1978, p. 415).

19 See: J. Rückert: *Idealismus, Jurisprudenz und Politik bei Friedrich Carl von Savigny, op. cit.*; D. Nörr: *Savignys philosophische Lehrjahre. Ein Versuch*, Frankfurt a.M., Klostermann, 1994.

20 Behler, *op. cit.*, p. 80.

21 Savigny, *Vorlesungen über juristische Methodologie 1802–1842*, ed. by A. Mazzacane, Frankfurt a.M., Klostermann, p. 87 (p. 88, pour les citations suivantes).

"new vision", he believes he's discovered (or hopes he has) at the foundation of Hugo's Treaty which he reviews in 1806, by a process of empathetic interpretation (*einfühlendes Verstehen*), the guiding principle of his own conception: "At the basis of this book one can find a superior idea, according to which the whole of legal science itself is nothing but history of law, so that an isolated study of the history of law cannot be distinguished by any other study of the science of law except by a certain difference in the distribution of light and shadow[22]". This new vision of the *science* of law must necessarily pass by a new approach to the *history* of law that should no longer be "external" but comprehend „the whole of the internal history of law"[23]. The notes of one of young Savigny's students, a certain Jakob Grimm, do not say otherwise: "The ordinary notion of History of Law is limited – one offers solely an external history instead of an internal one, when the system must be considered as being in constant evolution[24]."

*

This philological turn in German thinking, aiming at the renewal of all knowledge domains, was, in Savigny's work, at the root of a historisation of the science of law. The main condition of this historisation is a new vision of history as *internal,* i. e. as a history that is no longer regarded as a "collection of moral and political examples[25]" but as the spontaneous development of a "conscience", or a "spirit" that one must penetrate intuitively, through a "living intuition"; thus, this effort to reach out to the spirit of past times takes part in the formation or edification (*Bildung*) of the spirit of this subject of knowledge itself[26]. On the other hand this philological turn inspired, at the same time, „a new way of understanding the connection between the modern and the ancient". For the philologists Heyne, Wolf and Humboldt „the aim is no longer to study the Greeks in order to transpose them to modern times, but to understand them in their own present as a complete totality[27]"; in the same way, in Savigny's work, the aim is no longer to maintain a purely mimetic relationship to roman antiquity or to establish roman law as an exemplary model that, in this great "collection of moral and political examples" one should try to reproduce or to imitate; an imitation in the formal sense would precisely imply an external link between the imitating and the imitated, whilst the paradigm of an internal history strives to construct an organic community between the whole past and the whole present of the people that is currently undertaking this effort of the spirit[28], a free imitation, not

---

22 See the above-mentioned recension in Savigny, *Vermischte Schriften*, t. 5, *op. cit.*, p. 2.

23 *Ibid.*, p. 5.

24 Savigny, *Juristische Methodenlehre*, G. Wesenberg (ed.), Stuttgart, Koehler, 1951, p. 17.

25 Savigny, "Ueber den Zweck dieser Zeitschrift", *Zeitschrift für geschichtliche Rechtswissenschaft* I, 1815, p. 3. French translation: "Sur le but de la présente revue", in *L'esprit de l'École historique du droit, Annales de la Faculté de Droit de Strasbourg*, nouvelle série, n° 7, 2004.

26 Certainly, Savigny could say, with Friedrich Schlegel, that history "if it is not restricted to a mere list of names, dates and extraordinary events, if it knows how to encompass and depict the spirit of great eras, of great men and of events, is itself a true, sure and for every one intellegible philosophy, which gives all kinds of richest advices"; it is the best mean in order to "elevate and ennoble (…) the inner man". (F. Schlegel, *Tableau de l'histoire moderne*, vol. 1, from the french translation of Cherbuliez, Paris et Genève, Renduel, Cherbuliez, 1831, pp. 1–3.)

27 Quotations in J. Quillien, *op. cit.*, p. 17.

28 Obviously, the german people of the 19th century is not the *biological* or *natural* continuity of the roman people, but, for Savigny and Puchta, the *legatee* of its spirit.

of external forms but of the way of spiritual activity. One must therefore consider the globality of an era in itself, as a perfect total, as well as its connection to other eras which implies that this accomplished perfection does not lie entirely in the era itself. This is exactly what Savigny said in his famous phrase: "That which can be considered as individual is also, when seen from a different perspective, part of a higher All[29]." From this starting point, he can consider that the affirmation that an ancient form of law is essentially superior to modern law in a way that would allow it to legitimately dominate present and future is to "fail to understand and to completely disfigure the historical vision of the legal science": "on the contrary, the essence of this vision consists precisely of the uniform recognition of the value and autonomy of each era, and simply insists that the living connection that links the present to the past must also be acknowledged; without knowledge of it we can only perceive the external manifestation, and not the internal essence of contemporary law[30]". While being autonomous from one point of view, these periods are at the same time intimately connected to each other; they exist in a state of freedom, but also in a state of dependence and necessity: "So, each era must acknowledge the existence of something that is at once necessary and free[31]". Thus the present time is not purely and simply in a state of dependence established by a formally mimetic relationship, in a state of dependence to a model that must be imitated. Ernst Behler[32] demonstrated the importance, for the historical conscience, of the belated (only towards the second half of the 18th century, especially through Herder) importation in Germany of the "Quarrel of the Ancients and the Moderns". Now, the romantics reacted against Herder's "relativist conception", which regards history as a vast continuous movement driving human affairs, and that leads him, as through a linear historical logic, to the conclusion that he is obviously "closer to Shakespeare than to the Greeks"[33]. The romantics' historical conscience is precisely not that of a simple linear *continuum*, whether progressive or regressive, that keeps putting an ever greater distance between the beginning and the present. "The problem of our literature", wrote Fr. Schlegel to his brother in 1794, "seems to me to be the reunion of what is essentially modern with what is essentially ancient[34]". There can be no true perfection in art, wrote Behler in this perspective, except „in a living connection to Antiquity[35]" – a *living connection,* that is a connection that is spiritual, and thus free[36].

The resemblance can obviously not be denied. Savigny's history of law is not the history of a loss, of a remoteness; it is the history of constant improvement that can only be achieved through the summoning of the Roman origins and their destiny in an effort to revive the *spirit.* For Fr. Schlegel, the imitation of the ancients should not consist in the reproduction of an external form but – and that is a higher ambition – in a gesture aiming to reclaim a *spirit[37]*, - in other words an *internal* form. In the same way, Savigny's updating of roman law is not based on a mere external description of its rules and solutions but on a recapturing of the spirit of the classical roman

29   "Ueber den Zweck dieser Zeitschrift", *op. cit.,* p. 3.
30   Quotations in Savigny, *System des heutigen Römischen Rechts,* tome 1, Berlin, Veit, 1840, pp. xiv–xv.
31   Savigny, "Ueber den Zweck dieser Zeitschrift", *op. cit.,* p. 3.
32   Behler, *op. cit,* pp. 23 *sq.*
33   *Ibid.,* p. 27. Quotation from Herder's essay *Shakespeare* (1772).
34   *Ibid.,* p. 29, I underline.
35   *Ibid.*
36   "Free in relation with the Antiquity", says Friedrich Schlegel (*ibid.,* p. 106).
37   *Ibid.*

law scholars, i. e. at the same time on a penetration into their conceptuality (that can only be achieved through systematization), and the reclaiming of their method, their approach to legal concepts.

*

It is only on the basis of this fundamental thesis that we can comprehend, first of all, the importance that this intimate connection between history and system had for Savigny: systematization is precisely this operation of actualizing, of reviving the spirit of historical law. Once again there is an obvious parallel to Fr. Schlegel's project of an "historical system", based on an absolute correlation between historical and systematical components[38]. "History", wrote Schlegel, "is philosophy in the making, and philosophy is accomplished history[39]". We must note at here that philosophy is not History with a capital H, but the accomplishment of *a* history, it is just a *moment* of that history. Besides, philosophy can only have a systematical form, external or internal. It was this correlation that allowed Savigny to contemplate this connection between historical science and philosophical science of law, a connection that he demanded, as we saw, since 1802.

The possibility of an internal history of law that could be associated to a philosophy of law presupposes that we abandon the kantian position which considers history as a simple *cognitio ex datis,* essentially separated from the true sciences, the latter being, as *cognitio ex principiis,* systematizable, in other words: liable to be unified under an idea[40]. It is precisely this kantian caracterisation, which refuses to consider history as a true science, that Thibaut (1772–1840), Savigny's main adversary in the Codification quarrel, insisted on in his *Encyclopädie*: "History in and of itself is not one of the sciences, since no systematic order is possible within it". It was also on the basis of a similar position that Anselm Feuerbach rejected the claims of the Historical School of Law.[41]

Joachim Rueckert is therefore right to insist on the fact that the concept of history that Savigny employed was a concept that originated from „the German idealism *after* Kant"[42]. This *internal* history that Savigny's programm aspires to implies a concept of history which goes further back than Herder; it originates from the first romantics and Schelling, whose thought was, according to Habermas, "more historical than that of all of his contemporaries", among which one must also consider Hegel[43].

We must remember once again at this point this phrase of capital importance contained in the opening article of the Journal for Historical Jurisprudence of 1815: "Every era must recognize something given which however is at once necessary and

---

38 Behler, *op. cit.*, p. 95.

39 *Athenaeum*, Fragment 325, in: Lacoue-Labarthe, Nancy, *op. cit.*, p. 147.

40 See Kant's *Architectonik* in the *Kritik der reinen Vernunft*.

41 "Einige Worte über historische Rechtsgelehrsamkeit und einheimische deutsche Gesetzgebung" (1816), reprint in H. Hattenhauer (ed.), *Thibaut und Savigny*, München, Franz Vahlen, 1973, pp. 221 *sq.*

42 J. Rückert, "Juristische Methode und Zivilrecht beim Klassiker Savigny (1779–1861)", in Rückert (ed.), *Fälle und Fallen in der neueren Methodik des Zivilrechts seit Savigny*, Baden-Baden, Nomos, 1997, p. 39.

43 Habermas, *Das Absolute und die Geschichte* (1954), quoted in P. David, *Schelling. De l'absolu à l'histoire*, Paris, PUF, 1998, p. 5.

free[44]." It is difficult not to see in this characteristic figure of a unity between necessity and freedom an allusion to the idealist concept of history just as it has been developped in Schelling's work. More than this, it is the true foundation of an *internal* history of law according to Savigny: necessity is not just an external and causal factor of history, it is also a condition for a true and real freedom of human beings. History is not an exhibition of moral behaviours, but the reconstruction of an internal development which is at once necessary and free.

Because it is also, in the latter's work, about the moment when "necessity and liberty must be united", when „necessity and liberty are intertwined, creating a single and unique essential being *(Wesen)*"[45]. Already in his *System of transcendental idealism* of 1800, Schelling clearly states that "History's main characteristic" is „that it presents liberty and necessity as a union", and that "it can only be possible *through* this union"[46].

Behind the apparent paradox of these formulas, one cannot help but recognize the idea that, if history was nothing but the reign of an erratic liberty, of the "arbitrary" according to Savigny's vocabulary, it would be nothing but a succession of chaos and ruptures, not only without any specific direction but also a succession of chaos and ruptures of which one cannot possibly give an orderly account. On the contrary, if history were nothing but the reign of pure necessity, it would consist of monotonous identical reproduction, and would be thus the exact opposite of history as we know it. We can therefore formulate the following hypothesis: this very moment of the union of the necessary and the free is the moment of human action, the true moment of the "Subject". Because, in the wake of Fichte, for whom "Me" is pure action, absolutely active[47], Schelling wrote: "The essence of the human being is action"[48]. As a conscience, the human being is action, and "all thought is an act[49]". However, every thought is accompanied by an "I think", that presupposes a rapport to oneself that is more primal than any thought. Thus, the absolute original act is self-consciousness, that is the act through which the subject sees itself as an object: "The fact that subject and object of thought are one in self-conscience can only be understood by everyone in the very act of self-consciousness[50]." The latter is thus the point where „subject and object immediately become one"[51]. This identity of subject and object in the act of self-consciousness is the foundation of Self[52]. Hence: the Self is the identity of the objective and the subjective, an identity that renders possible the paradoxical statement according to which "The self as such can only be without limits when it is limited, and inversely, the self as such can only be limited when it is without limits" [53]. It is on this paradox that the Self *as a process* is founded,

44   Savigny, „Ueber den Zweck dieser Zeitschrift", *op. cit.*, p. 3.
45   Schelling, *Philosophische Untersuchungen über das Wesen der menschlichen Freiheit und die damit zusammen-hängenden Gegenstände* (1809), SW I, 7, p. 385 (french translation: *Recherches philosophiques sur l'essence de la liberté humaine et les sujets qui s'y rapportent*, in Schelling, *Œuvres métaphysiques 1805–1821*, Paris, Gallimard, 1980, p. 168).
46   Schelling, *System des transcendentalen Idealismus*, SW I, 3, p. 593.
47   See: M. Vetö, *Fichte. De l'action à l'image*, Paris, L'Harmattan, 2001, p. 30.
48   Schelling, *Einleitung zu: Ideen zu einer Philosophie der Natur* (1797, 2nd ed. 1803), SW I, 2, p. 13.
49   Schelling, *System des transcendentalen Idealismus*, SW I, 3, p. 365.
50   *Ibid.*
51   *Ibid.*, p. 364.
52   "The concept of the I happens through the act of the self-consciousness; apart from this act, the I is therefore nothing": *ibid.*, p. 366.
53   *Ibid.*, p. 382.

because this paradox is not conceivable if we regard the Self as a substance-subject always identical to itself. The identity of the subjective and the objective can only be understood from the viewpoint of the Self regarded as activity; this implies not only the subjective affirmation of what should be, but also the objective negation of what should no longer be. It is therefore to be regarded as a process of becoming[54].

This little, very summary, detour through the metaphysics of conscience is essential, as it allows us to understand how the post-Kantian elaboration of the theme of self-conscience provides evolution, time and history with a foundation in Schelling's idealism. From this starting point, one can understand Schelling's assertion, clearly formulated in his *Stuttgart Private Lessons*: "In truth, time is contained in *every thing* itself. There is no external, universal time; all time is subjective, in other words it is an internal time that every thing contains in itself and that does not exist outside itself[55]."

The main thesis here is that the history of law in Savigny's work can, as an *internal* history, only be understood on the basis of a subjective notion of time, a notion developed in German idealism on the basis of the fundamental theme of self-conscience.

We can therefore only comprehend Savigny's construct of the image of law by associating it to this subjective notion of time and of the process of becoming. That way we can understand the true significance of the following phrase: "*Der eigentliche Sitz des Rechts (ist) das gemeinsame Bewußtsein des Volkes*": "The true seat of the Law is the collective consciousness of the people"[56]. The people are an "active, personal subject[57]". If the metaphysical presuppositions established above are exact, we come to the conclusion that Law, as a subjective phenomenon, is essentially history, because it is the expression of an active subject; because its knowledge is the knowledge of the history of a conscience, and it is directed to this internal history that Savigny speaks of. Therefore, in order to understand Savigny's project on the basis of its philosophical foundations, we must ascribe to the concept of "consciousness", foundation of the concept of "law", all the metaphysical significance that was ascribed to it, at that time, by the idealists and especially Schelling.

*

I'd like to insist briefly on three consequences of this construction of law as history, on the basis of metaphysics of the subject.

First of all, what we call "the sources of law", to the number of three according to Savigny – custom, legislation and science – must be distinguished from the actual origin of law, its *Entstehungsgrund*, that is the popular consciousness. These "sources", that are thus the derivations of an original stream, are just modes of revelation of a

---

54   *Ibid.*, p. 383.
55   *Stuttgarter Privatvorlesungen*, SW I, 7, p. 431.
56   Savigny, *Vom Beruf unsrer Zeit für Gesetzgebung und Rechtswissenschaft*, Heidelberg, Mohr und Zimmer, 1814, p. 11. "The seat of the production of the law is this natural whole (*Naturganze*), because it is this common popular spirit, which moulds the individuals, in which the force lies that can meet the need mentioned above." (*System des heutigen Römischen Rechts*, vol. 1, *op. cit.*, p. 19.) "Like a language, the law is living in the popular consciousness." (*ibid.*, p. 9.) "Positive law is living in common consciousness of the people, therefore we call it a *popular law*." (*ibid.*, p. 14). The "foundation of every positive law" has "its existence, its actuality in the common consciousness of a people." (*ibid.*, p. 35).
57   *System des heutigen Römischen Rechts*, vol. 1, p. 18.

law that already exists, whose fermentation is constant but obscure[58]; an invisible but real law that Savigny calls "positive" law. But people as a direct bearer of custom, legislators, and lawyers, as "representatives" of the people[59], are not external instances of the consciousness they express. Therefore, the work of these "sources" is the work of the self-consciousness of the popular subject. Their activity is a process of *self-auto-revelation*.

Secondly, if jurisprudence is one of the organs of a people's self-consciousness, and if this consciousness produces the law of a people, then jurisprudence works with a law that is not external to it, as a distinct object; it strives for the realization of this law. Savigny's jurisprudence is therefore not a "positivist" one in the contemporary sense of the term, if scientific positivism implies a principle of strict separation between subject and object of knowledge. The science of law, where it has been developed, is one of the driving forces – and could possibly be the main driving force – of the true history of law, in other words of law itself. If the realization of law has to go through this obscure fermentation process and through the act of its revelation, then the science of law is, properly speaking, a way of production of law, and even the most important way of production, because it reveals, unveils this law to the consciousness in the most complete and most clear manner, grasping it in its proper organic order, as a system[60]. For this reason, and on the basis of its own principles, it makes sense to rank the legal science among the sources of law.

We can finally see the importance, in Savigny's work, of the question of methodology; its scope is far wider than the simple problem of applying rules to concrete situations[61] – it is much more to be regarded as a reflection on legal action, which alone allows the intimate communion of spirits that goes beyond external literal analogies. Hence the more precise clarification of the relationship of the Historical school legal scholar to Roman Law: "If the main ailment affecting the state of our law consists of an ever growing distance between theory and practice, then there can be no other remedy than the re-establishment of their natural unity. And it is precisely to this effect that the Roman law can be of great service, if we have the intention of using it correctly. In Roman law scholars, this natural unity is still apparent and intact, and still acts in the liveliest fashion[62]." This "natural unity" that characterized the action of roman jurists significantly corresponds to this "peak of the period when art was naturally formed" that Schlegel alludes to when evoking the summits of ancient art[63]. The effort of the legal historian should aim to reclaim, that is to comprehend, the legal art of the Romans, and not just contend itself with exposing and comparing its "practical rules": "In fact, the question lies deeper"[64]: "In order for knowledge of Roman law to guide us to the aim that we have established here, there is only one thing to do: we have to read ourselves and think of ourselves in the

---

58 Puchta uses a strong metaphor: the *Volksgeist* is like a "dark workshop" in which the law would have been prepared. See: *Enzyklopädie*, in *Cursus der Institutionen*, vol. 1, p. 27 (french translation in *L'esprit de l'École historique du droit*, Annales de la Faculté de droit de Strasbourg, nouvelle série, n° 7, 2004, pp. 35 *sq.*).

59 Savigny, *Vom Beruf unsrer Zeit*, op. cit., p. 12.

60 That is why Savigny's struggle against codification must be understood as a struggle for the superiority of science compared with custom and, especially, legislation.

61 See: Rückert, "Savigny et la méthode juridique", art. cit.

62 Savigny, *System* I, Vorrede, p. XXV.

63 Quoted in Behler, *op. cit.*, p. 29.

64 Savigny, *System* I, Vorrede, p. XIX.

writings of the ancient jurists[65]". This phrase contained, in the most consolidated fashion, already back in 1840, two themes that are essential not only to Savigny's thought, but also to that of the first Romantics.

One can indeed detect watermarked in it the figure of the *Selbstdenker,* he who thinks by himself but with the Other – or, even better: he who thinks *through* the Other or *as* the Other (*hineindenken*). Thinking with, or through the Other is the "only way" that would allow the thinker to avoid succumbing to his own arbitrary tendencies, by rejecting the position of separation in favor of that of a community of thought – that is where he could find the point of convergence of necessity and liberty. This leitmotif runs through the whole of the Preface of Savigny's System, that opens with a eulogy of the legal scholars' intellectual liberty and the refusal to be subjected to the authorities of thought: thinking with or through the Other is not to submit oneself, to place oneself under the Other, but to raise oneself to the Other's level, the only place that renders critical thinking possible[66]. But being thus linked to the "Other", this freedom of thought is not a purely arbitrary act. The hermeneutic approach, thus extended, becomes an example of the effort to reach the point where liberty and necessity become one.

We can detect then, in this phrase, the desire to insist on reflection by the use of the reflexive pronoun "ourselves" (*uns*): read *ourselves* and think *ourselves* in classical literature. He who thinks by himself in the other is emblematic figure of the reflecting critic. We reach the conclusion that, in this light, the historicist approach is not that of the external observer of a long gone past. The legal historian of the Historical school of law must, according to Savigny, constantly strive for the actualization of Roman law. This effort needs reflective critique. Critique and reflection form the essence of Savigny's historical method. It is precisely by this method that the legal scholar can accomplish his mission: "Every era's most sensible activity should be destined to try to decipher, rejuvenate and refresh this given material with an intimate necessity"[67]. The legal historian is certainly past-oriented; however, as an *updater* of law, he cannot contend himself with being past-oriented in an attitude of pure contemplation. He acts *within* and *on* the law. His action is not as such bound solely to the present moment; being an essentially historical activity, it converses with the future as well. "The historian", said another extract of the *Atheneaum,* "is a prophet facing the past[68]". We can thus perfectly understand that theory and contemplation cannot be separated from practice and action. Savigny's insistence on the union of theory and practice is, or at least such is our thesis, linked to his conception of history.

*

This historical necessity acts on the subject and as a subject. Its seat is the conscience. The history of law is history of the conscience of law, and law is in its essence nothing but this conscience as it develops through history. Hence the jurist's mission, which consists entirely of the re-appropriation of this conscience. And this

---

65   *Ibid.,* p. XXVII.
66   This is also the reason why, in the preface to his System, Savigny stresses the point that the historical school does not have as an intent to subject the present law to the old Roman law (*ibid.,* pp. XIV *sq.*).
67   "Ueber den Zweck dieser Zeitschrift", *op. cit.,* p. 264.
68   Lacoue-Labarthe, Nancy, *op. cit.,* p. 107.

mission can be nothing other than an effort of the conscience, in other words the effort through which popular legal conscience becomes the jurist's own clear conscience. One can thus understand why, when studying the ancient scholars, the contemporary legal scholar must study himself and why he has to study himself as a "we". He renders the historical legal conscience present to the contemporary conscience – he re-presents it. The *method* acquires therefore much greater than ordinary significance in Savigny's work; for him, *method* is much more than a set of rules aiming to determine our understanding – it is much more a personal exercise aiming to develop our conscience. It is an "introduction to the personal study of the jurisprudence"[69] (*Anleitung zu einem eigenen Studium der Jurisprudenz*), it is a method of formation[70] of the spirit that can only be educated through the reflective study of the ancient masters.

According to Savigny, "the historical method triumphs when we succeed in offering a simple and immediate intuition (*Anschauung*) to the object of our study, resembling the intuition of something that we have ourselves experienced[71]". At this point we can understand perfectly how the historical "method" requires the intimate appropriation, by the subject, of the object of knowledge. The historical "object" becomes accessible to the subject when the latter is sufficiently trained in this mode of "immediate intuitive understanding". We find here again the recognition of the value of intuition – "living" intuition –, comparable to the value that is ascribed to it in the Schelling's doctrine on science. This conception of the historical method is linked to Savigny's reflexion on legal hermeneutics, i. e. on the way that we may obtain access to, "reconstruct" within us the sense, or, more precisely, "the inherent meaning of the law", through a process of interpretation regarded as a "free spiritual activity"[72].

Savigny's thought was entirely oriented to revealing the hidden associations that arrange the historical world; that give it form, shape and meaning. Such is also the meaning of the hermeneutics towards which points the "philological turn" adopted by German thought around 1800, in a profound and powerful movement. Such is Savigny's secret that the commentator must reveal.

---

69   *Vorlesungen über juristische Methodologie*, op. cit., pp. 14–19.
70   The word "formation" means here the same as the German term *Bildung*: the process of culture and education by which an individual spirit takes shape.
71   "Ueber den Zweck dieser Zeitschrift", *op. cit.*
72   See: *System* I, *op. cit.*, §§ 32, 33.

Hiroshi Kamemoto

How Should Legal Philosophers Make Use of Economic Thinking Implications of R.H. Coase's Economic Theory

1. Two Types of 'Law and Economics'

Economic policy involves a choice among alternative social institutions, and these are created by the law or are dependent on it. The majority of economists do not see the problem in this way. They paint a picture of an ideal economic system, and then, comparing it with what they observe (or think they observe), they prescribe what is necessary to reach this ideal state without much consideration for how this could be done. The analysis is carried out with great ingenuity but it floats in the air. It is, as I have phrased it, "blackboard economics."[1]

I think 'Law and Economics' as an academic subject can take two forms. The first is the Coasian type, which studies how legal system influences the working of economic system. It belongs to economics, and could be called economic 'Law and Economics.' The second type, by contrast, is engaged by jurists including legal philosophers. It aims at mastering economic way of thinking and making use of it to understand, interpret, and propose law. It could be called juristic 'Law and Economics'.

I shall argue that the latter type is unnecessary or may be harmful, although economics is very useful for legal science. To support this assertion, I shall take Coase's theory as one of the best achievements of economic 'Law and Economics', and make clear how it has been misunderstood by all jurists of 'Law and Economics' as well as almost all economists.

2. Why Juristic 'Law and Economics' Is Not Necessary

If jurists' objective in referring to economic theory is to improve law by way of understanding some of the functions of law from an economic point of view, it is obviously better to learn economics from genuine economists than from jurists of 'Law and Economics'.

Some jurists of 'Law and Economics' might insist that 'Law and Economics' be a division of law which picks out those part of law that connect inseparably with economy and apply economic theory to answer legal problems. This view, however, would make us lose sight of the fact that *every* legal phenomenon can be analyzed from an economic point of view.

---

1   R.H. Coase, *The Firm, the Market, and the Law*, the University of Chicago Press: Chicago and London, 1988, p. 28.

3. Why Juristic 'Law and Economics' Is Sometimes Harmful

Economics as a science is neutral to any ideology. It argues neither for nor against so-called market economy. In fact both economists who supported socialist planned economy and those who supported free enterprise system believed in the same micro-economic theory. There are no top-class economists such as Milton Friedman and F.A. Hayek who use Pareto or Kaldor-Hicks efficiency in order to vindicate free market system.

Nevertheless some jurists of 'Law and Economics' such as Richard Posner have contributed to making widely known the falsehood that micro-economics endorses market economy. It is said market equilibrium is efficient, because it maximizes consumer's and/or producer's surplus. But the well-known graph of demand and supply curves you see in every standard textbook is no more than a model for beginners in learning economics. It cannot be an object of vindication. There is no market or market economy as an institution or system in such a graph.

4. Transaction Cost and Law

It is Coase who called on economists to pay attention to the significance of market as an institution. He says "Markets are institutions that exist to facilitate exchange, that is, they exist in order to reduce the cost of carrying out exchange transaction."[2]

Any exchange transaction always entails some positive cost, though standard economics assumes transaction cost is zero. Coase says as follows:

> [F]or their operation, markets ... require the establishments of legal rules governing the rights and duties of those carrying out transactions ... Such legal rules may be made by those who organize the markets, as it is the case with commodity exchanges ... Agreement [of the rules] is facilitated in the case of commodity exchanges because the members meet in the same premises and deal in a restricted range of commodities; and enforcements of the rules is possible because the opportunity to trade on the exchange is itself of great value and the withholding of permission to trade is a sanction sufficiently severe to induce most traders to observe the rules ... When the physical facilities are scattered and owned by a vast number of people with very different interests, as is the case with retailing and wholesaling, the establishment and administration of private legal system would be very difficult. Those operating in these markets have to depend, therefore, on the legal system of the State.[3]

Markets in this description have concrete forms and substance, and are not abstract concepts as in the explanation of price mechanism. In Coase's theory it is explained by considering transaction costs why there are many kinds of markets and why forms of markets are so different. More interesting for legal philosophers, it makes clear why private legal systems are sometimes established and administrated by private people in spite of the fact that legal systems are a kind of public goods. If the cost of self-regulation of the market, which I think is a kind of transaction cost, is

---

2   Ibid., p. 7.
3   Ibid., p. 10.

lower than the gain from the working of the market, the market would be regulated by the practitioners themselves of the market. If, on the contrary, the former is higher than the latter, state law would be necessary to maintain and promote market exchange for the public good.

5. Externality and Reciprocity

Coase's theory of transaction cost should be treated in the context of market exchange. But in fact it is discussed in the context of externality. An externality is "the effect of one person's decision on someone who is not a party to that decision."[4]

I think externality as a technical term in economics is a strange one because economists study how economic actions of independent agents such as firms and consumers influence indirectly, as it were, economic actions of other independent agents. If we understood externality in the sense of the definition above, externalities would emerge in almost all economic behaviors. When a person out of work is seeking a job, she would give other job seekers negative externalities. When a shop shows prices of its commodities, it would give positive externalities to the potential purchasers including those who would not buy them. The shop owner takes such a behavior seeing that it is more profitable than alternative behaviors. To explain her behavior we do not need such a concept of externality.

Too often as it is ignored, Coase rejects the concept of externality and uses the words "harmful effects"[5] instead of negative externalities in a case of pollution, for example. He emphasizes reciprocal character of the problem. People including economists would suppose a factory owner is liable for the damages, if the smoke from it has harmful effects on neighbors. But if this legal policy were adopted, the neighbors in turn would damage the factory owner. Coase says as follows:

To avoid the harm to B would be to inflict harm on A. The real question that has to be decided is, Should A be allowed to harm B *or* should B be allowed to harm A? The problem is to avoid the more serious harm.[6]

It matters not only whether the factory owner in production does not consider the costs for neighbors but also whether the neighbors do not consider the costs for the factory when they continue to live there.

Coase objects to so-called Pigovian taxes for the same reason. The basic idea of Pigovian tax is the following. If a factory harms the neighbors through smoke, for example, and the neighbors do not have rights to the same amount as the damages suffered in effect, the production of the factory would be too much because it would continue to produce without regard to the costs for the neighbors. To prevent such a state of affairs government should impose on the factory a tax equal to the damages suffered by the neighbors.

But this policy may not be optimal according to Coase. When such taxes are imposed, the factory will try to decrease the harms through a smoke-preventing device, for example, to avoid taxes as long as the cost for it is lower than the amount of the taxes. If the number of neighbors increases, the factory will be willing to pay more cost to prevent smoke for the same reason. The neighbors, however, would

4   Ibid., p. 24.
5   Ibid., p. 95 *et passim.*
6   Ibid., p. 96. Italics are added by me.

not consider the cost borne by the factory. As a result the population of neighbors would be too big. Coase contends that it is better to tax not only the factory but also neighbors, if the factory ought to be taxed.[7]

Many economists as well as jurists of Law and Economics are thinking like a lawyer, who thinks the polluter alone is liable, when they see the case of negative externalities such as pollutions. It is strange to me.

6. Coase Theorem

As far as zero transaction costs are assumed, the value of production is maximized, whoever has the rights to the resources under discussion.[8] This is Coase theorem well-known among even jurists who are not interested in Law and Economics. It implies that the distribution of rights does not influence at all the allocation of resources under the zero-transaction-costs assumption. But many economists who perhaps have not read Coase's essays add that the distribution of rights influence the distribution of incomes. Almost all jurists of Law and Economics follow them. Coase objects to such an interpretation of his own theory.[9]

Let us suppose first that a rancher produces something with cattle and a neighboring farmer produce crops, and that some crops would be destroyed by the roaming of the cattle. Suppose second that among the factors employed for the rancher's production only the ranch gives rise to the rent, and among the factors employed for the farmer's production only the farm gives rise to the rent. The term "rent" means "the difference between what a factor of production earns under discussion and what it could otherwise earn".[10] Suppose finally that the lands of the ranch and the farm are rented from the same owner.

When the damage the cattle bring to crops is smaller than both the rent of the ranch and the rent of the farm, both the rancher and the farmer would continue to operate, whether the rancher is liable for the damage or not. When the rancher is liable, the sum he is willing to pay for renting the land would decrease by an amount of the value of the damage. If the rancher is not liable, the sum the farmer is willing to pay for renting the land would decrease by an amount of the value of the damage. The wealth of each producer (and also the land owner) is, therefore, the same regardless of liability rules. This is the case when the relative sizes of those rents and the value of damage are otherwise. The rentals adjust themselves to the change of liability rules so as to keep the wealth of each party the same as before.

The conclusion that wealth is constant whoever has the rights is correct even if the liability rule would be changed in the future. For zero transaction costs imply that parties could have any detailed contracts without costs for the future change of rules.

---

7   Ibid., pp.151–152 and 181.
8   Ibid., p. 158. An assumption of perfect competition is not necessary, because under the zero-transaction-costs assumption any seller can always find without costs the buyer who is willing to pay the highest price.
9   See ibid., pp. 163–170 for the following.
10   Ibid., p. 163.

7. Coasian World

Coase theorem can be derived from common sense, so to speak, in standard economics. Zero transaction costs imply that every seller of her own rights to some resources can always and immediately find the purchaser who is willing to pay the higher sum than any other purchasers. As a result the value of production is maximized. As to the right to pollute or stop pollution, this is also the case, for it is a kind of right to resources, not different in essence from the other kinds of rights to goods.

Coase's contribution to economics is that he emphasizes positive transaction costs and non-applicability of Coase theorem in reality.

> The world of zero transaction costs has often been described as a Coasian world. Nothing could be further from the truth. It is the world of modern economic theory, one which I was hoping to persuade economists to leave.[11]

Being a theoretical economist as he is, Coase recommends economists to investigate transaction costs in reality. The idea of transaction cost will help them study real costs. We cannot say anything about which legal rule is better than the alternatives until we know how much it costs to adopt it. It does not mean jurists have to examine the costs by themselves, but they can use the achievements of positive economists. Many jurists of Law and Economics, however, seem to be discussing what the best rule is from an economic point of view without even the rough data. It is true that we can use and need some assumptions to construct models for analyzing reality, but we need minimal data at least in order to make some proposal about law, if we should talk about law in action rather than law in books or law on blackboards.

8. Implications of Coase's Economic Theory for Legal Philosophy

Let me repeat and supplement important implications for legal philosophers derived from Coase's theory.

First, Coase's theory makes clear how and when private and State laws are generated in terms of transaction costs. Private legal systems are created when the parties frequently meet at the concentrated places, and breaking rules are easily detected and sanctioned by the members themselves. If the transaction costs of establishing and maintaining the legal system are lower than the gain from employing it, private law will emerge. State legal systems are presumed to be necessary, if it is difficult to set up and keep such a private legal system because of the higher transaction costs.

Second, what economists call public goods can be supplied even by private people or groups. Legal systems are a kind of public goods. Coase demonstrates how lighthouses in England have been supplied and funded.[12] He objected the payments of costs from the general tax, which is the way of financing many academic economists recommend. If the fees for using lighthouses are collected from the people in general through the national taxation system, the administration of lighthouses would be as inefficient as other works of states.

---

11   Ibid., p. 174.
12   See ibid., pp. 187–213.

Third, it may be the best from an economic point of view for the state to do nothing, even if there were pressing social problems that people think the state should deal with. If the costs are greater than the benefits brought about by implementing a proposed policy, it is better to abandon such a policy. I would like to call costs for constructing new legal and political systems "institutional costs".[13] I regard them as a kind of transaction costs in a wider sense. It may be difficult to estimate them accurately. It is nevertheless true that institutional changes cost much value. Conscientious jurists and legal philosophers who propose institutional improvements often forget this obvious fact. Every action, good or bad, costs something positive. This has been a common sense in economics.

Finally states as well as private firms do economic activity. By this I mean not national company but every activity of states. As far as government manages to get financial resources and supplies services, all actions of government can be analyzed in terms of economics.

Economics cannot always treat all costs. Institutional improvements involve costs it is difficult for economists to estimate. Some of them cannot be described in terms of the value of production. We can nevertheless learn something important from economists who are always thinking about costs, although they often forget considering transaction costs when they discuss market in abstraction or on blackboard.

---

13   Cf. Steven N. S. Cheung, *Will China Go 'Capitalist'?*, Institute of Economic Affairs, 1982, pp. 30–47.

Adrian Künzler

The Jurisprudence of Welfare Maximization[*]
Embracing Complexity and Uncertainty in the Environmental, Health and Safety Context

The application of cost-benefit analysis to regulation is widely believed to provide for a disciplined method of rationally assessing the consequences of proposed courses of action. This article exposes a critical flaw in the neoclassical welfare economic paradigm of cost-benefit assessment and argues that it is insufficient to apply a single value framework to reality. Taking account of the complexity and uncertainty of certain aspects of real-world phenomena, the article describes the way some common understanding of an underlying concept of 'reality-based' regulatory law and economics can be reached. The article thereby indicates how related behavioral sciences can deepen our understanding of regulation.

I. Introduction

The global financial crisis of 2007–2011 has generated calls for *conceptual* re-examination of regulatory policy, its attitude towards the efficiency of markets and the role of legal, social, and ethical norms in a market economy.[1] It has prompted policymakers and scholars to re-examine the assumptions underlying a variety of the legal arena's current neoclassical economic theories and the goals of regulatory agendas.[2] It has been claimed that a great number of today's economic and environmental problems reflect *regulatory failures* and *inadequate regulatory oversight*.[3]

Legal scholars specializing in various fields of regulation have echoed the assumption that domestic regulatory policies must incorporate more of the *complexity* underlying the industrial economy.[4] One debate that has remained latent over the last half-dozen years concerns the role of *cost-benefit analysis* as a technique to render regulatory policy apparently more neutral and objective. Although the conventional wisdom holds that cost-benefit analysis provides for a more 'scientific' approach to legal policy, Professor Douglas A. Kysar has recently written that cost-benefit analy-

[*]   This essay is based on the IVR Young Scholar Prize Lecture given at the World Congress of the IVR in Frankfurt am Main (Germany) on August 19, 2011. The final version of this article benefitted from insightful comments made by Professor Walter Ott at Zurich University School of Law and Professor E. Donald Elliott at Yale Law School. Essential support received for this research from the Swiss National Science Foundation and the Yale Law School is gratefully acknowledged.

[1]   What went Wrong with Economics, *Economist* July 18 (2009), 11–12; see also John Cassidy, *How Markets Fail. The Logic of Economic Calamities*, 2009.

[2]   The Other-Worldly Philosophers, *Economist* July 18 (2009), 65–67; George A. Akerlof / Robert J. Shiller, *Animal Spirits. How Human Psychology Drives the Economy and Why It Matters for Global Capitalism*, 2009.

[3]   Raghuram G. Rajan, *Fault Lines. How Hidden Fractures Still Threaten the World Economy*, 2010, 154–182; see also Christine A. Varney, Vigorous Antitrust Enforcement in this Challenging Era, May 12 (2009), 4–5, >http://www.justice.gov/atr/public/speeches/245777.htm<.

[4]   See, Douglas A. Kysar, The Jurisprudence of Experimental Law and Economics, *J. Institutional & Theoretical Econ.* 163 (2007), 187.

sis is „a policy-making approach that achieves its appearance of case-specific rationality at the price of insensitivity to context and to longer-term, systemic rationality."
According to Kysar, „policymakers cannot be content with the local equilibriums
identified by conventional cost-benefit analyses but instead must aim to alter – over
time and in rather dramatic macroscale ways – the economic and technological
forces that combine to structure any given policy context with its microscale snap-
shot that seems to admit of only one 'optimal' solution."[5] Professors Richard L.
Revesz and Michael A. Livermore echo this sentiment, with a slightly different emphasis, writing that „cost-benefit analysis is […] biased against regulation." They ascribe „the roots of the antiregulatory bias within cost-benefit analysis" to „historical
rather than conceptual" reasons and contend that it stems from „the shunning of
cost-benefit analysis by proregulatory interests […] which had the unintended effect
of leaving antiregulatory interests free to shape the use of the technique toward their
purposes."[6] Numerous other scholars have engaged in the debate over the proper
role of regulation in the economy arguing in favor and against the application of
cost-benefit analysis on a variety of different grounds.[7]

Outside of the academy, cost-benefit analysis is often used by governments to
evaluate the desirability of a new regulatory framework or a given intervention in the
free play of market forces. It is heavily used in today's government when deciding on
whether a new business regulation should be introduced, a new road should be built,
or a new drug through the state healthcare system should be offered. What is more,
the assumption that the principle of cost-benefit analysis allows us to analyze what
might happen under varying policies and conditions with respect to social or economic welfare may seem so intuitive that for the most part scholars have failed to
test the application of the welfare-maximization approach against the question of
whether it provides for *useful* simplifications or *over*simplifications. In the context of
the environmental, health and safety laws this has been recognized – because a value
must be put on human life or on the environment: The cost-benefit principle requires us for example to install a guardrail on a dangerous stretch of mountain road
if the dollar cost of doing so is less than the implicit *dollar value* of the injuries,
deaths, and property damage thus prevented.[8]

This argument yields important implications for the study of cost-benefit analysis to regulation in general. This article argues that the cost-benefit analysis principle
may create useful simplifications of the economy that allow us to analyze a vast
number of market conditions helping us to avoid devising the most realistic models
that detail all individuals and their whimsical behavior, and all institutions, that
would be hopelessly complex and of little value in analysis. The cost-benefit principle has been used as a *method* for analyzing markets,[9] as an apparently neutral technical apparatus for studying the relationship between competition and market out-

5   Douglas A. Kysar, *Regulating from Nowhere. Environmental Law and the Search for Objectivity*, 2010, X.
6   Richard A. Revesz / Michael A. Livermore, *Retaking Rationality. How Cost-Benefit Analysis Can Better
     Protect the Environment and Our Health*, 2008, 10.
7   For a recent sustained critique, arguing that cost-benefit analysis is fundamentally flawed, see, Frank
     Ackerman / Lisa Hinzerling, *Priceless: On Knowing the Price of Everything and the Value of Nothing*, 2004.
8   Robert H. Frank, Why Is Cost-Benefit Analysis So Controversial?, *J. Legal Stud.* 29 (2000), 913.
9   See, Steven M. Teles, *The Rise of the Conservative Legal Movement: The Battle for Control of the Law*, 2008,
     91.

comes and plays a pervasive role in relevant legal discourse.[10] It integrates the distinctive grammar of economics into the law, producing a richer conception of appropriate legal argument. However, I argue that the application of the wealth-maximization principle to regulation is not actually capable of pursuing an 'economically *correct* regulatory policy' that unreservedly allows us to deeper investigate into economic relationships, and that conclusively enables regulators to reduce welfare costs through decision errors by better discriminating between welfare enhancing and welfare diminishing behavior.

This article's argument also informs ongoing policy debates regarding the application of alternative (economic) approaches to regulation. To claim that the wealth-maximization principle is based on a 'scientific' view of the economy and therefore always generates *better* outcomes or results or provides for a *more objective* regulatory framework is to fall victim to the illusion that through the application of a single value framework to reality, such as rational choice or welfarism, the necessity of making value judgments can be avoided.[11] Rather, *scientific theory* points to the fact that the economy and the legal decision-making environment may be too complex to support the level of purity and clarity that cost-benefit analysis alone is able to achieve with respect to the ultimate interpretation of results. Its exclusive application ignores the facts that individual preferences are necessarily plural, that market outcomes are necessarily uncertain, and that legal judgments are necessarily pragmatic. Within the context of realistic legal decision tasks, any attempt to replicate such research methodology may fail to capture what is distinctively complex about the assigned tasks; vested interests have to be confronted, conflicting aims have to be reconciled. Above all, the existence of 'complex organized phenomena' has to be acknowledged and the fact that effective government is a matter of getting the balance right between autonomy and coordination. Hence, policymakers and courts need to embrace the fact that cost-benefit analyses are based on pre-scientific decisions, or, are *axiomatic* in character.[12] Such analyses may not be judged – as is done in the natural or social sciences – on their 'truth', but on their effectiveness in terms of the conclusions they permit to be drawn. Such a *pragmatic jurisprudential framework* presupposes a debate as to whether the consequences of a particular method are *desirable or undesirable.*[13] It sometimes offers a better conceptual fit for scientific approaches in law than the purely positivistic framework of social science and, at the same time, allows for careful consideration of *constitutional rights* and the idea that the *preferences of the citizens* should be the relevant normative criteria for appropriate decisions about the objectives of regulatory policy.

In the pragmatic spirit of 'reality-based economics', the first section of the article sets out to explore the bounds and limits of cost-benefit analysis in the environmental, risk and safety contexts. First, it examines the question of whether the welfare-maximizing approach is operable if the complexity and uncertainty of real-world

---

10 Bruce A. Ackermann, Law, Economics, and the Problem of Legal Culture, *Duke L.J.* 6 (1986), 929–947.

11 See, e.g., Efficiency and Beyond, *Economist* July 18 (2009), 68–69.

12 See on axioms in general Walter Ott, *Der Rechtspositivismus. Kritische Würdigung auf der Grundlage eines juristischen Pragmatismus,* 1992, 117–162, above all at 163, 164–168; with respect to the axiomatic character of economic approaches in competition law, see, Adrian Künzler, *Effizienz oder Wettbewerbsfreiheit? Zur Frage nach den Aufgaben des Rechts gegen private Wettbewerbsbeschränkungen,* 2008, 285–289.

13 See below III.B; illustrative examples are provided by Kysar (Fn. 4), 187 and Ott (Fn. 12), 165–166, 171; see with respect to the present context Künzler (Fn. 12), 284, 288–288.

conditions are given appropriate attention (II). It goes on to show that unless value judgements are made, even cost-benefit analysis is unworkable (III). There follows a discussion of the cornerstones of a 'reality-based' concept of regulatory economics (IV). The article concludes with a summary of findings (V).

II. The problem of establishing a criterion for determining economic welfare

A. Balancing welfare-enhancing and welfare-reducing efficiencies

The cost-benefit analysis process involves – whether explicitly or implicitly – a balancing of the total expected costs against the total expected benefits of one or more actions in order to choose the best or most profitable option. In this way, prospective legal rules are appraised by efficiency criteria, such as social- or consumer welfare, efficient allocation of production factors or, in short, their economic outcomes. From a scholarly perspective, advocates of cost-benefit analysis support the use of *scientific evidence* to improve regulatory decisions.[14] Starting out from the neoclassical welfare-economic principle of *preference autonomy*, and the associated postulate that governmental interventions in individual preferences are only justified when they *demonstrably* have a welfare-enhancing effect (Coase), under the cost-benefit analysis approach, such interventions are only legitimate if their positive welfare effects are *empirically verifiable*. And intervention is only endorsed if welfare losses are fairly certain to be avoided. Otherwise there is a risk that government interventions will themselves inhibit the 'free play of market forces'.[15] Furthermore, this view is founded on the premise from neoclassical welfare economics that economic welfare is the outcome of the *revealed* preferences (wants) of individual subjects. Preference autonomy is ascribed an *instrumental* significance for economic welfare:[16] governmental interventions in the preferences of economic actors can lead to welfare losses, because they distort the *subjective valuation* of parties to a market transaction. Only in the absence of preference-interference – empirically verifiable circumstances excepted – can (individual) economic welfare actually be realized. Under the welfare-maximization approach, therefore, an assessment of health, environmental, risk and safety regulations with reference to their impacts on economic welfare should be conducted in the following way: if welfare is increased, the regulation under assessment must be declared permissible; otherwise, i. e. if welfare is diminished or in

---

14   At least, this ideal lies at the core of the concept of consumer surplus as a monetary measure of the maximum gain that an individual can obtain from a product at a given market price. First introduced by Jules Dupuit and later used by Alfred Marshall, the concept is defined as the difference between the maximum amount that an individual would be willing to pay for a good and the actual amount paid, see, Alfred Marshall, *Principles of Economics*, 1920, Book III Chapter VI §1; see also Revesz/Livermore (Fn. 6), 14, whose aim is to render cost-benefit analysis more neutral: "[…] conducted properly, cost-benefit analysis can help quantify areas of uncertainty to improve decision-making. If anything, formal cost-benefit analysis is especially useful in confronting imperfect information; it allows us to clarify the contours of our uncertainty and the distribution of potential outcomes, thereby improving our ability to make smart choices in the face of the unknown."

15   For an account on how market forces can be used to improve environmental regulation, see, E. Donald Elliott / Gail Charnley, Toward Bigger Bubbles. Why Interpollutant and Interrisk Trading are Good Ideas and How We Get from Here, *Forum For Applied Research and Pub. Policy* 13 (1998), 48–54.

16   See, e.g., Louis Kaplov / Steven Shavell, *Fairness versus Welfare*, 2002, 15–38; see also Richard A. Epstein, *Simple Rules for a Complex World*, 1995, 53–70.

cases of welfare-economic neutrality – or indeed uncertainty – the regulation must be prohibited.[17]

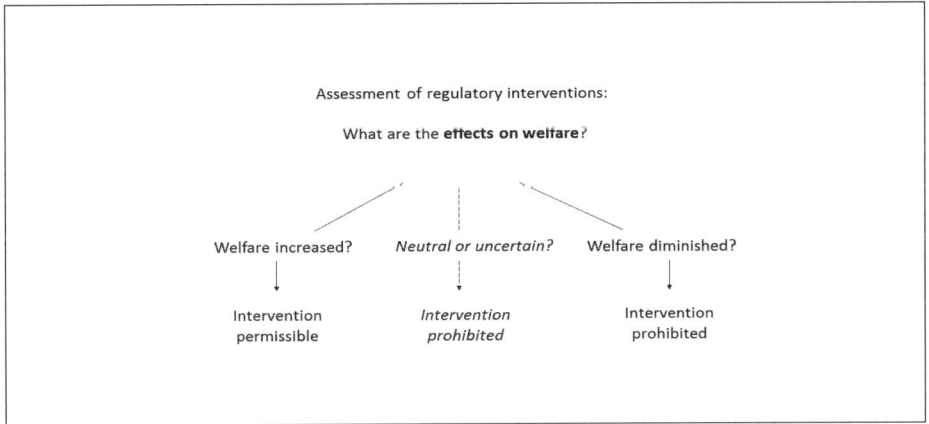

Fig. 1, Mechanism of Cost-Benefit Analysis:

According to this, it becomes clear that the welfare-maximization approach embodies the quest for an 'economically correct regulatory policy', or a 'more objective approach'. The maximization of economic welfare is deemed to be the supreme objective of regulation and there is widespread agreement on the desirability of minimizing false positives and false negatives. What is more, cost-benefit analysis, which uses more precise criteria and information than the traditional juridical approach is deemed to reduce the welfare costs through decision errors by better discriminating between the costs and benefits of regulation.[18]

B. Risk tradeoff analysis and discounting human lives

To be sure, cost-benefit analysis is a powerful tool for assessing regulation and may rightly be regarded as systematic thinking about decision-making. Who can oppose, economists sometimes ask, efforts to think in a systematic way about the consequences of different courses of action? The alternative, it would appear, is unexamined decision-making. But defining cost-benefit analysis so simply leaves it with few implications for actual regulatory decision-making. Presumably, therefore, those who urge regulation to make greater use of the technique have a more extensive prescription in mind.[19] Without questioning many of cost-benefit analysis' underlying assumptions here, the remainder of this article deals with the issue of whether it is justified to presume that the type of governmental interventions outlined above shall be prohibited in cases of *welfare-economic neutrality* – or *uncertainty*, respectively. Risk tradeoff analyses and discounting human lives are illustrative examples:

17   Note, however, that *in practice* this might be different: the fact that regulatory agencies sometimes use cost-benefit analysis only at the end of an assessment process might have the effect that in case of welfare-economic neutrality or uncertainty the regulation is declared permissible.

18   Revesz/Livermore (Fn. 6), 19.

19   For a comprehensive treatment of the implications of implementing cost-benefit analysis to competition law, see, Künzler (Fn. 12), 12.

In the environmental, health and safety context, the issue of whether regulatory decisions tend to minimize only *certain* risks has been discussed under the heading of *risk tradeoff analysis*. According to critics of this concept, cost-benefit analysis should pay attention not only to how regulation reduces a target risk but also to how it exacerbates others, how it raises countervailing risks.[20] A countervailing risk, for example, is in the nature of a harmful side effect of a pharmaceutical drug.[21] Or if a particular regulation would save an endangered species but would have the collateral effect of wiping out another, that collateral cost should be included in the initial analysis.[22] – In turn, taking account of countervailing risks has brought about criticism that cost-benefit analysis tends to look only at *negative* collateral consequences. In order to be balanced, the critics of this concept argue, cost-benefit analysis must acknowledge the ancillary *benefits* as well.[23] – However, if all possible effects should be considered, in practice it eventually becomes inevitable for health-risk assessments to be conducted on the basis of insufficient scientific data.[24] What ways, then, can regulators find to overcome such uncertainty so that their risk assessments can be completed? Need regulators expend resources to track all the positive and negative effects if the causal chain between benefit and rule is too attenuated? Or might it be sufficient to establish parity between ancillary benefits and countervailing risks?[25]

Moreover, in order to ensure that all flows of benefits and costs are expressed on a common basis in terms of their 'present value', such benefits and costs need be given a monetary value. As a result, the question of how decisionmakers measure the benefit of for example a saved life becomes critical. The standard way to measure the benefit of a saved life is to look at people's willingness to pay to avoid health and safety risks, which is then used to estimate the value of statistical life.[26] As willingness-to-pay studies of the value of human life have been conducted almost exclu-

---

20   See, e.g., John D. Graham / Jonathan Baert Wiener, Confronting Risk Tradeoffs, in: *Risk versus Risk: Tradeoffs in Protecting Health and the Environment*, ed. by John D. Graham / Jonathan Baert Wiener, 1995, 1–40; Robert W. Crandall / John D. Graham, The Effect of Fuel Economy Standards on Automobile Safety, *J.L. & Econ.* 21 (1989), 97, 101–115.

21   Aspirin, for example, may be taken to alleviate a headache, but it can also lead to a stomach ache. Therefore, in order to justify the use of Aspirin, the beneficial effects must outweigh the negative side effects.

22   The Supreme Court has referred to risk-tradeoff analysis in Whitman v. American Trucking Ass'ns, Inc., 531 U.S. 457 (2001). In that case, the plaintiffs sued the EPA to overturn a rule setting allowable levels of air pollution. In a concurrence, Justice Stephen Breyer maintained that risk-tradeoff analysis should be used by the EPA, finding that "the statute also permits the Administrator to take account of comparative health risks", id. at 495. Similarly, in a part of his decision in American Trucking that was not appealed by the EPA to the Supreme Court, Judge Williams decided the EPA had a duty to analyze the negative health impacts of its proposal to lower ozone levels, such as increases in skin cancer.

23   Aspirin, for example, has the unanticipated side effect of upsetting stomachs, but it also has the unanticipated benefit of preventing heart attacks and strokes. See for such criticism M. Shelef, Unanticipated Benefits of Automotive Emission Control: Reduction in Fatalities by Motor Vehicle Exhaust Gas, *Sci. Total Envtl.* 146/147 (1994), 93.

24   According to Cass R. Sunstein, Health-Health Tradeoffs, *U. Chi. L. Rev.* 63 (1996), 1423, 1541–1542, countervailing risks can be categorized into three groups: direct risk tradeoffs, substitution effects, and lulling effects. In all three cases, benefits accrue, both in the form of direct and ancillary benefits.

25   Revesz/Livermore (Fn. 6), 63 suggest the latter.

26   Kip W. Viscusi, The Value of Risks to Life and Health, *J. Econ. Literature* 31 (1993), 1912. The technique is generally traced to Thomas C. Schelling, The Life You Save May Be Your Own, in: *Problems in Public Expenditure Analysis*, ed. by Samuel B. Chase, Jr., 1986, 127 and E.J. Mishan, Evaluation of Life and Limb: A Theoretical Approach, *J. Pol. Econ.* 79 (1971), 687, 695–705.

sively in the context of industrial accidents, where the worker faces a risk of being either fatally injured by a piece of machinery and dying instantaneously, or surviving unscathed,[27] economists have devoted considerable attention to defining a relationship between the value of a life lost today and the value of a life lost years from now. Such temporal models, also known as *life-cycle models,* study the distribution of an individual's utility throughout his life.[28] Under this methodology, however – because younger people will on average lose more life years when they die –, younger people's lives are assigned a greater value than that of older people.[29] Also, the choice of the discount rate, the corresponding life-year value matters.[30] Nevertheless, in practice, there is disagreement as to whether all life-years should be valued equally no matter when they occur during the life cycle or whether they should be weighed differently. Also, should quality adjusted life-years – the quality of life losses from less-than-perfect health – be taken into account? If so, should a particular measure of different health states be adjusted to how different people adapt to health setbacks?

The discounting issue becomes even more prominent when environmental, health and safety benefits occur in the *future,* rather than at the time of the regulation. In one context, the target risks have long latency periods. Decades can pass between the exposure to a contaminant and the manifestation of the related disease.[31] In another context, regulatory benefits accrue to future generations.[32] And while the discounting issues under such circumstances are multi-faceted and complex, it is worth noting that a tendency has been observed according to which proponents of cost-benefit analysis favor discounting benefits that occur in the future – both in the latency and future generation contexts – whereas in contrast, environmentalists and others favorably disposed toward regulation are inclined to oppose such discounting.[33]

Hence if – in cases of uncertainty – price is taken as the sole means of measuring and balancing the costs and benefits of regulation, this inevitably involves *differentiated weighting* of the various factors concerned. The regulatory policy-maker, by using weighting factors to compensate for such disparities, faces a choice which can ultimately only be justified politically. On what basis are the said weighting factors to

27   See, Maureen L. Cropper/Frances G. Sussman, Valuing Future Risks to Life, *J. Envtl. Econ. & Mgmt.* 19 (1990), 160 with reference to further evidence.

28   See, Sherwin Rosen, The Quantity and Quality of Life: A Conceptual Framework, in: *Valueing Health for Policy: An Economic Approach,* ed. by George Tolley / Donald Kenkel / Robert Fabian, 1994, 221.

29   Revesz/Livermore (Fn. 6), 77 argue that this outcome is both inconsistent with economic theory and flatly contradicted by empirical data on how people value risk.

30   See, Richard L. Revesz, Environmental Regulation, Cost-Benefit Analysis, and the Discounting of Human Lives, *Colum. L. Rev.* 99 (1999), 941, 974–981; Kip W. Viscusi, The Value of Life in Legal Contexts: Survey and Critique, *Am. L & Econ. Rev.* 2 (2000), 195–222.

31   The issue of discounting was salient during the EPA's consideration of the asbestos ban. The affected industries challenged the regulation issued by EPA in Corrosion Proof Fittings v. EPA, 947 F.2d 1201 (5th Cir. 1991). The challenges prevailed on the claim that the EPA had not appropriately discounted the benefits of the regulation over the latency period. In his opinion, Judge Smith argued that "although various commentators dispute whether it ever is appropriate to discount benefits when they are measured in human lives, we note that it would skew the results to discount only costs without according similar treatment to the benefits side of the equation. [...] Because the EPA must discount costs to perform its evaluations properly, the EPA also should discount benefits to preserve an apples-to-apples comparison.", id. at 1218.

32   For the standard account, see, John Hartwick, Intergenerational Equity and the Investing of Rents from Exhaustible Resources, *Am. Econ. Rev.* 67 (1977), 972–974; Robert M. Solow, An Almost Practical Step toward Sustainability, *Resources Pol.* 19 (1993), 162–172.

33   See, Revesz/Livermore (Fn. 6), 95–96 with reference to further literature.

be defined? And what goals should be pursued by introducing such weighting factors? Whichever route is taken, it determines the result finally obtained. But depending on the option chosen, the assessment of the case in question will not always be
the same. This arrangement runs the risk of degrading the welfare-economic balancing model to a decision rule subject to arbitrary manipulation. Suddenly it is no
longer a matter of balancing quantifiable factors. It is rather a matter of a policy debate on the role of protecting the pro-regulatory interests allegedly restrained from a
certain practice or protecting the anti-regulatory interests alleged to be restraining
other parties, played out under the guise of an economic efficiency analysis.

III. The problem of value neutrality

A. Welfare maximization under parameter uncertainty

The problem of obtaining all the necessary data in a given case seems to render the
goal of maximizing social and economic welfare an almost insurmountable task. It
also gives rise to the question of whether welfare maximization under parameter uncertainty is actually *desirable*. There is an additional question mark hanging over this
goal under such circumstances in light of the difficulty of making interpersonal
comparisons of utility:
    Assuming that even if the advantages and disadvantages of some particular
practice could somehow be established and empirically recorded with precision the
proposed balancing of welfare effects does not make it possible to draw any general
conclusions as to the *actual* differences in utility for society. In view of the impossibility established in studies by Lionel C. Robbins[34] and Kenneth Arrow[35] of interpersonal comparisons or aggregation of utility perceptions, it cannot be taken for
granted that for example a price rise of $ 50 for a given product X – in order to
compensate, say, for the environmental implications of manufacturing – necessarily
means that buyer A suffers an individual loss valued at $ 50. It may well be that
buyer A values his individual loss of utility more highly than buyer B's corresponding utility loss. The subjective valuations of a $ 50 loss by buyer A and B need not be
identical. This applies equally in relation to the benefits obtained by the new regulation, or in relation to the possibly very heterogeneous group of consumers as a
whole. For consumer A, a price rise of $ 50 may perhaps imply a higher subjective
loss of utility than for consumer B. For the loss of utility associated with a certain
price rise is greater for someone without much income or wealth than for someone
with a very high income and plenty of assets.[36] From the difference produced by

---

34   Lionel C. Robbins, *An Essay on the Nature & Significance of Economic Science*, 1937, 138.
35   Kenneth Arrow, *Social Choice and Individual Values*, 1963, 9.
36   An effect of the law of diminishing marginal utility. Differences in subjective valuation also result
      from income or endowment effects, see, explanations in Russell B. Korobkin / Thomas S. Ulen,
      Law and Behavioral Science: Removing the Rationality Assumption from Law and Economics,
      Calif. L. Rev. 88 (2000), 1051, 1113–1144; Daniel Kahneman / Jack L. Knetsch / Richard H. Thaler,
      The Endowment Effect, Loss Aversion, and Status Quo Bias, *J. Econ. Perspectives* 5 (1991), 193, 194,
      197; see also Korobkin/Ulen, id. at 1107. One further difficulty is that individual impressions of
      utility are obviously not constant over time. People tend towards time-inconsistent behavior, i.e. an
      event that is more immediate is assessed differently from an event that is more remote in time, see,
      Ted O'Donoghue / Matthew Rabin, Behavioral Economics, Public Policy, and Paternalism. Study-
      ing Optimal Paternalism, Illustrated by a Model of Sin Taxes, *Am. Econ. Rev.* 93 (2003), 186–191;

changing a single variable, therefore, it is quite difficult – if not impossible – to draw conclusions about the scale of the individual's actual utility gain or loss, and hence the welfare gain or loss for society as a whole. Against this backdrop, Ian M. Little's comment still seems topical today: „The […] utilitarian thesis was that one could add up the welfares of different individuals to arrive at the welfare of society. That idea has now to be abandoned."[37]

Thanks to the introduction of the Pareto and the Kaldor/Hicks criterion, the new welfare economics today operates on the basis of an ordinal concept of utility which only compares different states in terms of 'better', 'worse' or 'equally good' and thus avoids interpersonal utility comparisons *in theory* at least. Even so, *in practice* the problem often remains unresolved. For regulatory agencies and courts there may be no option but to convert individual perceptions of utility into *monetary units*, i. e. with reference to an 'objective' scale that does not, however, permit any direct conclusions to be drawn about actual utility assessments.[38] However, in order to draw such conclusions as to the *actual* differences in utility for society, all parties affected by a particular intervention or non-intervention would have to be *asked* which measure they would feel indifferent about, which would be plainly an impossible and highly impractical exercise.[39]

It can be concluded from these reasons that cost-benefit analysis is – at least in cases of deep uncertainty – incomplete – or *imprecise*.[40] To diagnose the welfare effects of a particular change in conditions for given individuals, it would be necessary to determine the *actual* utility for each individual and include this in the economic calculation of welfare. But the purely monetary measurement of advantages and disadvantages does not allow to determine whether, in a concrete case, for example, a loss to person A of, say $ 1,000 in property damage as a result of oil spills is compensated by a gain of, say, $ 1,200 in increased turnover resulting from an additional oil cleanup mandate for person B. If price is still used as the sole means of 'measur-

Shane Frederick / George Loewenstein/Ted O'Donoghue, Time Discounting and Time Preference: A Critical Review, *J. Econ. Literature* 40 (2002), 351, 351–401; Korobkin/Ulen, id. at 1119; Matthew Rabin, Psychology and Economics, *J. Econ. Literature* 36 (1998), 11, 38.

37 Ian M. Little, *A Critique of Welfare Economics*, 1957, 52.

38 The problem may (partially) be circumvented by e.g. making estimates on the basis of previously conducted surveys or using other valuation techniques such as willingness-to-pay studies. However, because such studies are often rare agencies revert to discounting as a 'second-best' approach, see, Revesz (Fn. 30), 957–960. In the field of health economics, use of variants such as cost-utility analysis and quality-adjusted life years are used to analyze the effects of health policies. However, even if with such methods, unlike with cost-benefit analysis, the benefits do not have to be expressed in *monetary* terms, a *numerical value* (e.g. quality-adjusted life years) has to be assigned. Although in this way, the endowment effect may be avoided because e.g. of different time discounting and time preferences amongst individuals, the problem of interpersonal comparisons of utility is not entirely resolved.

39 With regard to willingness to pay and the use of average values of a statistical life Revesz/Livermore (Fn. 6), 83 therefore state: "If the average is used for the value of a statistical life, people with high willingness to pay receive 'too little' regulation, people with low willingness to pay receive 'too much' regulation, and the average person gets a 'just right' level of regulation. In many cases, it will not be possible to finely calibrate regulation, so this phenomenon is simply a byproduct of the inability to individually tailor regulations."

40 Several peer-reviewed studies have pointed out to possible inaccuracies of cost-benefit estimates, see, Bent Flyvbjerg/Mette Skamris Holm/Soren Buhl, Underestimating Costs in Public Work Projects. Error or Lie?, *ABA J. 68* (2002), 279–295 (regarding costs in transportation infrastructure planning); Bent Flyvbjerg / Mette Skamris Holm/Soren Buhl, How (In)accurate are Demand Forecasts in Public Work Projects? The Case of Transportation, *J. Am. Planning Ass'n* 71 (2005), 131–146 (regarding benefits in transportation infrastructure planning).

ing' welfare effects in society, then this will implicitly involve excluding other welfare relevant determinants from the economic welfare calculus. Cost-benefit analysis therefore presupposes a *particular definition of 'economic welfare'* – thereby potentially excluding important welfare-relevant determinants.

B. Cost-benefit analysis and the search for scientific objectivity

In light of the preceding remarks, the question remains of whether the cost-benefit analysis principle itself is based on scientific evidence – given the fact that it is an empirically based concept – and is, in that sense, 'objective'. As pointed out above, the welfare-maximization principle presupposes, among other things, that there is general agreement on the *meaning of 'social or economic welfare'*, and that it is possible to predict whether regulatory interventions will promote or impede this concept of 'social or economic welfare' in future. In light of this, one is tempted to ask whether *this particular concept of 'social or economic welfare'* is based on a factual (empirical) observation expressing an element of scientific knowledge, or whether the concept is merely a conventional stipulation, or a postulate:

Our colloquial understanding of 'social or economic welfare' is primarily associated with *freedom of action* or *preference autonomy*.[41] It is assumed that preference autonomy brings forth a series of macroeconomic benefits, which cannot be defined conclusively beforehand but are only achieved indirectly, by means of protecting the freedom of action of individuals.[42] Freedom of action leads to the advancement of technical progress, adaptation of production factors to changes in economic data, assimilation of offers to buyer preferences, optimal resource allocation, spreading of the risk of free enterprise among market participants, selection of efficient enterprises, stabilization of prices, neutralization of economic power, etc. On the other hand, 'social or economic welfare' – as understood by proponents of the cost-benefit analysis paradigm – is not defined indirectly through freedom of action of individuals, but *directly and conclusively* with reference to welfare impacts that can be determined and measured in monetary terms. The critical divergences between the neoclassical principle of 'social or economic welfare' and the open-ended freedom of action paradigm therefore reside in a *definition*.[43]

Now, the fact alone that the expression 'social or economic welfare' is *not* assigned a firmly bounded meaning shows that *no* scientifically verifiable factual observation with regard to 'social or economic welfare' based on reality is possible: to claim that for example the purely monetary concept of 'social or economic welfare' of the cost-benefit analysis approach is scientifically 'true' would be untenable because any such observation relies upon a *conventional stipulation* defining what economic welfare really is. In other words: any attempt to verify the concept of 'social or economic welfare' empirically on the basis of experience and with reference to physical and/or mental realities (prices, quantities, preference autonomy, market par-

41   See, e.g., Epstein (Fn. 16), 53–70.
42   According to Epstein (Fn. 16), 72 this is manifested clearly in the nature of contracts: "The basic mechanism of contract is very simple, powerful and universal. It essentially involves your surrendering something that you value in exchange for something else that you value even more. If both sides allow the trade to occur, there will be an enormous increase in overall well-being, unless there are some systematic losses to third parties […]".
43   See, Künzler (Fn. 12), 61–63.

ticipants' choices and fall-back options, etc.) is immediately met with the problem that it is necessary to know *in advance* what factors have to be considered relevant to welfare. In order to know what 'social or economic welfare' is, it is necessary to pre-suppose experiences that differ from other experiences in that they represent experiences which can be attributed to 'social or economic welfare'. However, this already takes for granted the concept of 'social or economic welfare' which is the very aim of the inquiry.[44] For how can certain behaviors be said to have welfare impacts without even knowing what 'social or economic welfare' actually and precisely means? Hence, empirical studies *on their own* cannot result in a certain definition of 'social or economic welfare'. A verifiable or falsifiable factual observation is generally only possible when the material to be investigated is already precisely delimited; in other words, when the situation to be described has already been identified.[45] A verifiable or falsifiable definition of 'social or economic welfare' is therefore only possible if 'social or economic welfare' were clearly delimited by linguistic usage (i. e. if there exists a habitual language use), or if a conventional stipulation – *an axiom* –[46] already precisely circumscribes the material to be (empirically) investigated.[47] However, there is no sufficiently clear linguistic usage or other universally valid definition regarding the concept of 'social or economic welfare'. Thus *no* factual observation with regard to reality is possible.

It follows that the concept of 'social or economic welfare' is based on a *pre-scientific decision*,[48] meaning it should not be judged on its truth but on its *effectiveness* in terms of the conclusions it permits to be drawn.[49] This 'pragmatic' interpretation of the wealth-maximization principle presupposes a level-headed debate in a spirit of tolerance.[50] It is not conducive to such a debate when two factions try to 'disprove' the other's views and insist on the rightness of their own position. The decisive issue is rather to understand the approach underlying a particular view, and to think through the consequences, i. e. the advantages and disadvantages of each proposed solution. In other words, it is necessary to inquire where a particular approach will lead, what its implications are. Crucially it must have the power to solve particular practical problems. This means abandoning a value-free approach,[51] for when it comes to the question of which consequences of a regulatory policy are desirable or undesirable, having to make value judgments or respect value judgments imposed by the legal regime is unavoidable.

---

44   A general problem of the theory of science, see, Ott (Fn. 12), 150–151; Karl Popper, *Realism and the Aim of Science. The Post-Script to the Logic of Scientific Discovery*, 1983, 24–26; with respect to the present context Künzler (Fn. 12), 281–282.

45   Ott (Fn. 12), 151.

46   Note, however, the vulnerability of this metaphor: while a *stipulative definition* proposes a linguistic usage, an *axiomatic stipulation* serves as a starting point for deducing and inferring other (theory dependent) truths or (mathematical) statements.

47   See generally Ott (Fn. 12), 151; with respect to the present context Künzler (Fn. 12), 283–284.

48   See generally Ott (Fn. 12), 163; with respect to the present context Künzler (Fn. 12), 284.

49   For a critical overview on Popper's falsifiability criterion of demarcation in economics, see, Bruce J. Caldwell, Clarifying Popper, *J. Econ. Literature* 29 (1991), 1, 1–33.

50   Bruce A. Ackerman / Richard B. Stewart, Reforming Environmental Law: The Democratic Case for Market Incentives, *Colum. J. Envtl. L.* 13 (1988), 171, 189; see more generally Ott (Fn. 12), 167.

51   Ackerman/Stewart (Fn. 50), 189; Ott (Fn. 12), 171.

IV. Cornerstones of a reality-based framework of regulatory policy

The preceding parts of this article have revealed that cost-benefit analysis does not necessarily stand for a scientifically sound approach. At least in cases of uncertainty, the orientation towards welfare maximization remains a postulate that is based on value judgments. Any policy recommendation based on that principle suggests a degree of precision that cannot scientifically be proven. Therefore, considerable doubts remain if concrete policy recommendations should be made. On the other hand, it cannot be inferred from this that there are other approaches which are necessarily able to achieve better results. Hence, it would be false to assume that other approaches are superior to the cost-benefit analysis approach. However, as uncertainty about parameters describing preferences implies not only uncertainty about the dynamics of the predicted outcomes but also implies uncertainty about cost-benefit analysis' utility-based welfare criterion, it seems worth considering how the welfare-maximization approach can be complemented where *uncertainty* plays a central role or where *'hard cases'* have to be decided. Section IV.A. roughly outlines the legal implications of cost-benefit analysis in such circumstances. Section IV.B. delineates the epistemological background of complexity theory and section IV.C. makes specific propositions on how to better handle complexity issues. I argue that in cases of extreme uncertainty cost-benefit analysis should be accompanied by a *balancing of interests* and that such a balancing does not necessarily imply more stringent regulation or presumably welfare-reducing policy measures.

A. Legal implications of cost-benefit analysis

The rigorous assumption from neoclassical welfare economics that governmental interventions in individual preferences are only justified when they *demonstrably* have a welfare-enhancing effect is based on the implicit view that „what we don't know won't hurt us".[52] However, in situations of deep uncertainty, this might mean to *overlook unintended consequences.* The Food and Drug Administration (FDA) for example has made its risk-assessment burden lighter by suggesting that novel scientific processes in the case of cloning, genetic modification and nanoengineering are not in themselves cause for regulatory scrutiny or distinction. Rather, they should only become relevant if they lead to demonstrated differences in the physical or compositional characteristics of end products as compared to conventional counterparts.[53] Introducing nanomaterials or genetically modified organisms widely into field environments however means ignoring the *irreversible nature* of such actions.[54] On the other hand, the proposition from advocates of neoclassical welfare economics to simply price and incorporate the value of this precaution into the welfare-economic

---

52   Kysar (Fn. 5), 91; see also Revesz/Livermore (Fn. 6), 1.
53   See, Douglas A. Kysar, Preferences for Processes: The Process/Product Distinction and the Regulation of Consumer Choice, *Harv. L. Rev.* 118 (2004), 525 with further references.
54   Kenneth J. Arrow / Anthony C. Fisher, Environmental Preservation, Uncertainty, and Irreversibility, *Q. J. Econ.* 88 (1974), 312, 317 argue that "[…] if we are uncertain about the payoff to investment in development, we should err on the side of underinvestment, rather than overinvestment, since development is irreversible. Given an ability to learn from experience, underinvestment can be remedied […] whereas mistaken overinvestment cannot, the consequences persisting in effect for all time."

optimization calculus so that cost-benefit analysis can continue in the usual way[55] would „invite exclusionary, technocratic decision making in the face of grave uncertain collective choices, precisely the context that [...] instead requires inclusiveness, transparency, and candid acknowledgment that ethical choices are being undertaken."[56] The veil of apparent scientific rigor, therefore, has to be lifted and the blunt reality of indeterminacy needs to be addressed. In situations of deep uncertainty, „the resulting permissive approach [that] comports well with the tendency of liberal market democracies to permit private action unless and until a public justification has been demonstrated [entails the problem that] this predisposition has been presented in a scientific vernacular, as an assumption about the empirical tendencies of nascent technologies, rather than as what it properly is – a preference for *distributing the burden of uncertainty* in a particular way, according to political values."[57]

B. Regulating complexity

The view that analysts can keep with the classical scientific tradition, and refuse to accommodate the implications of complexity theory in the very scientific models that are used to generate ranges of costs and benefits, is hardly tenable if *recent epistemological principles* are given appropriate attention. In the sciences, it is recognized today that a distinction has to be made between calculable *risk* – risk to which a numerical probability can be assigned, and of which the likelihood, direction, and magnitude by which actual outcomes may deviate from the estimated (mean) risk can also be estimated – and *uncertainty*, to which a numerical probability and distribution cannot be assigned with any confidence that it is correct.[58] In his essay, „The General Theory of Employment", John M. Keynes defined uncertainty as follows:

> „*By 'uncertain' knowledge, let me explain, I do not mean merely to distinguish what is known for certain from what is only probable. The game of roulette is not subject, in this sense, to uncertainty [...]. The sense in which I am using the term is that in which the prospect of a European war is uncertain, or the price of copper and the rate of interest twenty years hence, or the obsolescence of a new invention, or the position of private wealth-owners in the social system in 1970. About these matters there is no scientific basis on which to form any calculable probability whatever. We simply do not know.*"[59]

This distinction is closely intertwined with the notion of *simple* and *complex phenomena* which had been discovered by the mathematician Warren Weaver and the economist

---

55   Id. at 319; see also Revesz/Livermore (Fn. 6), 16–19.

56   Kysar (Fn. 5), 92; for further critique of the 'unprecautionary principle', see, Wendy E. Wagner, The Precautionary Principle and Chemical Regulation in the U.S., *Hum. & Ecological Risk Assessment* 6 (2000), 459, 466–68.

57   Kysar (Fn. 5), 91 (emphasis added).

58   The distinction is explicit in John M. Keynes, The General Theory of Employment, *Q. J. Econ.* 51 (1937), 209; see also Frank H. Knight, *Risk, Uncertainty, and Profit*, 1921, 19–20; The term "risk", as it is usually used in economics refers simply to the probability of some event's occurring, rather than, as is common in ordinary language, referring to the probability times the consequence (i.e., the expected cost), as when one says that e.g. mountain climbing is risky.

59   Keynes (Fn. 58), 213–214.

Friedrich A. von Hayek in the course of the last century:[60]

Simple phenomena consist of few variables which stand in deterministic (fixed) relations with one another. The most extreme case involves only two variables, of which the state or the change of one is the cause of the state or the change of the other. Consequently, as long as one knows the state or the change of the causal variable, it is possible to derive a prognosis for the effect variable. Further, if the causal variables are controllable, then the effect variables can also be controlled. So the first variable depends entirely on the second, and not on (a large number of) other factors. Accordingly, the behavior of the first variable can be described with a sufficient degree of precision simply by considering its dependency on the second variable, ignoring the more trivial effects of other factors. Simple relations of this kind are found mainly in the classical natural sciences of the 17th to 20th centuries, e.g. in Newton's laws of mechanics.

In contrast to that, *complex phenomena* consist of a large number of variables which relate to one another in a 'systematic' way. These relations are not invariant but can change in space and time. The character of such phenomena depends not only upon the attributes and the relative frequency of the individual component elements, but also upon the way in which the individual elements are interconnected. *Complexity* is a particular characteristic of the phenomena studied in economics and the social sciences, but also in such disciplines as biology, medicine or psychology. To derive specific predictions about certain events in these subject areas, one needs complete information on every single element of the phenomenon in question. The ability to make specific and concrete statements about such phenomena would presuppose an unattainable amount of knowledge about singular conditions. Without this knowledge it is only possible to make what are known as *pattern predictions*; that is to say, what can be learned relates only to certain general attributes and to the short- and medium-term direction of the operative processes, at the most. Nevertheless, this knowledge can still be useful in some cases for influencing these process attributes and the direction of the process. On the other hand, it is impossible to recognize the individual stages of these processes in advance, let alone their ultimate outcome. Furthermore, it is impossible to obtain prognostic knowledge of the kind that would allow the prediction of specific occurrences.

In current research and applied practice it is common for such complex phenomena to be treated *as if* they were simple phenomena. This is partly because, today, the knowledge of simple fixed relations and their application for prognosis and control has become the goal of all disciplines and their hallmark of quality. A 'science' that cannot attain this standard 'yet' is deemed to be backward. These 'backward' sciences attempt to align their methods, their interpretation of results and the use of their findings for prognosis and control with conventions from the natural sciences.[61] Keynes highlighted this phenomenon with respect to maintaining adherence to the optimization-policy framework:

> *„Nevertheless, the necessity for action and for decision compels us as practical men to do our best to overlook this awkward fact and to behave exactly as we should if we had behind us a good Benthamite calculation of a series of prospective advantages and*

---

60   Warren Weaver, *Wirtschaft und Komplexität*, 18 ORDO. Jahrbuch für die Ordnung von Wirtschaft und Gesellschaft 163 (1967).

61   On the reductionist view of neoclassical welfare economics, see, Ackerman (Fn. 10), 940–941 (1986).

disadvantages, each multiplied by its appropriate probability, waiting to be summed.''[62]

But when it comes to solving complex problems, the relevance of these methods is dubious: in the real world, ascertaining all the necessary data to capture a complex phenomenon is a difficulty that is virtually insuperable. Consequently, if one wants to consider more recent epistemological principles in regulatory policy, one has to pay due regard to the fact that in the case of many of the phenomena subject to environmental, health, risk and safety regulation, decision makers should abandon the pretense of actually attempting to locate and pursue an 'optimal' outcome. As these involve the interdependent actions of millions of factors, whose structures are *not constant* but *variable* in space and time,[63] decisionmakers „should present for collective consideration an unalloyed depiction of what is, and is not, known about the possible consequences of human action, so that the political community can consider directly whether it wants to entertain […] irreversible […] harm as part of its unique legacy."[64] In other words, if the implications of complexity theory are accommodated properly into the scientific models that are used to assess costs and benefits, such an accommodation often will mean that scientists are only able to offer a series of *qualitatively described scenarios* that might flow from policy choices, without probability estimates assigned to them, rather than *quantitatively* depicted but ultimately unhelpful cost-benefit ranges.[65]

C. Assigning the burden of proof according to real-world conditions

1. Balancing of interests and the principle of proportionality

The *assignment of an implicit burden of proof* to regulatory agencies that predictably biases decisions against the protection of the environment and against health or safety „might be appropriate within the ivory towers of the university, where scholars aim to bolster the scientific credentials of welfare economics by portraying it as the 'objective implementation of benefit-cost analysis, based on established economic theory and empirical research'. In the real world of policy making, however, decisions [often] must be made in advance of comprehensive knowledge."[66] Therefore, when assigning the burden of proof, irreversibilities and the problem that future individuals – or even just agents who are imperfectly situated to assert their rights or interests in the manner that today's liberalism often demands of them have to be taken into account.

As shown above, recent epistemological principles such as uncertainty and complexity theory offer possible answers to resolving these problems: regulatory agencies should, in cases of deep uncertainty adopt measures that are *proportionate* to the threat perceived and that are open to revision as knowledge develops.[67] For the

---

62   Keynes (Fn. 58), 214.
63   Weaver (Fn. 60), 163.
64   Kysar (Fn. 5), 97–98.
65   Clive L. Spash, *Greenhouse Economics: Value and Ethics*, 2002, 115, 127; Kysar (Fn. 5), 97.
66   Kysar (Fn. 5), 214–215.
67   Commission of the European Communities, Communication from the commission on the precautionary principle (2000), *available at* >http://ec.europa.eu/dgs/health_consumer/library/pub/pub07_en.pdf<.

reasons set out, they should not be hampered by a *default assumption* against any kind of government regulation in advance of complete scientific demonstration of harm. Consequently, *in cases of deep uncertainty*, cost-benefit analysis has to be accompanied by a *balancing of interests* which presupposes 1) identification of potentially negative effects resulting from a phenomenon, and 2) a scientific evaluation of the risk which because of the insufficiency of the data, their inconclusive or imprecise nature, makes it impossible to determine with sufficient certainty the risk in question. When an activity raises threats of harm to human health or the environment, precautionary measures should be taken *even if some cause-and-effect relationships are not fully established scientifically*.

2. Measures resulting from reliance on the proportionality principle

In the kind of situations described, the question remains of *how* decision-makers have to respond. Above all, they have to decide *whether or not to act*. The appropriate response in a given situation is the result of a political decision, a function of the risk level that is 'acceptable' to the society on which the risk is imposed. For regulatory agencies this problem becomes more manageable when, as Professor E. Donald Elliott has suggested, viewed diachronically (over time) rather than analytically assessing what relative weights should properly be given to facts (risk) and values (precaution) synchronically and in the abstract.[68] Thus the practical question that every regulator in such situations must ask is:

> „*Shall I act to address this particular problem now, basing my decision on what is currently known (or, more accurately, believed to be known)? Or shall I instead defer action until a later date, when more may be known, but at the cost of what occurs in the meantime?*"[69]

Viewed from this practical, diachronic perspective – which is the situation that a regulator actually faces in trying to decide on concrete actions – the problem of the relative weights to be assigned to fact (risk) and to value (precaution) may become much more tractable:

> „*As a matter of common sense, a regulator may be well advised to wait until later to act if, but only if, (a) it seems unlikely that much preventable harm will occur in the meantime, but (b) it also seems likely that enough useful information will be developed in the meantime so that making a better decision in the future will be substantially less difficult than it is today.*"[70]

Only with the help of a balancing of interests can such an assessment be made „[...] because these quantities are incommensurable (i. e., they exist in different realms and implicate different values), and because they involve predictions about the future [...]."[71]

---

68   E. Donald Elliott, Global Climate Change and Regulatory Uncertainty, *Ariz. J. Int'l Comp. L.* 9 (1992), 259, 261.

69   Ortwin Renn / E. Donald Elliott, Chemical Regulation in the United States and Europe, in: *The Reality of Precaution: Comparing Risk Regulation in the United States and Europe*, ed. by Jonathan B. Wiener / Michael D. Rogers / James K. Hammitt / Peter H. Sand, 2011.

70   Id.

71   Id.

3. Nature of the action ultimately taken

With respect to maximizing overall welfare, the implicit assumption by cost-benefit analysis that the inevitable uncertainty described must be construed *against* government interventions is based on the grounds that according to the neoclassical welfare-economics concept of 'social or economic welfare' 'in case of doubt' overall well-being cannot be enhanced by interfering with individual preferences.

However, a *balancing of interests* in such cases – as opposed to cost-benefit analysis – involves making value-judgments which affect legally protected interests. And by no means must these value-judgments necessarily correspond to the values of welfare economics. Rather, such value-judgments might be prescribed in the constitution and in a particular statute by the legislator.[72] In case of doubt, these must be respected and applied to the concrete case when the balancing test is carried out.[73] Moreover, in cases of doubt, a „balancing of interests" may add a *second* and a *third dimension* to the linear, one-dimensional decisionmaking system that is assumed by an approach according to which economic conditions are translated predictably into economic conclusions that call for prescribed economic measures, and environmental conditions can be translated predictably into environmental conclusions that call for environmental measures, and so forth.[74] And although such a „balancing of interests" is an expression of the general principle of proportionality, which is particularly significant in relation to the restriction of basic rights in constitutional law, these kinds of interference with the preferences of those concerned are widely acknowledged in 'reality-based economics'. Colin F. Camerer, Samuel Issacharoff, George Loewenstein, Ted O'Donoghue and Matthew Rabin use the term 'asymmetric' or 'benign' paternalism:

> „*A regulation is asymmetrically paternalistic if it creates large benefits for those who [are subject to] errors, while imposing little or no harm on [others]. Such regulations are relatively harmless to [the latter], while at the same time advantageous to those [subject to] suboptimal choices.*"[75]

One of the main aims of this kind of governmental regulation is to bring interventions in individual preferences in line with the goal of reducing 'false positives' and 'false negatives', i. e. with the goal of maximizing macrosocietal welfare. At the same time, it allows for decision-making criteria which do justice to *real-world* conditions.[76]

---

72 Künzler (Fn. 12), 64–65.
73 A notion that has been referred to as 'environmental constitutionalism', see, Kysar (Fn. 5), 229–254.
74 Kysar (Fn. 5), 71.
75 Colin F. Camerer / Samuel Issacharoff / George Loewenstein / Ted O'Donoghue / Matthew Rabin, Regulation for Conservatives: Behavioral Economics and the Case for 'Asymmetric Paternalism', *U. Pa. L. Rev.* 151 (2003), 1211–1212.
76 Id. at 1221; Christine Jolls, Governing America: The Emergence of Behavioral Law and Economics, *Max Weber Lecture Series* (2010), 1–4, *available at* >http://www.law.yale.edu/documents/pdf/ Faculty/Jolls_TheEmergenceofBehavioralLawandEconomics1.pdf<; Richard H. Thaler / Cass R. Sunstein, *Nudge. Improving Decisions about Health, Wealth, and Happiness*, 2008, 5 sum up this kind of governmental interventions under the heading of 'libertarian paternalism': "The libertarian aspect of our strategies lies in the straightforward insistence that, in general, people should be free to do what they like [...]. To borrow a phrase from the late Milton Friedman, libertarian paternalists urge that people should be 'free to choose'. We strive to design policies that maintain or increase freedom of choice. When we use the term libertarian to modify the word paternalism, we simply mean liberty-preserving. And when we say liberty-preserving, we really mean it. Libertarian paternalists want to

V. Concluding remarks

This article is not a petition against cost-benefit analysis in regulation but a plea for the application of *reality-based* economic concepts and analysis methods.[77] The underlying hypothesis of the neoclassical welfare-economics approach, that economic welfare can only be measured on the scale of 'economic efficiency', is not unreservedly tenable. And it is reasonably clear that this no longer reflects the 'majority view' within economics, either. In fact, it is now well recognized in the discipline of economics that social and economic welfare is not conceptually limited to material values, that outcomes are not always predictable, and that the states of equilibrium studied by the neoclassical economists sometimes bear little resemblance to the complexity and uncertainty of reality. The problem of traditional economic models lies in the inherent contradictions that arise when they are being applied to reality. They tend to downplay if not ignore the need to decide on the real 'pre-givens' of regulatory policy by relying on the 'objectivity' of a certain paradigm of macrosocietal phenomena. At the same time, support is sought in speculative yet very concrete individual predictions. What this fails to recognize is the degree of *responsibility* incumbent upon regulatory policy-makers for the theories they develop.[78] Expectations are being created which the regulatory system is incapable of fulfilling from the outset, for many decisions on the basis of the neoclassical welfare-economic calculus may have, in reality, considerable external implications.

However, once it is borne in mind that a more 'reality-based approach' resorts to a variety of epistemological principles, on closer examination there is far less of a discrepancy between a reality-based regulatory policy and scientific advances than when neoclassical welfare economics is taken as an absolute standard. As stated at the outset, 'reality-based economics' is not as unified as neoclassical welfare economics, but that is an *advantage* rather than a disadvantage, because it means that different theories can be used to explain *different aspects* of the subject matter. In summing up, a *pragmatic approach* seems unavoidable, or, as Arthur C. Pigou mentions in the early pages of 'The Economics of Welfare' comparing economists to doctors, who are interested in scientific knowledge „for the healing that knowledge may help to bring."[79] To a doctor, the key thing about treating a disease is not the elegance of the analysis underpinning the diagnosis he makes, but whether the treatment he recommends works. Reality-based lawyers and economists have the same outlook.

---

make it easy for people to go their own way; they do not want to burden those who want to exercise their freedom."

77   See, Jolls (Fn. 76), 1–4.

78   Wernhard Möschel, Wettbewerb zwischen Handlungsfreiheiten und Effizienzzielen, in: *Recht und spontane Ordnung. Festschrift für Ernst-Joachim Mestmäcker zum 80. Geburtstag*, ed. by Christoph Engel / Wernhard Möschel, 2006, 355, 365; Ott (Fn. 12), 167; Künzler (Fn. 12), 289.

79   Arthur C. Pigou, *The Economics of Welfare*, (Transaction ed.) 2009, 5.

Stanley L. Paulson*

The Very Idea of Legal Positivism

Introduction

Much in recent discussions on legal positivism suggests that the controversy surrounding the notion turns on the distinction between inclusive and exclusive legal positivism.[1] As a point of departure in distinguishing them, the separation principle is helpful.[2] At the most general level, the separation principle – as Kenneth Einar Himma neatly puts it – denies 'that there is necessary overlap' between the law and morality.[3] The separation principle counts, then, as the contradictory of the morality principle, according to which there *is* 'necessary overlap' between the law and morality, however this might be explicated.[4] What the legal positivist's denial of the morality principle comes to can be refined, we are told, by appealing to the distinction between inclusive and exclusive legal positivism. Inclusive legal positivism leaves open the possibility that in a given legal system there may or may not be necessary overlap between the law and morality, while exclusive legal positivism recognizes no possibility of necessary overlap.[5] Again – this time in Matthew H. Kramer's words – '[t]he *separability* of the legal realm and the moral realm, as opposed to their ineluctable *separation*, is the condition [that the inclusive legal positivist] seeks to highlight.'[6]

One can arrive at a broader perspective by opening up the field to cover not only inclusive and exclusive legal positivism but also *non*-positivism, represented by the defence of the morality principle,[7] according to which, again, there is necessary

---

* Special thanks to Bonnie Litschewski Paulson for wise counsel on every aspect of my work on Kelsen and to Robert Alexy for stimulating discussion and for his gracious hospitality in Kiel.

1   An excellent discussion, chock full of arguments, is Kenneth Einar Himma, 'Inclusive Legal Positivism', in *The Oxford Handbook of Jurisprudence and Legal Philosophy*, ed. Jules Coleman *et al.* (Oxford: Oxford UP, 2002), 125–65. See, too, the detailed statements in Matthew H. Kramer, *In Defense of Legal Positivism* (Oxford: Oxford UP, 1999); Kramer, *Where Law and Morality Meet* (Oxford: Oxford UP, 2004).

2   H.L.A. Hart, 'Positivism and the Separation of Law and Morals', *Harvard Law Review*, 71 (1957–8), 593–629, repr. in Hart, *Essays in Jurisprudence and Philosophy* (Oxford: Clarendon Press, 1983), 49–87.

3   Himma, 'Inclusive Legal Positivism' (n. 1), 125.

4   The claimed 'necessary overlap' between the law and morality is understood in a great variety of ways, as illustrated by prominent examples in the recent literature. See e.g. Gustav Radbruch, 'Statutory Lawlessness and Supra-Statutory Law' (first publ. 1946), trans. Bonnie Litschewski Paulson and Stanley L. Paulson, *Oxford Journal of Legal Studies*, 26 (2006), 1–11; John Finnis, *Natural Law and Natural Rights* (Oxford: Clarendon Press, 1980), 2nd edn. (Oxford: Oxford UP, 2011); Finnis, *Philosophy of Law* (Collected Essays, vol. IV) (Oxford: Oxford UP, 2011); Robert Alexy, *The Argument from Injustice* (first publ. 1992), trans. Bonnie Litschewski Paulson and Stanley L. Paulson (Oxford: Clarendon Press, 2002); Lon L. Fuller, 'The Forms and Limits of Adjudication', *Harvard Law Review*, 92 (1978–9), 353–409, repr. (with omissions) in Fuller, *The Principles of Social Order*, ed. Kenneth Winston, 2nd edn. (Oxford: Hart Publishing, 2001), 101–39.

5   See Joseph Raz, *The Authority of Law* (Oxford: Clarendon Press, 1979); Raz, *Ethics in the Public Domain* (Oxford: Clarendon Press, 1994), at 210–27 *et passim.*

6   Kramer, *In Defense of Legal Positivism* (n. 1), 114 (emphasis added).

7   The nomenclature 'legal non-positivism' is congenial in suggesting a generic reading of the term, such that legal positivism and legal non-positivism together exhaust the field. That is, on the generic reading 'legal positivism' and 'legal non-positivism' are correctly read as contradictories. For an illuminating statement of various legal theories, grouped together under the 'positivist' and 'non-

overlap between the law and morality. It is clear that any two of these three views stand in a relation of contrariety.[8] For example, the cover statements giving expression to non-positivism and inclusive legal positivism cannot both be true, but they might well both be false, and then the cover statement giving expression to exclusive legal positivism would be true.

Say what you will about inclusive *versus* exclusive legal positivism – some defend the distinction, others dismiss inclusive legal positivism as a non-starter.[9] I want in any case to argue that a more fundamental distinction within the positivist camp lies elsewhere. The distinction I have in mind is that between legal positivism *qua* naturalism and legal positivism without naturalism. Even though, for reasons institutional in nature, legal positivism has largely been discussed in a vacuum, there is a standing presumption that there are ties between legal positivism and 'positivism writ large' in the greater philosophical tradition – or, as it would be put in present-day philosophical circles, ties between legal positivism and naturalism. What sorts of ties? In the first two parts of the paper, I offer an answer. In Part One, I draw on John Austin's legal philosophy and argue that it reflects the greater philosophical rubric, positivism writ large or – my substitution again – naturalism. And, in Part Two of the paper, I address and defend my substitution of naturalism for positivism writ large.

Specifically, in Part One of the paper, two theses are of special interest. My first thesis: Austin's naturalism – his reduction of ostensibly juridico-normative concepts to matters of fact (namely, to habit) – is, as he contends, sufficient to make out his case on the nature of law. My second thesis: If Austin's naturalism has him claiming that *every* aspect of the law lends itself to restatement in factual terms, then it is scarcely surprising that the makes no claims respecting a non-contingent link between the law and morality. He has *ex hypothesi* no occasion to make such a claim – indeed, were he to make such a claim, it would be inconsistent with the naturalistic claim. Taken together, these two theses make a point, I should like to think, of genuine significance. That is, if these two theses are indeed correct and if Austin's legal philosophy is representative of traditional legal positivism, then the celebrated separation principle is not doing the lion's share of the work in legal positivist circles after all. Rather, the separation principle is simply a corollary of naturalism, the overriding view.

In Part Two of the paper, I take up the substitution of naturalism for positivism writ large. In first thinking about how to sort out species of legal positivism, I assumed I would be working with positivism writ large as the greater philosophical stage on which legal positivism finds its place. A fair bit of reading disabused me of this notion. To be sure, to speak of positivism writ large might well be appropriate if I were directing my remarks to developments in philosophy in, say, the mid-nineteenth century. At that point in time, the older Hegelian consensus in Europe had been altogether displaced by scientific positivism. I am thinking, for example, of Hermann von Helmholtz, known for his pioneering work in physics and physiology,

positivist' rubrics, see Alexander P. d'Entrèves, 'Two Questions about Law', in *Existenz und Ordnung. Festschrift für Erik Wolf zum 60. Geburtstag*, ed. Thomas Würtenberger *et al.* (Frankfurt: Klostermann, 1962), 309–20, repr. in d'Entrèves, *Natural Law*, 2nd edn. (London: Hutchinson, 1970), 173–84.

8   See Robert Alexy, 'On the Concept and the Nature of Law', *Ratio Juris*, 21 (2008), 281–99, at 285–7.

9   For criticism, see e.g. Stefano Bertea, 'A Critique of Inclusive-Positivism', *Archiv für Rechts- und Sozialphilosophie*, 93 (2007), 67–81; Scott Shapiro, 'Law, Morality, and the Guidance of Conduct', *Legal Theory*, 6 (2000), 127–70. Kramer replies to Shapiro in *Where Law and Morality Meet* (n. 1), at 45–75.

as well as for his efforts in recasting Kant's theory of knowledge in a modern, that is, positivistic idiom.[10] All of this in the mid-nineteenth century.[11] By contrast, 'positivism' is a term of abuse in philosophical circles today. Jürgen Habermas writes that positivism in philosophy proceeds from 'scientistic presuppositions',[12] and Bernard Williams writes that 'to fall back on positivism' with an eye to avoiding interpretation is 'an offence against truthfulness'.[13]

In our time, the view that continues to enjoy a great reception in philosophical circles is naturalism. Willard Van Orman Quine, the 'father of contemporary naturalism' as one writer calls him,[14] understands naturalism as the appeal to the sciences. Naturalism, Quine tells us, assimilates epistemology to 'empirical psychology'.[15] Quine's view is not, however, the only view of naturalism. Naturalism is greater than Quine, thanks not least of all to the extraordinary role he played in begetting it in its contemporary form. Quine's view counts today as one prominent characterization of naturalism, and David Hume's view counts as another. I return to Hume in Part Two of the paper.

Finally, in Part Three of the paper, I turn to legal positivism without naturalism. Here the overriding figure is Hans Kelsen. While Kelsen is of course defending the separation principle, his position represents a wholesale rejection of naturalism, which, he insists, is wrong-headed. Thus, the idea that the separation principle is but a corollary of naturalism can scarcely be attributed to him.

My greater thesis, then, is that Austin and Kelsen represent two poles within legal positivism, namely, legal positivism *qua* naturalism and legal positivism without naturalism. The position represented by Hans Kelsen's colossus[16] is, I think, peculiar to him. By contrast, any of a host of other figures in the jurisprudential tradition can be substituted for John Austin, a point to which I return.

Part One: John Austin

It is no accident that Austin's statement of the separation principle is found in a footnote to the text of Lecture V – a fairly lengthy footnote, to be sure, where Austin carefully sets the stage for a reply to William Blackstone.

10   See e.g. Hermann von Helmholtz, 'Über das Sehen des Menschen' (lecture in Königsberg 1855), in Helmholtz, *Vorträge und Reden*, 4th printing, 2 vols. (Braunschweig: Friedrich Vieweg, 1896), vol. 1, 85–117.
11   Helmut Holzhey offers a three-fold characterization of philosophical positivism at mid-century: first, knowledge stemming from the sciences is privileged, while the philosopher's claims respecting knowledge are disputed, second, knowledge of reality (*Wirklichkeitserkenntnis*) is restricted to what can be drawn from sense experience, and, third, thought is understood solely in terms of the 'subjective' function of interpretation along with the ordering of the elements of sense experience. Helmut Holzhey, 'Der Neukantianismus', in Helmut Holzhey and Wolfgang Röd, *Die Philosophie des ausgehenden 19. und des 20. Jahrhunderts [Teil] 2. Neukantianismus, Idealismus, Realismus, Phänomenologie* (Munich: C. H. Beck, 2004), 30.
12   Jürgen Habermas, *Knowledge and Human Interests* (first publ. 1968), trans. Jeremy J. Shapiro (Boston: Beacon Press, 1971), 88.
13   Bernard Williams, *Truth and Truthfulness* (Princeton: Princeton UP, 2002), 12.
14   Penelope Maddy, *Second Philosophy. A Naturalistic Method* (Oxford: Oxford UP, 2007), 4. A single important figure in contemporary legal philosophy writes *expressis verbis* within the framework of Quinean naturalism, namely: Brian Leiter, *Naturalizing Jurisprudence* (Oxford: Oxford UP, 2007).
15   See n. 31 below.
16   The editor of the *Hans Kelsen Werke* (Tübingen: Mohr Siebeck, 2007 ff.), Matthias Jestaedt, estimates that Kelsen's published writings run to 17,500 pages.

> Sir William Blackstone ... says in his 'Commmentaries', that the laws of
> God are superior in obligation to all other laws ... that human laws are of
> no validity if contrary to them ... Now, he *may* mean that all human laws
> ought to conform to the Divine laws. If this be his meaning, I assent to it
> without hesitation ... But the meaning of this passage of Blackstone, if it
> has a meaning, seems rather to be this: that no human law which conflicts
> with the Divine law is obligatory or binding; in other words, that no human
> law which conflicts with the Divine law *is a law* ... Now, to say that human
> laws which conflict with the Divine law are not binding, that is to say, are
> not laws, is to talk stark nonsense.[17]

Relegating to a footnote what we, influenced by H.L.A. Hart, are accustomed to calling the separation principle suggests that the real thrust of Austin's position lies
elsewhere. As indeed it does. Austin, in Lecture VI, devotes a good bit of attention
to the straightforward reduction of the doctrine of sovereignty to concatenations of
fact. His lines on habitual obedience are familiar:

> The superior which is styled sovereignty ... is distinguished ... by the fol-
> lowing marks or characters: – 1. The *bulk* of the given society are in a *habit*
> of obedience or submission to a *determinate* and *common* superior ... [and]
> 2. That certain individual, or that certain body of individuals, is *not* in a
> habit of obedience to a determinate human superior.[18]

And, lest the significance of the appeal to habit be missed, Austin repeats the point a
number of times in Lecture VI.[19]

With this scheme of Austin's, we have the makings of the central argument I
wish to attribute to him. If his conceptual repertoire is traceable back to the doctrine
of sovereignty and if sovereignty is reducible in turn to concatenations of fact, then,
Austin is arguing, this is *sufficient* to explain the ostensibly normative material of the
law. This being so, he has no occasion to appeal to morality. In other words, Austin
has in effect built right into his reduction the thesis that there cannot be 'necessary
overlap' between the law and morality. And there is no reason for the proponent of
such a theory to pay special attention to a separation principle, which has no standing as an independent doctrine in the theory.

Before continuing with Austin, I want to underscore the general import of what
I am drawing from his theory. Given the prominence of the separation principle as
the underlying notion in the myriad Anglo-American defences of legal positivism
over the past half century, its absence – with a single important exception – from the
lively European debate over legal positivism a hundred years ago strikes one, at any
rate on first glance, as puzzling.[20] The straightforward explanation, however, is this.
A host of *fin de siècle* European legal theorists, roughly identifiable as positivists, made
the very sort of move that Austin made. That is, they claimed that facts of nature are

---

17   John Austin, *Lectures on Jurisprudence* (first publ. 1863), 5th edn., 2 vols., ed. Robert Campbell (Lon-
      don: John Murray, 1885), vol. 1, Lecture V (at pp. 214–15) (emphasis in original), also in John Aus-
      tin, *The Province of Jurisprudence Determined* (first publ. 1832), ed. H. L. A. Hart (London: Weidenfeld
      and Nicolson, 1954), Lecture V (at pp. 184–5) (emphasis in original).
18   Austin, *Lectures* (n. 17), Lecture VI (at p. 220) (emphasis in original); Austin, *Province* (n. 17), Lecture
      VI (at pp. 193–4).
19   See Austin, *Lectures* (n. 17), Lecture VI (at e.g. pp. 222, 223–4, 227); Austin, *Province* (n. 17), Lecture
      VI (at e.g. pp. 195, 198–9, 202–3).
20   The exception to the rule is Hans Kelsen, and I take up his position in Part Three.

sufficient to explain ostensibly juridico-normative material, and since morality cannot, then, be necessary, they had no occasion to talk about it. In a word, their move was naturalistic.

A good illustration is found in the work of Georg Jellinek, the most influential figure in public law theory (*Staatsrechtslehre*) on the European Continent a hundred years ago, translated in his own day into major indo-European languages. In some circles, it is presumed that Jellinek is a 'normativist', a 'Neokantian'. A closer look at the texts, however, shows clearly that Jellinek's celebrated doctrine, 'the normative force of the factual', reduces without remainder to matters physiological or psychological. And this is a reduction of Jellinek's own making. As he puts it, the 'normative import' of the factual counts simply as our physiological or psychological tendency to reproduce, in our minds, that to which we have become accustomed.[21] This is closer to Hume than to anything in Neokantianism.

Again, my thesis is that Austinian naturalism – the move from the ostensibly normative material of the law to concatenations of fact – is standard fare for legal positivists generally. While my thesis may appear to be obvious – and I would be pleased if it did – it is hardly the received opinion. For example, in his celebrated paper 'Positivism and the Separation of Law and Morals'[22] and again in *The Concept of Law*,[23] Hart sets out five different doctrines under the rubric of legal positivism – command, separation, analysis, judicial decisions as logical deductions, and noncognitivism. He attributes the first three of these to Jeremy Bentham and Austin. The doctrine that I claim is fundamental – naturalism – does not turn up on Hart's list, and it is not implied by anything that does turn up there.

Back to Austin, as promised. I have spoken of tracing the whole of Austin's conceptual repertoire to the doctrine of sovereignty and of reducing sovereignty in turn to concatenations of fact. A comparable argument can be generated by looking to Austin's command doctrine, implicit in the doctrine of sovereignty.[24] The doctrine of command, on one reading of Austin's treatise, can be understood in terms of three components: the commander's intention that a party act (or forbear from acting) in a particular way, the commander's expression of this intention to the party, and – central to the doctrine – the commander's power to impose a sanction should the commandee fail to comply with the directive.[25] The power to impose a sanction is not, however, to be understood as a property of the commander, for a commander, characterized in the Austinian theory in terms of the power to impose sanctions, might not have such power over the particular party to whom he issues his di-

---

21   Jellinek writes: 'To seek the basis of the normative force of the factual in its conscious or unconscious reasonableness would be utterly mistaken. The factual can be rationalized later, but its normative import lies in an underived property of our nature, on the strength of which something we are already accustomed to is physiologically and psychologically easier to reproduce than something new.' Georg Jellinek, *Allgemeine Staatslehre*, 2nd edn. (Berlin: O. Häring, 1905), 330, 3rd edn. (1914), 338. The reduction to fact, in Jellinek's work at this juncture, is captured effectively by Michael Stolleis, *Public Law in Germany 1800–1914* (first publ. 1992), trans. Pamela Biel (New York and Oxford: Berghahn, 2001), 442–3.

22   See Hart, 'Positivism and the Separation of Law and Morals' (n. 2), 601–2 at n. 25, repr. in Hart, *Essays in Jurisprudence and Philosophy* (n. 2), 57–8 at n. 25.

23   See H.L.A. Hart, *The Concept of Law*, 2nd edn. (Oxford: Clarendon Press, 1994), 302, at note pertaining to p. 185.

24   See Austin, *Lectures* (n. 17), Lecture V (e.g. at p. 177); Austin, *Province* (n. 17), Lecture V (e.g. at p. 132).

25   Austin, *Lectures* (n. 17), Lecture I (at p. 91, and see p. 89); Austin, *Province* (n. 17), Lecture I (at p. 17 and see pp. 13–14).

rective, as in the case of a sovereign's putative command to another sovereign. The power to impose a sanction is to be understood, in other words, as a relation between commander and commandee or, more generally, between superior and inferior.[26] Austin gives expression to the relation – we might call it the 'power relation' – when he writes:

> The term superiority signifies might: the power of affecting others with evil or pain, and of forcing them, through *fear* of that evil, to fashion their conduct to one's wishes.[27]

Fear, a brute fact, is the operative notion here, and the argument proceeds just as before. If Austin's 'correlative terms' of obligation and sanction are traceable back to their correlative, the command,[28] and if the command is reducible in turn to concatenations of fact – in particular, to the commandee's fear – then, so Austin, this move is sufficient to explain the ostensibly normative material of the law. [29] And if this move is sufficient, there is no basis for claiming a non-contingent link between the law and morality.

It is useful to dwell for just a moment on the concept of fear. Just as no one would claim that sexual desire is acquired through reasoning or is the product of experience, so likewise for fear. Notwithstanding the fact that experience may shape our responses on both fronts, the phenomena themselves have a basis independent of experience.[30] Hume speaks of natural instinct. This mention of Hume brings me to Part Two, the substitution of naturalism for positivism writ large.

Part Two: The Substitution of Naturalism for Positivism Writ Large

I remarked in the Introduction that Quine, in the name of naturalism, would have us appealing to the sciences. Epistemology becomes 'empirical psychology'.[31] Although there are great differences between Quine's naturalistic enterprise and David

---

26   Austin, *Lectures* (n. 17), Lecture I (at pp. 96–7); Austin, *Province* (n. 17), Lecture I (at pp. 24–5).
27   Austin, *Lectures* (n. 17), Lecture I (at p. 96) (emphasis added) (see also p. 90: 'that which is not feared is not apprehended as an evil'); Austin, *Province* (n. 17), Lecture I (at p. 24) (emphasis added) (see also p. 16).
28   On 'correlativity', see Austin, *Lectures* (n. 17), Lecture I (at pp. 89, 96, see also pp. 91–2); Austin, *Province* (n. 17), Lecture I (at pp. 14, 24, see also pp. 17–18).
29   As noted by Hart, Austin also has a second interpretation of the command. It turns on his definition of obligation 'as the "chance or likelihood" that one who has been commanded to do or abstain from doing something would suffer some evil in the event of disobedience'. See H.L.A. Hart, 'Analytical Jurisprudence in Mid-Twentieth Century: A Reply to Professor Bodenheimer', *University of Pennsylvania Law Review*, 105 (1956–7), 953–75, at 965; H.L.A. Hart, 'Legal and Moral Obligation', in *Essays in Moral Philosophy*, ed. A.I. Melden (Seattle: University of Washington Press, 1958), 82–107, at 95–9; Hart, *The Concept of Law* (n. 23), 282 note at (c), 290 note pertaining to p. 83. For Austin's own text on 'chance or likelihood', see Austin, *Lectures* (n. 17), Lecture I (at p. 90); Austin, *Province* (n. 17), Lecture I (at p. 16).
30   I owe the example to H.O. Mounce, *Hume's Naturalism* (London and New York: Routledge, 1999), 62.
31   'Naturalism does not repudiate epistemology, but assimilates it to empirical psychology. [The] epistemological question [is] a question within science: [how humans] have managed to arrive at science from such limited information. Our scientific epistemologist pursues this inquiry.... Evolution and natural selection will doubtless figure in this account, and he will feel free to apply physics if he sees a way.' W.V.O. Quine, 'Five Milestones of Empiricism' (lecture of 1975), in Quine, *Theories and Things* (Cambridge, Mass.: Harvard UP, 1981), 67–72, at 72.

Hume's, there are similarities, too. For example, many regard Hume's theory of human nature in Book III of *A Treatise on Human Nature* as a study in moral psychology. As one prominent interpreter of Hume puts it, '[t]o a large extent, Hume's theory of human nature is not, in our terms, philosophical, but psychological'.[32] Hume's famous – some will say 'notorious' – dictum that 'reason is, and ought only to be the slave of the passions',[33] is most helpfully seen as his response to the elevated role played by reason in the rationalist philosophies of the Cartesian tradition.[34] Hume's tack is diametrically opposed. He looks inward:

> Take any action allow'd to be vicious: Wilful murder, for instance. Examine it in all lights, and see if you can find that matter of fact, or real existence, which you call *vice*. In which-ever way you take it, you find only certain passions, motives, volitions and thoughts. There is no other matter of fact in the case. The vice entirely escapes you, as long as you consider the object. You never can find it, till you turn your reflexion into your own breast, and find a sentiment of disapprobation, which arises in you, towards this action. Here is a matter of fact; but 'tis the object of feeling, not of reason. It lies in yourself, not in the object. So that when you pronounce any action or character to be vicious, you mean nothing, but that from the constitution of your nature you have a feeling or sentiment of blame from the contemplation of it.[35]

These notions – feeling, sentiment, instinct, the constitution of our nature – have one looking inward. And this, Hume would have us believe, is the source of our psychological explanations.

This view of 'Hume the naturalist' comes as a surprise to those who take their cues from a textbook account of Hume, which has him following his empiricist predecessors, Locke and Berkeley, while recognizing – and making the most of – the scepticism to which their view inevitably leads. The argument on behalf of scepticism is familiar. Empiricism has its source in sense experience. Beliefs that stem from sense experience do not lend themselves to justification. A justification requires an appeal to something independent, but there is no way of stepping outside sense experience in order to appeal to something independent of it. The result is scepticism.

This point, in explicit criticism of Hume's scepticism, stems, *inter alia*, from the philosopher Thomas Reid. Defending his own view, Reid argues that sensory experience is not '*what* we perceive' but rather that '*whereby* we perceive'.[36] Norman Kemp Smith – in path-breaking papers a hundred years ago and in an extraordinary

32   Terence Penelhum, 'Hume's Moral Psychology', in *Cambridge Companion to Hume*, ed. David Fate Norton (Cambridge: Cambridge UP, 1993), 117–49, at 119. Penelhum is not alone. See also Jerry A. Fodor, *Hume Variations* (Oxford: Clarendon Press, 2003), at 1–27 *et passim*, who suggests that Hume's naturalism anticipates current work in cognitive science.

33   David Hume, *A Treatise on Human Nature* (first publ. 1739–40, 2nd edn., ed. P.H. Nidditch (Oxford: Clarendon Press, 1978), II.iii.3. (at p. 415).

34   See Penelhum, 'Hume's Moral Psychology' (n. 32), 119–20, on which I have drawn here.

35   Hume, *Treatise* (n. 33), III.i.1. (at pp. 468–9) (emphasis in original).

36   See *The Works of Thomas Reid*, 8th edn., 2 vols., ed. William Hamilton (Edinburgh: James Thin, 1895), vol. 1, pp. 108, 112, 117, 121 *et passim*. The quotation in the text is Mounce's tidy summary statement, in Mounce, *Hume's Naturalism* (n. 30), 1, 54 (emphasis in original). Reid's philosophy is presented in rich detail in Keith Lehrer, *Thomas Reid* (London and New York: Routledge, 1989).

treatise on Hume some seventy years ago – stands Reid's interpretation of Hume on its head.[37] In Kemp Smith's splendid words: Hume 'is depicted as having done no more than deliver his successors from a bondage to which he himself remained subject. A strangely paradoxical verdict!'[38] Hume, on Kemp Smith's interpretation, was keenly aware of the scepticism inherent in traditional empiricism and sought to provide an alternative. The alternative, naturalism, is found in Book III of Hume's *Treatise*. Indeed, Kemp Smith goes on, the best way to read Hume is to begin with Book III of the *Treatise* before turning to Book I, whose scepticism will then properly be seen as qualified by Hume's naturalism.

Part Three: Positivism without Naturalism. The Case of Hans Kelsen

Where legal positivism *qua* naturalism is the point of departure, Hans Kelsen is the spoiler. Other legal positivists count as naturalists, arguing that since the facts are sufficient to explain ostensibly normative material, no non-contingent link between morality and the law can be necessary. Kelsen offers no such argument, for he, unlike all the others, is not arguing that ostensibly juridico-normative material is reducible to fact. Kelsen defends what he terms a normative legal philosophy.

Normativity,[39] Kelsen tells us, is his alternative to other approaches within legal philosophy, but – the rub – there has never been any agreement on what he means here. The interpretations of Kelsen's idea of normativity run the gamut, from a counter-factual interpretation of normativity[40] to a 'justified normativity' thesis. The justified normativity thesis is far and away the most ambitious reading of normativity in Kelsen's legal philosophy. It has been attributed to Kelsen in different forms with different sorts of argument by no fewer than four leading figures – Robert Alexy, Carlos Santiago Nino, Joseph Raz, and, a bit earlier, by Alf Ross –[41] with, so far as I can tell, each writer developing his own case independently of the others. I confine

---

37 See, in particular, Norman Kemp Smith, *The Philosophy of David Hume* (London: Macmillan, 1941). The early papers are 'The Naturalism of Hume (I.)', *Mind*, 14 (1905), 149–73, and 'The Naturalism of Hume (II.)', ibid. pp. 335–47.

38 Kemp Smith, *The Philosophy of David Hume* (n. 37), 3.

39 Normativity, for many purposes a concept in its own right, has enjoyed a good bit of attention in recent philosophy. See e.g. Joseph Raz, 'Explaining Normativity: On Rationality and the Justification of Reason', *Ratio* 12 (N.S.) (1999), 354–379, repr. in Raz, *Engaging Reason* (Oxford: Oxford UP, 1999), 67–89. See also Alan Millar, *Understanding People. Normativity and Rationalizing Explanation* (Oxford: Clarendon Press, 2004); John Skorupski, *The Domain of Reasons* (Oxford: Oxford UP, 2010). In the paper 'A "Justified Normativity" Thesis in Hans Kelsen's Pure Theory of Law?' in *Institutionalized Reason*, ed. Matthias Klatt (Oxford: Oxford UP, 2012), 61–111, I have explored at greater length the differences between normativity in recent philosophy and in Kelsen's theory.

40 In an overview of Kelsen's work, Robert Walter writes that coercive systems, legal systems in particular, are to be interpreted '*as if* they were normative'. Walter, 'Der gegenwärtige Stand der Reinen Rechtslehre', *Rechtstheorie*, 1 (1970), 69–95, at 70 (emphasis in original).

41 See Alexy, *The Argument from Injustice* (n. 4), at 95–123; Carlos Santiago Nino, 'Some Confusions surrounding Kelsen's Concept of Validity', *Archiv für Rechts- und Sozialphilosophie*, 64 (1978), 357–77, at 357–65, repr. in *Normativity and Norms. Critical Perspectives on Kelsenian Themes* [hereafter: *NN*], ed. Stanley L. Paulson and Bonnie Litschewski Paulson (Oxford: Clarendon Press, 1998), 253–61; Nino, *La validez del derecho* (Buenos Aires: Editorial Astrea, 1985), at 7–40 *et passim*; Joseph Raz, 'Kelsen's Theory of the Basic Norm', *American Journal of Jurisprudence*, 19 (1974), 94–111, repr. in *NN* (this note, above), 47–67, and in Raz, *The Authority of Law*, 2nd edn. (Oxford: Oxford UP, 2009) [hereafter: *AL*], 122–45; Alf Ross, 'Validity and the Conflict between Legal Positivism and Natural Law', *Revista Jurídica de Buenos Aires*, 4 (1961), 46–93 (bilingual printing), at 82, and see generally at 78–82, repr. in *NN* (this note, above) 147–63, at 160, and see generally at 159–61.

myself here to Raz, whose statement is in some respects the most extreme of the four. Raz begins by contrasting Hart's position with Kelsen's. H.L.A. Hart is a proponent of *social normativity*, understanding '[t]he normativity of the law and the obligation to obey it [as] distinct notions.' An altogether different understanding, Raz continues, is evident in the work of one who recognizes 'only the conception of *justified normativity*',[42] namely, Hans Kelsen. In characterizing justified normativity, Raz writes:

> [T]o judge the law as normative is to judge it to be just and to admit that it ought to be obeyed. The concepts of the normativity of the law and of the obligation to obey it are analytically tied together. Kelsen, therefore, regards the law as valid, that is, normative, only if one ought to obey it.[43]

Of course Raz sees the paradox in attributing justified normativity to Kelsen, a thesis that places Kelsen far closer to natural law theory than to anything found in traditional or naturalistic legal positivism. Indeed, Raz invites attention to the paradox, writing that although 'Kelsen rejects natural law theories, he consistently uses the natural law concept of normativity, i. e. the concept of justified normativity.'[44]

Interpreters of a philosopher will of course pursue what they deem to be the most promising reading of the philosopher's work. So far, so good, but with a caveat. Merit lies in pursuing what the philosopher actually wrote rather than in imposing on the philosopher's text an interpretation 'from without', so to speak. As Paul W. Franks puts it in his book on the post-Kantians, '[i]f we assume that historical figures are asking or answering our questions', we 'run the risk of both distorting what they say and missing an opportunity to learn from them, whether positively or negatively.'[45]

Raz, like Alexy, Nino, and Ross, can reply that he is drawing an interpretation from the text, not imposing an interpretation on it. The reply is a good one as far as it goes, but it gives rise to the question of just how representative the passages selected by Raz and the others are. As I have argued at length elsewhere, the passages selected are in fact not representative of Kelsen's work. And then the point made by Franks stands: We learn best from historical figures when we address the questions they themselves were asking and answering.

What, then, takes the place of justified normativity? My answer: Kelsen's project over many decades was, above all, an ambitious and far-reaching attempt, first, to show that naturalism in *fin de siècle* legal science is mistaken, and, second, to develop the rudiments of an alternative theory that would secure the autonomy (*Eigengesetzlichkeit*) of the law and, by the same token, the purity (*Reinheit*) of legal science. And this takes us full circle back to the question of normativity. Kelsen's alternative

---

42 Raz, 'Kelsen's Theory of the Basic Norm' (n. 41), 105 (emphasis added), in *NN* (n. 41), 60, in Raz, *AL* (n. 41), 137.

43 Ibid.

44 Raz, 'Kelsen's Theory of the Basic Norm' (n. 41), 110–11, repr. *NN* (n. 41), 67, and in Raz, *AL* (n. 41), 144.

45 Paul W. Franks, *All or Nothing. Systematicity, Transcendental Arguments, and Skepticism in German Idealism* (Cambridge, Mass., and London: Harvard UP, 2005), 5. Of course this idea is hardly new; I quote from Franks because his statement of the matter is unusually perspicuous. To the same effect, see John Rawls, *Lectures on the History of Political Philosophy* (Cambridge, Mass.: Harvard UP, 2007), at 251: '[I]n studying the works of the leading writers in the philosophical tradition, one guiding precept is to identify correctly the problems they were facing, and to understand how they viewed them and what questions they were asking.'

to naturalism yields a normativity thesis, and this should come as no surprise. He has to be committed to something that is normative in character lest he have no alternative to naturalism after all. In sharp contrast to the thesis of justified normativity, however, Kelsen's normativity thesis is part and parcel of his greater effort to develop an alternative to naturalism and thereby to lend respectability to legal science, underscoring its nomological dimension. I call Kelsen's thesis the *nomological* normativity thesis. As Kelsen understands the thesis, its import is underscored by a 'law-like', necessary or nomological connection at the very core of his legal philosophy. In what follows, my primary concern is to invite attention to this connection.

Kelsen's alternative to naturalism is captured in my reconstruction by the concept of peripheral imputation. 'To impute' (Latin *imputare*) means to bring into reckoning, to ascribe, to attribute. Kelsen's German verb is '*zurechnen*', and 'to impute' is a reliable translation, not least of all in light of Kelsen's own occasional use of the loan-word '*imputieren*' where '*zurechnen*' might have been expected.[46]

Kelsen has two doctrines of imputation. The first of these, central imputation, is by and large a reflection of the philosophical tradition, though Kelsen's use of central imputation is anything but traditional.[47] The second doctrine, peripheral imputation, is peculiar to Kelsen. Both doctrines purport to offer an alternative to causal explanation, and both, for this reason, are of unusual significance in Kelsen's legal philosophy – central imputation in Kelsen's very early work, and peripheral imputation thereafter. I shall confine my discussion to the latter, peripheral imputation, for this is the doctrine that underlies Kelsen's nomological normativity thesis.

Kelsen tells us that peripheral imputation links 'material facts' (*Tatbestände*). As he puts it in the *Allgemeine Staatslehre*, in what counts as an early statement of the doctrine: '[P]eripheral imputation always leads from one material fact to nothing other than another material fact.'[48] A comparable statement is found in the first edition of the *Reine Rechtslehre*. At the end of a section devoted to the doctrine of central imputation, Kelsen contrasts that doctrine with peripheral imputation. Central imputation, he writes,

> is an entirely different operation from the peripheral imputation mentioned earlier, where a material fact is connected ... to another material fact within

---

46   As Kelsen writes: 'It would be a serious misunderstanding if one wanted somehow to impute [*imputieren*] to these observations [on the legal authority of administrative agencies] the significance of a political mandate for the greatest possible restriction of the state's administrative activity.' Kelsen, *Hauptprobleme der Staatsrechtslehre* (Tübingen: J.C.B. Mohr, 1911), 503, and see at 138, 194, 209, repr. in *Hans Kelsen Werke*, ed. Matthias Jestaedt, vol. 2 (Tübingen: Mohr Siebeck, 2008), 650, and see at 244, 306, 322. See also Hans Kelsen, *Über Grenzen zwischen juristischer und soziologischer Methode* (Tübingen: J. C. B. Mohr, 1911), at 44.

47   Central imputation serves in Kelsen's very early work as an escape hatch from naturalism and psychologism. Later he turns to the basic norm, already evident in *Das Problem der Souveränität und die Theorie des Völkerrechts* (Tübingen: J.C.B. Mohr, 1920), and to a Neokantian transcendental argument, and these steps represent his effort to replace central imputation with something more satisfactory. To be sure, central imputation survives elsewhere in Kelsen's work. His most extensive discussion of both imputation doctrines – central and peripheral – is found in a lengthy essay: Kelsen, 'Unrecht und Unrechtsfolge im Völkerrecht', *Zeitschrift für öffentliches Recht*, 12 (1932), 481–608, see at §§ 1–2 (pp. 481–504), § 5 (pp. 525–9), § 7 (pp. 537–44).

48   Hans Kelsen, *Allgemeine Staatslehre* (Berlin: Julius Springer, 1925), § 12 (d) (p. 65).

the system, that is, where two material facts are linked together in the re-
constructed legal norm.[49]

Two questions arise. What exactly would Kelsen have us understand by material
facts? And how might peripheral imputation, linking material facts, be formulated?
As to the first question, Kelsen answers in terms of 'legal condition' and 'legal consequence', more precisely, in terms of the state of affairs counting as the legal condition in a particular instance and, in Hohfeldian parlance, the legal position that
emerges as its legal consequence. This seems to be an odd fit, for we do not ordinar-
ily think of a legal consequence as a material fact (*Tatbestand*). Rather, in a hypotheti-
cally formulated legal norm, a material fact falling within the scope of the antecedent
clause of the norm triggers the legal consequence, establishing, in Kelsen's doctrine,
the legal position of liability that counts as the legal consequence.

It is, however, material facts, thus understood, that Kelsen brings together in introducing peripheral imputation. He writes that '[i]f the mode of linking *material facts*
is causality in the one case, it is imputation in the other.'[50] What is more, he uses 'legal condition' and 'legal consequence' alongside 'cause' and 'effect' as the respective
relata of these very same ordering principles or relations, imputation and causality.[51]
That is, he understands their *relata* as species of the genus 'material fact'.

To shed light on Kelsen's expansion of the notion of material facts as the *relata*
of peripheral imputation, it is perhaps helpful to point to his effort to provide as
close a parallel as possible to the principle of causality. Since he assumes material
facts to be indisputably the *relata* in the case of causality, so likewise, he is arguing,
material facts serve as the *relata* in the case of peripheral imputation. Kelsen wishes
to underscore a law-like, necessary or nomological relation in the law running parallel to the law-like, necessary or nomological relation manifest in causality, and his
development of this parallel is a central part of his effort to reply to naturalism and,
by the same token, to turn the legal science of his day into something scientifically
respectable.[52] If it can be shown that aspects of the fundamental ordering principle
of the natural sciences are reflected *per analogiam* in the fundamental ordering principle of legal science, then, so Kelsen, the parallel will indeed enhance the status of legal science qua science.[53]

I turn now to the second question, which speaks to the formulation of peripheral imputation. One proposal for a formulation might read (with an 'and if …'
clause inserted between parentheses as a shorthand reference to the other conditions
associated with a legal proceeding):

---

49   Hans Kelsen, *Introduction to the Problems of Legal Theory*, a translation of the first edition of Kelsen's
     Reine Rechtslehre (1934) by Bonnie Litschewski Paulson and Stanley L. Paulson (Oxford: Clarendon
     Press, 1992) [hereafter: *LT*], § 25 (d) (pp. 50–1).
50   Kelsen, *LT* (n. 49), § 11 (b) (p. 23) (emphasis added).
51   See Kelsen, *LT* (n. 49), § 11 (b) (at pp. 23–4).
52   See generally Kelsen, *Über Grenzen zwischen juristischer und soziologischer Methode Grenzen* (n. 46), at 1–15
     et passim; Horst Dreier, *Rechtslehre, Staatssoziologie und Demokratietheorie bei Hans Kelsen*, 2nd printing
     (Baden-Baden: Nomos, 1990), at 1–15 et passim; Horst Dreier, 'Hans Kelsen's Wissenschafts-
     programm', *Die Verwaltung*, Beiheft 7: *Staatsrechtslehre als Wissenschaft*, ed. Helmuth Schulze-Fielitz
     (Berlin: Duncker & Humblot, 2007), 81–114.
53   I take up the parallel in the name of methodological forms, see the text at nn. 60–5 below.

Formulation I: If an act of a certain type takes place (and if …), then the actor or a surrogate[54] is liable for that act.

This formulation is ruled out, however, by Kelsen's stipulation that peripheral imputation links material facts, where the latter material fact is understood to be the liability imputed to the legal act. To adopt formulation I as a representation of peripheral imputation would be to confuse peripheral imputation with central imputation.

The alternative is a 'subjectless' counterpart to formulation I, that is to say, a formulation that does not include an ascription to a legal subject:

Formulation II. If an act of a certain type takes place (and if …), then that act is treated as 'liability ascribing'.

Its counterintuitive character aside, a point to which I return below, formulation II captures the import of peripheral imputation. A defensible formulation must reflect a necessary connection between the two material facts. And if the formulation is confined, as here, to the act and to liability – the liability imputed to the act – then the link is indeed necessary. As Kelsen writes:

If there is the necessity of an absolute 'must' when the law of nature links cause and effect, so there is the equally rigorous 'ought' when the law of normativity (*Rechtsgesetz*) sets out the synthesis of conditioning and conditioned material facts. In the sphere of the law or in 'legal reality', … delict is linked to punishment with the same necessity as, in the sphere of nature or in 'natural reality', cause is linked to effect.[55]

This is close to being right as a statement of Kelsen's position, though one wrinkle has to be ironed out. Kelsen cannot be claiming a necessary link between the delict and the actual imposition of punishment. That would not make good sense, for, as we know and as Kelsen makes perfectly clear elsewhere, 'in the system of nature, punishment may fail to materialize for one reason or another'.[56] It is not punishment but criminal liability – and by the same token civil liability – that figures in the law-like, necessary or nomological link. In the most general terms, liability serves in this formulation as the second *relatum*, the second 'material fact'. The relation of liability to the act to which it is imputed is a necessary relation. By contrast, the actual imposition of punishment in the criminal law and the actual execution of judgment in the civil law is a contingent matter.[57]

Still, formulation II seems counterintuitive in imputing liability to the act, not to the actor. We are accustomed to distinguishing between the imputation of liability

---

54   Here I am using 'surrogate' to cover all the variations on the theme of vicarious and collective liability, see the text at n. 58 below.

55   Hans Kelsen, '"Foreword" to the Second Printing of *Main Problems in the Theory of Public Law*', trans. in *NN* (n. 41), 3–22, at 5 (in the last latter sentence, the quotation marks are in the original text).

56   Kelsen, *LT* (n. 49), § 11 (b) (pp. 25).

57   The point made here can be compared with Hart's argument directed to Austin's claim that nullity is a sanction. Hart replies that nullity and sanction are conceptually distinct. Specifically, he points out that a nullity follows necessarily from the failure to satisfy the conditions of the legal arrangement (Jones purports to marry Sally, but the 'marriage' is null and void, for he is already married), whereas the actual imposition of a sanction is a contingent matter. See Hart, *The Concept of Law* (n. 23), at 33–5, and Austin, *Lectures on Jurisprudence* (n. 17) Lecture XXIII (at p. 457), Lecture XXVII, (at pp. 505 f.).

individually on the one hand and collectively on the other.[58] In the first case, the imputation of liability is either to the actor or, under the rubric of vicarious liability, to a surrogate. In the second case, liability is imputed, say, to the insurance company.

Why does Kelsen restrict himself to the imputation of liability to the act rather than to the actor? Kelsen's restriction can be explained, I think, by the contingent element presupposed in identifying the liable party. As understood in this or that jurisdiction, the character of the liable party – actor, surrogate, or collective body – is a contingent factor, a question of legal policy, not legal science. This point strengthens Kelsen's hand in insisting that the necessary link be limited to the imputation of liability to the act.

In any case, it is precisely this necessary relation between act and liability that represents the core of what I am calling Kelsen's nomological normativity thesis. The relation is nomological in being necessary or law-like, and it is normative in being non-causal. Further permutations stemming from imputation, thus understood, will then be forthcoming where liability is ascribed to a person, triggering the empowerment of a legal organ to follow through with whatever sanction is called for.

What remains now is to cast imputation in terms that invite attention to the underpinnings of the nomological normativity thesis. At some points in his work, Kelsen treats imputation as a Kantian or Neokantian category by analogy to the category of causation.[59] The transcendental argument that Kelsen adduces in the name of imputation *qua* category, however, is not sound. If Kelsen nevertheless utilizes imputation in his philosophy as in my sketch above, then its foundation requires a closer look. My suggestion is that Kelsen's concept of peripheral imputation be conceptualized as a *methodological form*, specifically, the methodological form peculiar to legal science. The notion is drawn from the work of the Baden Neokantian Heinrich Rickert.

In the last chapter of his treatise, *The Object of Knowledge*,[60] Rickert distinguishes the constitutive categories of objective reality – for example, the category of permanence – from the methodological forms of the various standing disciplines. Rickert's basic idea is that objective reality, constituted transcendentally, must be sharply distinguished from the processing (*Bearbeitung*) of the material given in objective reality. Objective reality, Kant's phenomenal world, is constituted by means of the categories of reality, while the processing of the material of objective reality is the work of the standing disciplines, which are grounded in their respective methodological forms. Rickert offers lawfulness (*Gesetzlichkeit*) as an example of a methodological form in the natural sciences.[61] In fact, the example has to be taken as the *genus* of methodological forms in the natural sciences generally, for it has application to all of them.

In *The Object of Knowledge*, Rickert begins with the constitutive categories of reality.

58   See Kelsen, *LT* (n. 49), § 13 (at p. 27); Hans Kelsen, *General Theory of Law and State*, trans. Anders Wedberg (Cambridge, Mass.: Harvard UP, 1945), at 59, 69–71; Hans Kelsen, *Reine Rechtslehre*, 2nd edn. (Vienna: Franz Deuticke, 1960) at § 28 (c) (pp. 125–6).
59   See Kelsen, *LT* (n. 49), § 11 (b) (at p. 23).
60   See Heinrich Rickert, *Der Gegenstand der Erkenntnis*, 2nd edn. (Tübingen and Leipzig: J.C.B. Mohr, 1904), at 205–28, Rickert, *Der Gegenstand der Erkenntnis*, 6th edn. (Tübingen: J.C.B. Mohr, 1928), at 401–32. See also Heinrich Rickert, *Die Grenzen der naturwissenschaftlichen Begriffsbildung* (first publ. 1902), 5th edn. (Tübingen: J.C.B. Mohr, 1929), at 283–4, 373–7, *et passim*.
61   See Rickert, *Der Gegenstand der Erkenntnis*, 6th edn. (n. 60), at 409–10.

> The unique significance of...the forms that have been discussed in terms
> of the examples of causality and permanence requires that they be given a
> special name, one that distinguishes them as original forms in contrast to
> methodological forms. Building on the expression 'objective reality', we
> could speak ... of 'objective forms of reality'. But we prefer ... the term
> 'constitutive'. In that these particular forms constitute what is presupposed
> as finished product or as real material of cognition, 'constitutive' designates
> exactly what we mean. Thus, the categories that shape the objective, real
> world from what is in fact given should be called the *constitutive categories of
> reality*.[62]

The methodological forms to which Rickert alludes are peculiar, respectively, to the
various standing disciplines. Referring in his treatise to Cartesian dualism, Rickert
writes:

> This *other* species of dualism, according to which the world is supposed to
> consist of two types of reality, each excluding the other – the world of *ex-
> tensio* and the world of *cogitatio* – is created by physics and by psychology,
> each with its respective methodological form.[63]

Physics has its own methodological form, and so does psychology.

Legal science, too, has its own methodological form, namely, imputation or, as
Kelsen sometimes puts it, the 'law of normativity'.[64] As he explains, looking back on
the theses he defended in *Hauptprobleme*:

> [T]he core problem becomes the *reconstructed legal norm*, understood as the
> expression of the specific lawfulness, the autonomy, of the law, as the legal
> counterpart to the law of nature (*Naturgesetz*) – the 'law of the law', so to
> speak, the *law of normativity* (*Rechtsgesetz*) ... What is obviously of importance
> in *Main Problems* is securing the *objectivity of validity*, without which there can
> be no lawfulness whatever, let alone the specific lawfulness, the autonomy,
> of the law. But without the expression of that autonomy, without the law
> of normativity, there can be no legal knowledge, no legal science. There-
> fore: objective judgment, not subjective imperative. 'The law of normativity
> is – outwardly – like the law of nature, in that it is directed to no one and
> valid without regard to whether it is known or recognized.' If the analogy
> between the law of normativity and the law of nature is still fairly limited
> here, this is in order to prevent the confusion of the two, indeed not to lose
> sight – because of the analogy – of the specific lawfulness, the autonomy,
> of the law as against the causal lawfulness of nature.[65]

---

62   Ibid. at 406–7 (quotation marks and emphasis in original), compare Rickert, *Der Gegenstand der Erk-
     enntnis*, 2nd edn. (n. 60), at 211.
63   Rickert, *Der Gegenstand der Erkenntnis*, 6th edn. (n. 60), 424 (emphasis in original), see also at 404,
     410, 411, 424, 426, *et passim*, and compare Rickert, *Der Gegenstand der Erkenntnis*, 2nd edn. (n. 60), at
     208, 210, 217, 221, *et passim*.
64   See the quotation immediately below.
65   Kelsen, '"Foreword" to the Second Printing of *Main Problems in the Theory of Public Law*' (n. 55), 5–6
     (emphasis in original). Kelsen's quotation within the quotation is from the *Hauptprobleme* (n. 46), at
     395, repr. in *Hans Kelsen Werke*, vol. 2 (n. 46), at 529 ('outwardly' appears in italics in the *Haupt-
     probleme* but not in the 'Foreword' quoted here). See also Kelsen, *LT* (n. 49), § 11 (b) (at p. 23–5).

The normative or non-naturalistic import of Kelsen's enterprise, the force of his law of normativity, plays itself out in the context of nomological legal science, understood as Kelsen's alternative to psychologism and naturalism in legal science. Specifically, the focus is on the methodological form of legal science – the relation of peripheral imputation. Where the antecedent condition obtains, this marks the imputation of liability to the act, a necessary relation. Where the ascription of liability to a person is made, this marks a change in that person's legal position. The change, Kelsen insists, is a normative change, not a causal change.

Concluding Remark

Coming full circle, back to the Introduction, I should like once again to allude to the distinction between inclusive and exclusive legal positivism, comparing it with the distinction between legal positivism *qua* naturalism and legal positivism without naturalism.[66] The first distinction has inclusive legal positivism riding piggyback on exclusive legal positivism. That is, in all those legal systems correctly characterized by means of the 'exclusive' variant, no distinction whatever is marked by inclusive legal positivism; it has, *ex hypothesi*, no application. The second distinction, however, that between legal positivism *qua* naturalism and legal positivism without naturalism, marks a difference in kind. That is, a characterization of a given legal system by appeal to legal positivism *qua* naturalism is in every instance different from a characterization of the same system by appeal to legal positivism without naturalism.

Kelsen, our proponent of legal positivism without naturalism, wages battle on two fronts, against natural law theory and against naturalism. And he responds on both fronts with doctrines that count as independent doctrines in his legal philosophy – 'independent' in that neither doctrine is derived from the other. He responds to natural law theory with the separation principle and to naturalism with the nomological normativity thesis. The import of these two doctrines is to be sharply distinguished from legal positivism *qua* naturalism, where the separation principle is simply a corollary of naturalism and where there is of course no nomological normativity thesis.

---

66   I am grateful to Robert Alexy for helpful discussion on this point.

Marijan Pavčnik

Methodologische Klarheit oder gegenständliche Reinheit des Rechts? Anmerkungen zur Diskussion Kelsen – Pitamic

1. Einleitung

Leonid Pitamic (1885–1971)[1] war ein Zeitgenosse Kelsens. Er studierte in Wien, wo er sich 1915 zum Privatdozenten für allgemeine Staatslehre und österreichisches Staatsrecht und 1917 noch für Rechtsphilosophie habilitierte. Kelsens Biograph Métall berichtet, dass Kelsen noch während des (ersten) Weltkriegs, als er begann die Frage der Souveränität zu erforschen, ein Privatseminar gründete, wo ein Kreis von jüngeren Forschern offen über rechtstheoretische Probleme diskutierte. Zu ihnen gehörten Adolf Merkl (1890–1970), Leonid Pitamic und Alfred Verdross (1890–1980), nach Kriegsende schlossen sich noch andere an.[2] Aus diesem Kreis entstand allmählich „Die Wiener Rechtstheoretische Schule", die „sich im wesentlichen unter dem unmittelbaren Einfluss Hans Kelsens entwickelt hat."[3] In Pitamics Fall spielten auch Merkls Theorie des rechtlichen Stufenbaues (zusammen mit dem sogenannten

---

[1] Pitamic wurde in Postojna geboren, die Grundschule und die ersten drei Klassen des Gymnasiums besuchte er in Gorica, dann zog er nach Wien, wo er als Zögling der Theresianischen Akademie sein Abitur ablegte und an der dortigen Universität sein Studium der Rechtswissenschaft abschloss. Sein Berufsleben begann er in den Jahren 1908 bis 1913, als er bei der Landesregierung in Ljubljana und bei den Bezirkshauptmannschaften in Krško, Litija und Postojna arbeitete. Im Jahre 1913 wurde er dem staatsrechtlichen Büro des Ministerratspräsidiums in Wien zugeteilt, wo er bis zum Zusammenbruch der Donaumonarchie blieb. In Ljubljana zählte er zu den Gründern der Juristischen Fakultät der Universität in Ljubljana. Er war ihr erster Dekan und ordentlicher Professor für öffentlich-rechtliche Fächer. Im Studienjahr 1925/26 war er Rektor der Universität in Ljubljana. In den Jahren von 1929 bis 1934 war er außerordentlicher Gesandter und bevollmächtigter Minister des Königreichs Jugoslawien bei der Regierung der Vereinigten Staaten in Washington. Nach seiner Rückkehr war er weiter an der Juristischen Fakultät in Ljubljana tätig, bis er 1952 pensioniert wurde. Pitamic war ab ihrer Gründung 1938 bis zum 21. Juni 1948, als er aus politischen Gründen vom Präsidium der Volksversammlung Sloweniens nicht als ihr Vollmitglied bestätigt wurde, Mitglied der Akademie der Wissenschaften und Künste in Ljubljana. Seit 1988 wird er in den Jahrbüchern der Akademie unter den verstorbenen Akademiemitgliedern angeführt. Bei der Akademieversammlung am 17. Dezember 1996 wurde er posthum rehabilitiert. 1996 setzten ihm die Universität Ljubljana und deren Juristische Fakultät vor dem Universitätsgebäude ein Denkmal in Form einer Büste. – Umfassender siehe *Adolf Merkl*: Prof. Dr. Leonidas Pitamic zum 70. Geburtstag, in: Österreichische Zeitschrift für öffentliches Recht, 7 (1956), S. 145–147; *Ivan Tomšič*: Leonidas Pitamic in memoriam, in: Österreichische Zeitschrift für öffentliches Recht, 23 (1972), S. 201–203, und *Marijan Pavčnik*: Leonid Pitamic (1885–1971), in: *Leonid Pitamic*: Na robovih čiste teorije prava/An den Grenzen der Reinen Rechtslehre (Herausgeber und Einführungsstudie: *Marijan Pavčnik*), Ljubljana 2005. Nachdruck: Ljubljana 2009 (im Folgenden abgekürzt als „*Pitamic*: An den Grenzen der RR"), S. 337–340. – Der Verfasser dieses Vortrags hat sich schon mehrfach mit Pitamic beschäftigt. Aus diesem Grund gibt es einige Überlappungen mit den früheren Aufsätzen; siehe insbesondere die Abhandlungen: 1. An den Grenzen der Reinen Rechtslehre, in: *Pitamic*: An den Grenzen der RR, S. 153–173, und 2. Leonid Pitamic, in: *Robert Walter / Clemens Jabloner / Klaus Zeleny* (Hrsg.): Der Kreis um Hans Kelsen. Die Anfangsjahre der Reinen Rechtslehre. Wien 2008, S. 325–350.

[2] *Rudolf Aladár Métall*: Hans Kelsen. Leben und Werk. Wien 1969, S. 29.

[3] *Métall*: Hans Kelsen (Fn. 2), S. 29. Siehe auch Der Kreis um Hans Kelsen (Fn. 1).

Fehlerkalkül) und Verdross' Naturrechtstheorie (zusammen mit seiner Ansicht über die Einheit des rechtlichen Weltbildes) eine bedeutende Rolle.

Im Vorwort zur zweiten Auflage von *Hauptprobleme der Staatsrechtslehre* schrieb Kelsen, Reine Rechtslehre sei „das gemeinsame Werk eines stetig sich erweiternden Kreises theoretisch gleich gerichteter Männer."[4] In diesen Kreis reihte Kelsen auch Pitamic ein und erkannte ihm zu, dass er wertvolle Beiträge zu der Frage, wie man die Grundnorm als Voraussetzung juristischer Erkenntnis definieren sollte, geleistet hatte.[5] Von einem engeren Kreis von Menschen, die gleiche Ziele anstrebten, spricht Kelsen auch im Vorwort zur ersten Auflage der *Reinen Rechtslehre*. Das Charakteristikum seiner „Schule" wäre, dass „hier jeder versucht, von anderen zu lernen, ohne darauf zu verzichten, seinen eigenen Weg zu gehen."[6] In Kelsens und Pitamics Fall konzentrieren sich diese Fragen um die methodologische und gegenständliche Reinheit des Rechts.

Im Folgenden werde ich zunächst Kelsens Rechtstheorie in der Zeit, auf die Pitamic in seinen Werken reagiert, kurz erläutern. Es folgt die Erörterung eines der Ausgangspunkte der Reinen Rechtslehre, nämlich der Denkökonomie, in der Kelsen in einem bestimmten Umfang Pitamics Auffassung annahm. Zweifellos war es die Frage der Grundnorm, in der Kelsen und Pitamic in unterschiedliche Richtungen gingen. Pitamic ging über die Reine Rechtslehre hinaus und versuchte einen gemeinsamen inhaltlichen Nenner zwischen Positiv- und Naturrecht zu finden. Er suchte den gemeinsamen Nenner in der Natur des Rechts. Das Endergebnis ist jedoch nicht, dass Kelsens und Pitamics Auffassungen einander ausschließen. Ihre Ansichten sind zweifellos unterschiedlich, doch sie können einander ergänzen, wenn man sie auf angemessene Weise verbindet. Der wesentliche Beitrag der Reinen Rechtslehre ist es, dass sie einen formalrechtlichen Rahmen entwirft, innerhalb dessen der Mensch inhaltlich schöpferisch sein kann.

2. Reinheit des Rechts

Es ist das grundlegende methodische Prinzip von Kelsens Theorie, dass sie „die Rechtwissenschaft von allen ihr fremden Elementen befreien" will.[7] Dieses metho-

---

4   *Kelsen*: Vorrede zur zweiten Auflage Hauptprobleme der Staatsrechtslehre entwickelt aus der Lehre vom Rechtssatze. Tübingen 1923, S. XXIII (im Folgenden abgekürzt als „Vorrede zur zweiten Auflage HP"; die erste Auflage aus dem Jahr 1911 wird nachfolgend als „HP" zitiert).

5   *Kelsen*: Vorrede zur zweiten Auflage HP, S. XV. An dieser Stelle wurden folgende Abhandlungen von *Pitamic* zitiert: Denkökonomische Voraussetzungen der Rechtswissenschaft, in: Österreichische Zeitschrift für öffentliches Recht, 3 (1917), S. 339–367 (im Folgenden abgekürzt als „Denkökonomische"); Eine „Juristische Grundlehre" (1918), in: Österreichische Zeitschrift für öffentliches Recht, 3 (1918), S. 734–757; Plato, Aristoteles und die Reine Rechtstheorie, in: Zeitschrift für öffentliches Recht, 2 (1921), S. 683–700, und Kritische Bemerkungen zum Gesellschafts-, Staats- und Gottesbegriff bei Kelsen, in: Zeitschrift für öffentliches Recht, 3 (1922), S. 531–544 (nachfolgend abgekürzt als „Kritische Bemerkungen"). Alle diese Abhandlungen sind nachgedruckt in: *Pitamic*: An den Grenzen der RR. Alle Abhandlungen, die in diesem Buch nachgedruckt sind, haben eine doppelte Seitenangabe: zuerst ist die Seite aus dem Erstdruck (in Klammern), dann folgt die laufende Nummer des Buches.

6   *Kelsen*: Vorwort zur ersten Auflage Reine Rechtslehre. Einleitung in die rechtswissenschaftliche Problematik. Leipzig und Wien 1934. Nachdruck: Scientia Verlag Aalen 1994 (im Folgenden abgekürzt als „RR 1"), S. IX.

7   *Kelsen*: RR 1, S. 1. – Über die Periodisierung von Kelsens Theorie siehe insbesondere *Stanley L. Paulson*: 1. Toward a Periodisation of the Pure Theory of Law, in: Letizia Gianformaggio: Hans Kelsen's Legal Theory. A Diachronic Point of View. Torino 1990, S. 11–47, 2. Introduction, in: Hans

dologische Programm ist bereits im Werk *Hauptprobleme der Staatsrechtslehre* klar umrissen. In der Vorrede zur zweiten Auflage sagt Kelsen sehr deutlich, dass es sich um „die Selbstständigkeit des Rechts als eines Gegenstandes wissenschaftlicher Erkenntnis" handelt.[8] Die Selbstständigkeit des Rechts ist ein Synonym für „die Reinheit der Lehre"[9], die am Recht nur als einer formellen seinsollenden Struktur interessiert ist. Die Reinheit der Lehre erfordert, dass man sie sowohl im Verhältnis zur soziologischen Betrachtung als auch im Verhältnis zur Naturrechtstheorie schützt. Im Verhältnis zur soziologischen Betrachtung muss sie deshalb geschützt werden, weil diese „sich des Rechtes wie eines Stückes *natur*gegebener Wirklichkeit nach *Kausal*-wissenschaftlicher Methode bemächtigen will", gegen die Naturrechtslehre muss man sie deshalb abgrenzen, weil diese ins Recht die Welt der ethisch-politischen Postulate einbringt.[10] Kelsens Positivismus ist kritisch und will deshalb mit Politik, Moral und Ideologie gar nichts zu tun haben.

Durch die Abgrenzung gegen soziologische und naturrechtliche Jurisprudenz wird die methodologische Reichweite der Reinen Rechtslehre eingeengt. Ihr Gegenstand ist, so Kelsen, das *positive Recht* und sie versucht „die Frage zu beantworten, was und wie das Recht ist, nicht aber die Frage, wie es sein oder gemacht werden soll."[11] Kelsens methodologischer Ansatz *ermöglicht* es *nicht*, positives Recht als einen integralen Teil der sozialen Wirklichkeit zu behandeln. Kelsens Ansatz lenkt uns in die Richtung von normativen Gesetzlichkeiten, die man durch Rechtsgesetz (als das Gegenteil vom Naturgesetz) erkennen kann.

Kelsens Rechtsgesetz akzeptiert den neukantianischen methodologischen Dualismus[12], der scharf zwischen der Welt von Sein (indikative Welt) und der Welt von

Kelsen: Introduction to the Problems of Legal Theory. Oxford 1992, S. XVII–XLII, 3. Introduction, in: Stanley L. Paulson, Bonnie Litschewski Paulson (Hrsg.): Normativity and Norms. Critical Perspectives on Kelsenian Themes. Oxford 1998, S. XXIII ff., 4. Four Phases in Hans Kelsen's Legal Theory? Reflections on a Periodization, in: Oxford Journal of Legal Studies, 18 (1998), S. 153–166, 5. Arriving at a Defensible Periodization of Hans Kelsen's Legal Theory, in: Oxford Journal of Legal Studies, 19 (1999), S. 351–364, 6. Konstruktivismus, Methodendualismus und Zurechnung im Frühwerk Hans Kelsens, in: Archiv des öffentlichen Rechts, 124 (1999) 4, S. 631–657, und 7. Der Normativismus Hans Kelsens, in: Juristenzeitung 61 (2006) 11, S. 529–536 (S. 530, Fn. 11). Vgl. *Carsten Heidemann*: Die Norm als Tatsache. Zur Normentheorie Hans Kelsens. Baden-Baden 1997, S. 23 ff., S. 43 ff. Für Pitamic, seine Entwicklung und seine kritische Behandlung der Reinen Rechtslehre ist vor allem die Zeit von HP bis RR 1 bedeutend. Über diese Zeit siehe auch *Matthias Jestaedt*: Von den „Hauptproblemen" zur Erstauflage der „Reinen Rechtslehren", in: Robert Walter / Werner Ogris / Thomas Olechowski (Hrsg.): Hans Kelsen: Leben – Werk – Wirksamkeit. Wien 2009, S. 113–135.

8   *Kelsen*: Vorrede zur zweiten Auflage HP, S. V.
9   *Kelsen*: Vorrede zur zweiten Auflage HP, S. V.
10   *Kelsen*: Vorrede zur zweiten Auflage HP, S. V.
11   *Kelsen*: RR 1, S. 1.
12   Darüber siehe z. B.: *Günther Winkler*: Sein und Sollen, in: Rechtstheorie – Beiheft 1 (1979), S. 177–193; *Stefan Hammer*: Kelsens Grundnormkonzeption als neukantianische Erkenntnistheorie des Rechts?, in: Stanley L. Paulson / Robert Walter (Hrsg.): Untersuchungen zur Reinen Rechtslehre. Wien 1986, S. 210–231; *Stanley L. Paulson*: Zur neukantianischen Dimension der Reinen Rechtslehre, in: Fritz Sander, Hans Kelsen: Die Rolle des Neukantianismus in der Reinen Rechtslehre. Hrsg. von Stanley L. Paulson. Aalen 1988, S. 7–26; *Horst Dreier*: Rechtslehre, Staatssoziologie und Demokratietheorie bei Hans Kelsen. 2. Aufl. Baden-Baden 1990, S. 83 ff.; *Stanley L. Paulson*: Lässt sich die Reine Rechtslehre transzendental begründen?, in: Rechtstheorie, 21 (1990), S. 155–179 (siehe besonders S. 168 ff.); *Stanley L. Paulson*: Vorwort zum Neudruck, in: Kelsen: RR 1, S. III–VIII; *Robert Alexy* u.a. (Hrsg.): Neukantianismus und Rechtsphilosophie. Baden-Baden 2002; *Ulfrid Neumann*: Wissenschaftstheorie der Rechtswissenschaft bei Hans Kelsen und Gustav Radbruch, in: Hans Kelsen. Staatsrechtslehrer und Rechtstheoretiker des 20. Jahrhunderts, hrsg. von Stanley L. Paulson und Michael Stolleis. Tübingen 2005, S. 35 ff., und *Axel-Johannes Korb*: Kelsens Kritiker. Ein Beitrag zur Ge-

Sollen (normative Welt) unterscheidet. Das Naturgesetz verbindet einen Tatbestand als die Ursache mit einem anderen als dessen Folge, das Rechtsgesetz verbindet die Rechtsbedingung mit der Rechtsfolge.[13] Die Verbindung zwischen der Rechtsbedingung und der Rechtsfolge ist das Prinzip der Zurechnung: wenn der Tatbestand T auftritt, *soll* die Rechtsfolge R folgen. Kelsen ist nicht daran interessiert, warum etwas rechtlich erlaubt, geboten oder verboten ist, ihn interessiert die normative Gesetzlichkeit, dass man auf eine bestimmte Weise handeln *soll* (Rechtsfolge), wenn man in bestimmte Umstände (welche Bedingungen zum Entstehen der Rechtsfolge sind) gerät. Dasselbe gilt für die Rechtsfolgen, die den rechtswidrigen Verhaltensweisen folgen *sollen*. Auch diesmal gilt Kelsens Interesse nicht der Natur der Rechtswidrigkeit oder der Natur der Sanktionen, sondern wieder lediglich der normativen Verknüpfung von Rechtsverletzung und Rechtfolge.

Eine „natürliche" Folgerung von Kelsens Ansatz ist es, dass das Recht ein System von Normen ist, die eine geschlossene Einheit bilden. Das Normensystem ist nicht durch Tatsachen und Werte, sondern nur durch Rechtsnormen derselben oder einer höheren Stufe begründet. Durch ein so verstandenes System von Rechtsnormen kann jedoch die Verfassung, die den hierarchischen Gipfel des positiven Rechts darstellt (wenn man sich lediglich auf Staatsrecht begrenzt), nicht normativ begründet werden. Die Verfassung wird rechtlich durch eine Grundnorm begründet, die als gedankliche Voraussetzung das bewusst macht, „was alle Juristen – zumeist unbewusst – tun, wenn sie (...) dieses positive Recht als eine gültige Ordnung" verstehen.[14] Es wird vorausgesetzt, dass Rechtsnormen als geltende Normen behandelt werden. Im Falle der Verfassung heißt das, dass „dasjenige, was das historisch erste verfassungsgebende Organ als seinen Willen geäußert hat, als Norm zu gelten habe".[15]

Kelsens methodische Reinheit ist so intensiv, dass sie nicht nur das Recht selbst als Normensystem bereinigt. Die Reinigung bezieht sich, wenigstens in einem bestimmten Sinn, auch auf Moral, andere Gesellschaftsnormen und Werte, die das Recht als Normensystem umgeben. Diese und andere Gesichtspunkte sind sicher bedeutend und sogar eine Notwendigkeit, wenn man das Recht auch aus anderen Blickwinkeln betrachtet. Von größter Bedeutung ist es, dass die spezifische Rechtserkenntnis rein sein muss. Es wäre unzulässig, die Ergebnisse explikativer Betrachtungen in normative Begriffskonstruktionen einzubringen.[16]

schichte der Rechts- und Staatstheorie (1911–1934). Tübingen 2010, S. 12–24.

13   *Kelsen*: RR 1, S. 22. Siehe auch HP, S. 3 ff.

14   *Kelsen*: RR 1, S. 67.

15   *Kelsen*: RR 1, S. 65. Vgl. auch *Kelsen*: Allgemeine Staatslehre. Berlin 1925. Nachdruck: Wien 1993, S. 249 ff. Siehe auch *Walters* und *Paulsons* Aufsätze, die in Fn. 36 angeführt sind. Über verschiedene Gesichtspunkte der Grundnorm vgl. auch *Ralf Dreier*: Sein und Sollen. Bemerkungen zur Reinen Rechtslehre Kelsens (1972), in: Recht – Moral – Ideologie. Studien zur Rechtstheorie. Frankfurt/Main 1981, S. 217–240, und Bemerkungen zur Theorie der Grundnorm, in: Die Reine Rechtslehre in wissenschaftlicher Diskussion. Schriftenreihe des Hans Kelsen-Instituts, Bd. 7. Wien 1982, S. 38–46; *Gerhard Luf*: Überlegungen zum transzendentallogischen Stellenwert der Grundnormkonzeption Kelsens, in: Werner Krawietz u.a. (Hrsg.): Theorie der Normen. FS für Ota Weinberger zum 65. Geburtstag. Berlin 1984, S. 567–581 (zitiert nach dem Nachdruck in: Gerhard Luf: Freiheit als Rechtsprinzip. Wien 2008, S. 57–71); *Robert Alexy*: Begriff und Geltung des Rechts. München 1992, S. 154 ff., und *Uta Bindreiter*: Why Grundnorm? A Treatise on the Implications of Kelsen's Doctrine. The Hague u.a. 2002.

16   *Kelsen*: HP, S. 42. Vgl. auch S. 496: „Aufgabe der juristischen Begriffsbildung ist es ja gerade, diese Schranken des Gesetzes – das formale Element – und nicht die innerhalb derselben stattfindende Tätigkeit zu erfassen! *Denn Recht ist Schutz und nicht das Geschützte, ist Schranke, nicht das Beschränkte!*"

3. Kelsens normativer Purismus und Pitamic

Es wäre nicht zutreffend, wenn man sagte, dass Pitamic von der Reinen Rechtslehre nicht angetan und begeistert war. Kelsens normativer Purismus hatte auf Pitamic überall dort einen sichtlichen Einfluss, wo es sich um Fragen handelte, die man ins Recht als normatives System einordnen konnte. Kelsens Ausgangspunkt, dass Sollen (die Norm) nur aus Sollen und nicht aus Sein hervorgehen kann, klingt bei Pitamic in der Behauptung nach, dass man (normative – Anm. M. P.) Rechtseigenschaften nur aus Rechtseigenschaften deduzieren kann: „Maßgebend ist nur das Verhältnis der durch positivrechtliche Formalzeichen bestimmten Gruppe der Normen zu ihr positivrechtlich über- und untergeordneten Gruppen, was jedoch mit der *Rechtskraft* der Norm identisch ist."[17] Fortan ist es für die Verfassung nicht mehr bedeutend, was sie regelt (das ist eine politische und gesellschaftliche Frage), sondern es ist nur rechtlich entscheidend, dass die Verfassung „jene Gruppe von Normen ist, die in der Rechtshierarchie (im Rahmen des Staatsrechts – Anm. M. P.) am höchsten steht und aus der alle anderen Normen und überhaupt Rechtstaten ihre Rechtlichkeit schöpfen."[18] Somit ist auch das Gesetz nicht ein Rechtsakt, der grundsätzlich die Rechte und Pflichten der Rechtssubjekte bestimmt, sondern es ist rechtlich lediglich ein Akt, in dem sich Normen befinden, die der Verfassung unmittelbar untergeordnet und zugleich anderem Recht im Staat übergeordnet sind.[19] Und dasselbe gilt wieder für die Verordnung, die nicht inhaltsmäßig interessant, sondern nur ein vollziehender Akt ist, der „von anderen Staatsorganen als den gesetz- und verfassungsgebenden erlassen wird."[20] Und so weiter, bis man zum letzten Akt kommt, der nur noch den Inhalt einer höheren Rechtsnorm im konkreten (gesellschaftlichen) Verhältnis verwirklicht.[21]

Die normative Ansicht weitete er auch auf den Staat, die Staatsorgane und die Verhältnisse unter ihnen aus. Pitamic stellte schon in seiner Abhandlung *Plato, Aristoteles und die reine Rechtstheorie* (1921) fest, dass Plato und noch stärker Aristoteles „bei Erforschung der Begriffe Staat, Staatsbürger, Gesetz etc. streng normativ vorgingen"[22] und fähig waren, methodischen Synkretismus zu vermeiden.[23] Am Beispiel von Aristoteles' Politik[24] begründet er, dass für den Staatsbegriff „die Idee des Staates als Ordnung, als Verfassungs- oder Rechtsordnung" wesentlich ist.[25] Für jede

---

Siehe auch *Kelsen*: Die philosophischen Grundlagen der Naturrechtslehre und des Rechtspositivismus, in: Philosophische Vorträge, veröffentlicht von der Kant-Gesellschaft, Pan-Verlag Rolf Heise, Charlottenburg, 1928, Heft 31, 73 Seiten. Zitiert nach dem Nachdruck im zweibändigen Werk: Die Wiener rechtstheoretische Schule, hrsg. v. Hans Klecatsky u.a., Wien 1968 (im Folgenden abgekürzt als „WS 1" bzw. „WS 2"), Bd. 1, S. 281–350 (S. 305): „Denn ein 'Verhältnis' ist nur zwischen Elementen eines und desselben Systems möglich."

17 *Pitamic*: Ustava in zakon (Verfassung und Gesetz), in: Slovenski pravnik, 36 (1922), S. 9.

18 *Pitamic*: Ustava in zakon (Verfassung und Gesetz, Fn. 17), S. 10.

19 *Pitamic*: Država (Der Staat). Celje 1927. Nachdruck: Ljubljana 1996 und 2009, S. 234. Siehe auch die englische Ausgabe: A Treatise on the State. Baltimore 1933. Nachdruck: Ljubljana 2008, S. 150.

20 *Pitamic*: Država (Der Staat, Fn. 19), S. 264.

21 Siehe *Pitamic*: Ustava in zakon (Verfassung und Gesetz, Fn. 17), S. 9–10, und Država (Der Staat, Fn. 19), S. 266.

22 *Pitamic*: Plato, Aristoteles und die reine Rechtstheorie (Fn. 5), S. 700.

23 *Pitamic*: Plato, Aristoteles und die reine Rechtstheorie (Fn. 5), S. 683.

24 *Aristoteles*: Politik, III, 1278b: „Staatsverfassung aber bedeutet Ordnung des Staates, der anderen Ämter und vor allem des wichtigsten über alle; das wichtigste nämlich über alle ist die Lenkung des Staates, Staatslenkung aber bedeutet die Staatsverfassung." Zitiert nach der Reclam Ausgabe (Stuttgart 1989); übersetzt von Franz F. Schwarz.

25 *Pitamic*: Plato, Aristoteles und die reine Rechtstheorie (Fn. 5), S. 688.

Verbindung ist „die Idee, das System, die Art der Verbindung, und nicht das Ver-
bundene als entscheidend erkannt."[26] Pitamic erkennt, dass gerade darin eine Parallele besteht zwischen der altgriechischen Auffassung, „die von den konstruktiven
Hilfsmitteln der modernen Jurisprudenz frei war", und der Reinen Rechtslehre, welche „die Verselbständigung, Verdinglichung, Hypostasierung dieser Hilfsmittel wieder auflöst und sie lediglich als *Hilfs*mittel juristischer Denkökonomie gelten lassen
will."[27]

Das Grundwerk, in dem Pitamic die normative Natur des Staates untersucht, ist
die Monographie *Država (Der Staat*, 1927).[28] Er vertrat die Erkenntnis, dass des Staates ständiger Kern „eine Rechtsvereinigung oder Rechtsorganisation von Menschen"
sei. Im Mittelpunkt des Staates stehen wieder Rechtsnormen, die besagen, welches
Gebiet, Volk und welche Gewalten zum Staat gehören und welchen Organisationen
diese Qualität nicht zusteht:

> Der Staat ist „die Rechtsorganisation von Menschen auf einem bestimmten
> Gebiet, die unmittelbar dem Völkerrecht untergeordnet ist und der alle
> Rechtsorganisationen auf diesem Gebiet untergeordnet sind mit Ausnahme
> jener, die selbst unmittelbar vom Völkerrecht abhängen."[29]

Für Pitamics Definition des Staates ist es charakteristisch, dass sie den Begriff der
Staatssouveränität als der höchsten Rechtsgewalt relativiert. Die Staatsgewalt ist die
höchste Gewalt auf einem bestimmten Territorium und bezüglich der Menschen, die
sich darauf befinden, nach außen ist sie jedoch dem Völkerrecht untergeordnet. Die
Staatssouveränität ist mit dem Bestehen des Völkerrechts unvereinbar. Der Staat ist
die höchste Rechtsgewalt nach innen, auf ihrem Territorium sind alle Rechtsorgani-
sationen, außer den internationalen, dem Staat und nur über ihn, also indirekt dem
Völkerrecht untergeordnet.[30] Dadurch erhält die Souveränität als Qualifikation des
Staates „ihre ursprüngliche Bedeutung, nämlich ‚höher' (lat. superanus – M. P.) an-
statt ‚höchster',".[31] Der Staat ist also die höchste Rechtsorganisation auf dem Staats-
territorium, höher als er ist jedoch das Völkerrecht, dem der Staat untergeordnet ist.
Völkerrechtliche Normen sind die Bedingung für die Festigkeit der zwischenstaatli-
chen Beziehungen.[32]

---

26 *Pitamic*: Plato, Aristoteles und die reine Rechtstheorie (Fn. 5), S. 688. Siehe auch *Alfred Verdross*:
Abendländische Rechtsphilosophie. 2. Aufl. Wien 1963, S. 44. Vgl. *Kelsen*: Gott und Staat, in: Logos,
11 (1922/23), S. 261–284. Zitiert nach dem Nachdruck in WS 1, S. 180.

27 *Pitamic*: Plato, Aristoteles und die reine Rechtstheorie (Fn. 5), S. 684.

28 Siehe auch die englische Ausgabe: A Treatise on the State (1933, Fn. 19). Siehe auch die Abhandlung Les déformations du raisonnement, sources d'erreurs dans les théories de l'Etat, in: Revue in-
ternationale de la théorie du droit, 1 (1926), S. 47–58; darin fasste er seine Auffassung vom Staat zusammen, die er ein Jahr später im Buch Država (Der Staat, 1927, Fn. 19) entwickelte.

29 *Pitamic*: Država (Der Staat, Fn. 19), S. 44.

30 *Pitamic*: Država (Der Staat, Fn. 19), S. 40.

31 *Pitamic*: Država (Der Staat, Fn. 19), S. 40. Pitamics Ansicht über die Souveränität des Staates stimmt
mit Kelsens Ansicht über die Zukunft des Völkerrechts überein; das Dogma der Staatssouveränität
muss die Souveränität des Einzelstaates überschreiten. Siehe *Hans Kelsen*: Das Problem der Souveränität und die Theorie des Völkerrechts. Tübingen 1920, S. 320. Siehe auch Abschnitt 6.2. dieses Beitrags.

32 *Pitamic*: Država (Der Staat, Fn. 19), S. 37. Vgl. auch *Kelsen*, der in seinem Werk Das Problem der
Souveränität (Fn. 31) *Pitamics* Abhandlung Die parlamentarische Mitwirkung bei Staatsverträgen in
Österreich (Leipzig, Wien 1915) zitierte und dabei darauf aufmerksam machte, dass *Pitamic* monis-
tisch konstruiert, wenn er das Verhältnis zwischen Staats- und Völkerrecht behandelt. Siehe Fn. 5
auf S. 176–177.

4. Die Suche nach der rechtlichen Grundnorm (Ausgangspunkt der Reinen Rechtslehre)

4.1. „Denkökonomische Voraussetzungen der Rechtswissenschaft"

Das Recht als ein System von Normen wäre utopisch, wenn es keinen entsprechenden Stützpunkt hätte.[33] Kelsen[34] und sein Kreis[35] suchten diesen Stützpunkt[36]:

> „Das Problem nun, das mir angesichts der strengen Normativität des Rechtes ungelöst zu sein schien, ergab sich daraus, dass *Kelsen* und ich und wir alle der offenkundigen, unabweisbaren Tatsache gegenüberstanden, dass zur Erkenntnis eines zeitlich und örtlich geltenden Rechtes die *Wirksamkeit* der Rechtsnormen, d. h. ihre tatsächliche, wenn auch nicht ausnahmslose Ausführung und Befolgung oder wenigstens die begründete Aussicht auf diese Wirksamkeit, beachtet werden muss."[37]

Eine Schlüsselrolle bei dieser Suche kam Pitamics Abhandlung *Denkökonomische Voraussetzungen der Rechtswissenschaft* (aus dem Jahr 1917) zu. Pitamic war ganz besonders daran interessiert, ob und wie man Kelsens Reinheit begründen könnte. In der genannten Abhandlung argumentierte er, dass man mit der normativen Methode allein nicht zum Ausgangspunkt eines konkreten Rechts kommen könne, wie es zunächst *Kelsens* Reine Rechtslehre versuchte. Pitamic wies schon zu jener Zeit darauf hin, dass man die Geltung des Rechts nicht nur über die gegenseitige Übereinstimmung einer niedrigeren Norm mit einer höheren oder einer jüngeren Norm mit einer älteren erkennen könne, sondern dass man dabei auch die Wirksamkeit des Rechtssystems als eines Ganzen berücksichtigen müsse. Er trat für das wissenschaftliche Prinzip ein, dass man den Verlauf der normativen Deduktion mit Hinsicht auf die gemäß

---

33 Vgl. schon *Walter Jellinek*: Gesetz, Gesetzesanwendung und Zweckmäßigkeitserwägung. Tübingen 1913, S. 28: „Der oberste Satz der Rechtsordnung dagegen ist so wenig wie das Naturgesetz eine Handlung; er ist ein unabänderliches Urteil über das Entstehen und Vergehen eines rechtlichen Sollens. (…) Nicht einer Handlung verdankt der Satz seine Geltung, sondern einer Denknotwendigkeit."

34 Siehe *Kelsens* Abhandlung Reichgesetz und Landesgesetz nach der österreichischen Verfassung (1914), die im Abschnitt 4.3. angeführt ist.

35 Ein besonderes Gewicht haben die Erörterungen von Alfred Verdross, der im Jahr 1916 auf das *Zweckmäßigkeitsprinzip* aufmerksam machte. Siehe *Alfred Verdross*: Die Neuordnung der gemeinsamen Wappen und Fahnen in ihrer Bedeutung für die rechtliche Gestalt der österreichisch-ungarischen Monarchie, in: Juristische Blätter, 44 (1915), S. 11–12, S. 121–123 und S. 134–137: „Vom Standpunkte der Rechtswissenschaft ist es daher eine jenseits der juristischen Erkenntnis liegende *Zweckmäßigkeitsfrage*, welche Konstruktionsbasis gewählt wird. *Zweckmäßigerweise* aber wird der juristische Konstrukteur auf das *soziologische Faktum* der wirkenden staatlichen Ordnungen aufbauend, nur solche Grundsätze zum Ausgangspunkte erwählen, denen ein Gegenwurf in der Wirklichkeit entspricht. Denn sonst verfolgt die Konstruktion keine praktischen Zwecke mehr und verwirklicht nicht ihre Aufgabe, die staatlichen Erscheinungen rechtlich zu deuten" (S. 134).

36 Siehe die ausführliche Entwicklungsgeschichte, die *Robert Walter* darstellte: Entstehung und Entwicklung des Gedankens der Grundnorm, in: Schriftenreihe des Hans Kelsen-Instituts, Bd. 18, Wien 1992, S. 47–59. Diese Abhandlung erschien in einer leicht ergänzten und geänderten Form auch in: Festschrift für Werner Krawietz zum 60. Geburtstag, hrsg. von Aulis Aarnio u.a., Berlin 1993 (siehe *Robert Walter*: Die Grundnorm im System der Reinen Rechtslehre, S. 85–99). Siehe auch *Stanley L. Paulson*: Die unterschiedlichen Formulierungen der „Grundnorm", in: Festschrift für Werner Krawietz (Fn. 36), S. 53–74, und *H. Dreier*: Rechtslehre (Fn. 12), S. 42–56.

37 *Pitamic*: Die Frage der rechtlichen Grundnorm, in: Völkerrecht und rechtliches Weltbild. Festschrift für Alfred Verdross. Wien 1960, S. 209. Nachdruck in: *Pitamic*: An den Grenzen der RR, S. 209.

einer anderen (kausalen) Methode verlaufende Entwicklung des Geschehens, also mit Hinsicht auf faktische Tatsachen, anschneiden müsse.

> Wie er selbst sagt, „muss bei dieser Wahl sowohl für das vergangene wie das gegenwärtige Recht ein gewisses *ökonomisches Prinzip* beobachtet werden; dieses Prinzip sieht vom *subjektiven* politischen Glauben vollständig ab und erschöpft sich in der *objektiven* Feststellung der materiellen Voraussetzungen für die Konstruktion solcher Rechtssätze, die in möglichster Übereinstimmung stehen mit wirkenden, das heißt mit jenen Sollvorstellungen, welche die Menschen auf jenem Gebiete und in jener Zeit tatsächlich motivieren, für welches und für welche wir das Recht erkennen wollen."[38]

Was die Natur dieses Prinzips betrifft, berief er sich auf den Philosophen und Physiker Ernst Mach:

> „Dieses Ziel, ein Gebiet mit dem geringsten Aufwand zu überschauen und alle Thatsachen durch *einen* Gedankenprocess nachzubilden, kann mit vollem Recht ein ökonomisches genannt werden."[39]

Pitamic sprach sich für *methodologische* Klarheit der Rechtstheorie aus, ohne im Gegenstand *Recht* ganz a priori nur seine Normativität zu sehen und ohne es ganz a priori von allen seinen nichtnormativen Elementen zu säubern. Pitamic unterscheidet scharf zwischen der deduktiv-normativen und der induktiv-kausalen Methode. Die Erstere bietet nur die Denkweise, mit der „die Normen eines *gegebenen* Rechtsstoffes in ihren Beziehungen zueinander widerspruchslos zu erkennen und im Verhältnisse zum tatsächlichen Geschehen anzuwenden sind."[40] Das Kernstück dieser Methode ist die normative Zurechnung, die nichts etwas Anderes ist als „die Verknüpfung eines Tatbestandes mit einem anderen Tatbestande auf Grund einer Norm".[41] Besonders kennzeichnend ist es, dass der Anwender der deduktiv-normativen Methode den Ausgangspunkt seiner Forschung voraussetzt, während man den Ausgangspunkt selbst (d. h. das Rechtsmaterial als den Gegenstand der Forschung) erst durch die induktiv-kausale Methode definieren kann. Die Letztere sucht den konkreten Ausgangspunkt, d. h. eine solche Rechtsordnung, die man „in ihren konkreten, zeitlich und örtlich bedingten *Inhalten*" findet.[42]

Dieser methodologische Dualismus, dem die Rechtswissenschaft nicht ausweichen kann, wird von Pitamic auf eine sehr bildhafte Weise illustriert:

> „Wenn *Kelsen* von einem als gegeben vorausgesetzten Standpunkte – einem Normenkomplex – ausgeht, aus dieser formalen, beliebige Inhalte zulas-

---

38 *Pitamic*: Denkökonomische, S. 366, und Nove smeri v pravni filozofiji (Neue Richtungen in der Rechtsphilosophie), in: Zbornik znanstvenih razprav, 1 (1921), S. 18. Siehe auch die Buchbesprechung: Hans Kelsen: Reine Rechtslehre (Leipzig/Wien 1934), in: Zeitschrift für öffentliches Recht, 15 (1935) 3, S. 414.

39 *Ernst Mach*: Die ökonomische Natur der physikalischen Forschung, in: Allmanach der Kaiserlichen Akademie der Wissenschaften, XXXII, Wien 1882. S. 302. Siehe auch S. 301, 303, 305, 306 und 316. Vgl. *Pitamic*: Denkökonomische, S. 339–367. Siehe die Fußnoten 1, 4, 5 und 11. – Siehe auch *Ernst Mach*: Erkenntnis und Irrtum. Leipzig 1905, S. 232: „*Eine vorläufige versuchsweise Annahme zum Zwecke des leichteren Verständnisses von Tatsachen, welche aber dem tatsächlichen Nachweis sich noch entzieht, nennen wir eine Hypothese.*"

40 *Pitamic*: Denkökonomische, S. 365–366. Mit dieser Methode führt man die juristische Konstruktion ausschließlich mit juristischen Begriffen durch (S. 367).

41 *Pitamic*: Denkökonomische, S. 342.

42 *Pitamic*: Denkökonomische, S. 344.

senden Voraussetzung rein deduktiv die Konsequenzen ableitet, so ist er gewissermaßen auf dem Gipfel irgend eines Berges, von dem er, sich normativ einen Weg bahnend, hinunter schreitet; *wie* man auf den Gipfel kommt, danach fragt er nicht. Die ,anderen' suchen erst die materiellen Voraussetzungen, den Ausgangspunkt der Normen zu gewinnen, sie suchen erst den Gipfel eines bestimmten Berges; sie bahnen sich den Weg hinauf, was nur mit der induktiven, kausal arbeitenden Methode möglich ist, da es sich ja … um die Konstatierung der in das Erkenntnisgebiet des Seins fallenden psychologischen Wirkungen von Sollvorstellungen handelt."[43]

Pitamic erklärt, dass man in der Reihe von Vorstellungen, die gemäß einer bestimmten Methode verlaufen, nie aus der unendlichen Reihe aussteigen kann, wenn man nicht mit Vorstellungen Halt gebietet, die nach einer anderen Methode verlaufen.[44] Die Rechtswissenschaft (und überhaupt jede Wissenschaft) kann auf eine solche endgültige Bestimmung nicht verzichten. Daraus entspringt die Notwendigkeit „von letzten Rechts*voraussetzungen*, die aber immer einen anderen Denkcharakter haben als die Rechts*normen*."[45] Und diese „letzte Voraussetzung" muss nicht mehr „als *sein sollend*, sondern als *seiend* vorgestellt werden."[46] Wie Pitamic sagt, geht es um „*den Sprung* (hervorgehoben von M. P.) über einen Abgrund, der in endloser Tiefe die Welt des Seins von jener des Sollens *logisch* trennt".[47] Kurzum: es handelt sich um ein ungelöstes, vielleicht sogar unlösbares erkenntnistheoretisches Problem, das man vielleicht durch einen menschlichen *Wert*sprung („*Wert*-" wurde von M. P. hinzugefügt) überbrücken kann, sodass „die normativ verlaufende Deduktion mit Rücksicht auf eine *Seinstatsache* (hervorgehoben von M. P.) abgeschnitten" ist.[48]

4.2. Der Gegenstand und die Methode der Forschung

Die von Pitamic gestellten Fragen betreffen einige Stellen, die für das Verständnis der Reinen Rechtslehre eine Schlüsselbedeutung haben und bis heute Gegenstand von zahlreichen Diskussionen sind. *Die Zentralfrage bezieht sich auch auf die Beziehung zwischen dem Objekt und der Methode bzw. zwischen der Methode und dem Objekt der Forschung.*[49] Kelsens Standpunkt, dass „die spezifische Methode den spezifischen Gegenstand bestimmt,"[50] ist für Pitamic unannehmbar und er weist ihn mit einer gemäßigteren Gegenfeststellung zurück, dass auch der spezifische Gegenstand die spezifische Methode, mit der man ihn erforscht, mitgestaltet. Pitamic erkennt ausdrücklich, dass „irgend etwas für die Wahl der Methode entscheidend sein muß."[51] Noch klarer: „Irgendwie muß also der Gegenstand doch von allem Anfang an gegeben, das heißt für den Verstand gegeben, also erkannt sein; andernfalls könnte er nicht für die Wahl der Methode maßgebend sein, da ja Wahl auch bereits ,Kenntnis' oder ,Er-

---

43   *Pitamic*: Denkökonomische, S. 344.
44   *Pitamic*: Denkökonomische, S. 355.
45   *Pitamic*: Denkökonomische, S. 356
46   *Pitamic*: Denkökonomische, S. 356.
47   *Pitamic*: Denkökonomische, S. 356
48   Siehe *Pitamic*: Denkökonomische, S. 356.
49   Vgl. insbesondere *Günther Winkler*: Rechtstheorie und Erkenntnislehre. Wien/New York 1990, S. 175 ff.
50   Siehe *Kelsen*: Der soziologische und der juristische Staatsbegriff. Tübingen 1922, S. 106.
51   *Pitamic*: Kritische Bemerkungen, S. 535.

kenntnis' voraussetzt." Der Umstand, dass man die normative Methode anwendet, bedeutet also, dass die Norm bereits hier ist. Der Gegenstand, den man erforscht, bietet sich somit irgendwie dem Forscher an, ohne dass er erst derjenige wäre, der diesen Gegenstand gestaltete.[52]

Das gleiche Gewicht hat auch die Frage, warum es gerade ein bestimmter und nicht ein anderer Gegenstand ist, der vom Forscher untersucht wird. Pitamic fragt sich: „Warum setze ich gerade *diese* Norm als gültig voraus, warum lasse ich sie eine ideelle Existenz führen, warum fälle ich gerade mit *dieser* und nicht mit einer anderen Norm ein Urteil über die Pflicht dieses konkreten Menschen."[53] Es liegt in der Natur der wissenschaftlichen Forschung, dass es keine beliebige Antwort auf diese Frage geben kann. Für Pitamic sind die „in der Sphäre des Sozialen liegenden psychologischen Seinstatsachen" diejenigen, die das bestimmen und „gerade diese und keine andere Norm als gültig voraussetzen."[54] Und das ist auch der Grund, dass für die Erkenntnis des Rechtes auch die induktiv-kausale Methode unbedingt erforderlich ist. Ihre Aufgabe ist es, „die materiellen Voraussetzungen für die Rechtskonstruktion zu beschaffen."[55]

Für Pitamic ist die Anwendung der induktiv-kausalen Methode berechtigt und ganz „legitim". Anderer Meinung waren Kelsen und Weyr, die Pitamic vorhielten, dass die Anwendung der induktiv-kausalen Methode „die völlige *Denaturierung juristischer Erkenntnis*"[56] bedeutet. Pitamic ist mit der Kritik nicht einverstanden, weil die Rechtswissenschaft es sich dadurch unmöglich machen würde, gerade jenen Forschungsgegenstand zu definieren, den sie mit der deduktiv-normativen Methode erforscht. Die Forschungen von Pitamic zeigten, dass die induktiv-kausale Methode immer dann nötig ist, wenn die „normative Welt des Rechts" (das Recht als Sollen) von den entsprechenden Seinstatsachen abhängt und darauf begründet ist. In der Abhandlung *Kritische Bemerkungen zum Gesellschafts-, Staats- und Gottesbegriff bei Kelsen* (1922) zählte er zu diesen Tatsachen auch die Frage der Sprache: „Normen bestehen aus Sprach- oder Schriftzeichen, deren Bedeutung eine rein *konventionelle* ist und die wie eine *Seinstatsache* (hervorgehoben von M. P.) zu erforschen und festzustellen ist."[57]

In diesem Sinne ist der Streit um Methode ein „*völlig steriler Streit*" (hervorgehoben von M. P.), schon deshalb steril, weil er nicht zwischen den Ausgangspunkten der Forschung und der normativen Rechtsforschung selbst unterscheidet.[58] Die Schlüsselfrage ist nicht, ob die zusätzliche Anwendung der induktiv-kausalen Me-

---

52 *Pitamic*: Kritische Bemerkungen, S. 535. Siehe auch diese Stelle auf derselben Seite: „Diese Norm ist nicht erst von mir zu konstruieren oder vorauszusetzen, denn dann wäre sie nur meine oder sonst eines Forschers Betrachtungsart, also Methode, sondern sie muß in den Vorstellungen anderer Menschen vorhanden sein, falls es sich um eine durch Normen verbundenen Gruppe handelt."

53 *Pitamic*: Kritische Bemerkungen, S. 539.

54 *Pitamic*: Kritische Bemerkungen, S. 539.

55 *Pitamic*: Denkökonomische, S. 367.

56 *Kelsen*: Buchbesprechung Leonidas Pitamic: Die parlamentarische Mitwirkung bei Staatsverträgen in Österreich (Leipzig, Wien 1915), in: Österreichische Zeitschrift für öffentliches Recht, 2 (1915–1916), S. 258. Ebenso auch *Franz Weyr*: Buchbesprechung Leonidas Pitamic Die parlamentarische Mitwirkung bei Staatsverträgen in Österreich (Leipzig/Wien 1915), in: Archiv des öffentlichen Rechts, 35 (1916), S. 346.

57 *Pitamic*: Kritische Bemerkungen, S. 546. Vgl. auch S. 547–548: „Der Bedeutungswandel in der Sprache hängt nun wieder vom Wandel in den gesellschaftlichen Anschauungen, also von sozialen Tatsachen ab." Siehe auch die Abhandlung Interpretation und Wortbedeutungswandel, in: Zeitschrift für öffentliches Recht, 18 (1938), S. 426 ff.

58 Vgl. *Pitamic*: Denkökonomische, S. 354.

thode „erlaubt" ist, sondern dass man die beiden Methoden nicht „konfundiert".[59] Es geht um methodologische Klarheit und Reinheit und nicht um Gegenstandsreinheit, die man lediglich mit der deduktiv-normativen Methode erforschen könnte. Wenn man auf die induktiv-kausale Methode verzichtete, würde das bedeuten, dass die Rechtswissenschaft wenigstens in einem bestimmten Umfang das zeitlich und räumlich gegebene Recht übersehen würde. Oder, wie Pitamic sagt, wir sehen „somit die Notwendigkeit der Berücksichtigung des Nicht-Normativen sowohl beim Ursprung der Grundnormen wie bei der Normeninterpretation; sind das aber praktisch nicht die maßgebendsten Momente?"[60]

4.3. Kelsens Reaktion

Kelsen berücksichtigte teilweise die Kritik von Pitamic.[61] Kelsen setzte als selbstverständlich voraus, dass man von positivem Recht nur dann sprechen kann, wenn seine Normen wenigstens im Durchschnitt gesellschaftlich wirksam sind, und versuchte eine entsprechende theoretische Lösung zu finden. Bis zu Pitamics Abhandlung *Denkökonomische Voraussetzungen der Rechtswissenschaft* (1917) ist es Kelsen nicht gelungen, diese Lösung so zu definieren, dass sie innerhalb der Grenzen der *Reinen* Rechtslehre bleiben würde. Kelsen hat sich der Problematik der Grundnorm genähert.[62] In der Abhandlung *Reichsgesetz und Landesgesetz nach österreichischer Verfassung* (aus dem Jahr 1914)[63] stellt er ausdrücklich fest, dass jede juristische Konstruktion „von bestimmten Normen als gültigen Rechtssätzen ausgehen" müsse.[64] Für Kelsen ist es typisch, dass die Auswahl dieses Ausgangspunktes keine juristische, sondern *eine politische Frage* ist und „daher vom Standpunkt juristischer Erkenntnis immer den Anschein von Willkürlichkeit haben" muss.[65]

Pitamic ist überzeugt, dass Kelsen seinen Gedanken über die Wirksamkeit des Rechts übernommen und in einer geänderten normativisierten Form ausgedrückt hat: zunächst über die Norm des Völkerrechts und dann noch als den Inhalt der Grundnorm. Kelsen hat, sagt Pitamic, „die erwähnte Idee vervollständigt, weil er

---

59 *Pitamic*: Denkökonomische, S. 367.
60 *Pitamic*: Kritische Bemerkungen, S. 548. Siehe auch die Buchbesprechungen: Hans Kelsen: 1. Das Problem der Souveränität und die Theorie des Völkerrechts (Tübingen 1928) und 2. Der soziologische und der juristische Staatsbegriff (Tübingen 1928), in: Zeitschrift für öffentliches Recht, 7 (1928), S. 641 ff., und „Reine Rechtslehre" (1935, Fn. 38), S. 413 ff.
61 *Kelsen*: Vorrede zur zweiten Auflage HP, S. XV. An dieser Stelle wurden vier Abhandlungen von *Pitamic* zitiert: siehe Fn. 5. – Die Sekundärliteratur, die Pitamics Beitrag zu den Problemen der Bestimmung der Grundnorm berücksichtigt, ist in den folgenden Aufsätzen von *Pavčnik* zitiert: 1. An den Grenzen der Reinen Rechtslehre (Fn. 1), S. 166–167, Fn. 67 und 73, 2. Leonid Pitamic (Fn. 1), S. 332–333, Fn. 19, 30 und 33, und 3. Die Frage der rechtlichen Grundnorm (Pitamics Brief an Hans Kelsen), in: ARSP, 96 (2010) 1, S. 96, Fn. 37. Siehe auch *Aleš Novak*: Metamorfoze Kelsnove temeljne norme in Leonid Pitamic (Methamorphoses of Kelsen's Basic Norm and Leonid Pitamic), in: Zbornik znanstvenih razprav, 68 (2008), S. 203–232.
62 *Walter*: Entstehung (Fn. 36), S. 49.
63 *Kelsen*: Reichsgesetz und Landesgesetz nach österreichischer Verfassung, in: Archiv des öffentlichen Rechts, 32 (1914), S. 202–245, 390–438.
64 *Kelsen*: Reichsgesetz und Landesgesetz (Fn. 63), S. 216.
65 *Kelsen*: Reichsgesetz und Landesgesetz (Fn. 63), S. 217. Siehe auch S. 413–414: „Es ist stets eine metajuristische, im Grunde eine politische Frage, welche Norm man derart als letzte oder oberste ansehen will, daß man auf eine weitere juristische Rechtfertigung ihrer Geltung verzichtet. Irgendwo muß jede juristische Betrachtung auf einen solchen letzten Punkt stoßen, auf dem das ganze System der juristischen Konstruktion ruht, gleichsam von außen her gestützt." Vgl. auch S. 435 ff.

das, was ich nur als das Erkenntnisprinzip für konkrete Staatsrechte vorschlug, als *Norm* ins Völkerrecht einbrachte."[66] Kelsens erkenntnistheoretisches Prinzip wurde „zum Inhalt einer *Rechts*norm erhoben" und soll damit als *juristisches* Prinzip fungieren. „Dadurch, daß das *Faktische* zum Inhalt einer Norm wird, erfährt es", so Kelsen, „einen ganz eigenartigen Bedeutungswandel, es wird sozusagen denaturiert, schlägt in sein Gegenteil um, wird selbst zum Normativen."[67] Pitamic wird durch diese Lösung nicht zufriedengestellt, weil dadurch „das *grundlegende* erkenntnistheoretische Problem nur um eine Stufe zurückgeschoben wird und wieder im Völkerrecht auftreten muss."[68]

Er drückt dieselben Bedenken auch angesichts der Grundnorm aus, wie sie von Kelsen in der ersten Auflage des Werkes *Reine Rechtslehre* (1934)[69] formuliert wurde. Pitamic kommentierte es so:

> „Diese Ordnung ist also das ‚empirische Material, das sich der rechtlichen Deutung darbietet'. Dieses Material muss also bereits vorliegen, bevor die Grundnorm, die ja ihren konkreten Inhalt aus diesem Material schöpft, angewendet werden kann. Das Ausleseprinzip für dieses Material ist aber keine Norm, sondern das ‚tatsächliche Verhalten von Menschen', also ein Seinsfaktum, das außerhalb der normativen Sphäre liegt; daher enthält auch die ‚Ordnung', die durch den früher erwähnten Tatbestand erzeugt wird, an und für sich kein rechtliches Sollen; diese Qualität soll ihr ja erst durch die Grundnorm verliehen werden. Nun ist aber eine bloß *hypothetische* Norm nicht imstande, Seinstatsachen als gesollt zu autorisieren oder zu rechtfertigen, da sie ja als ‚hypothetisch' selbst Rechtfertigung bedarf."[70]

Die Entwicklung von Kelsens theoretischen Standpunkten bestätigt die Fundiertheit der Angaben von Pitamic, dass Kelsen (in einem bestimmten Umfang[71]) seine kriti-

---

66   *Pitamic*: Nove smeri (Neue Richtungen, Fn. 38), S. 18. Vgl. auch die Buchbesprechung Kelsen: Das Problem der Souveränität (Fn. 60), S. 641–642.

67   Siehe *Kelsen*: Das Problem der Souveränität (Fn. 31), S. 99 und S. 240–241: „Was dort als ein mehr oder weniger erkenntnistheoretisches Prinzip angegeben wurde: der Grundsatz, jene Ursprungsnorm zu wählen, aus der sich in deduktiver Entfaltung eine Rechtsordnung ergibt, mit der das tatsächliche Verhalten der Menschen, deren Handeln den Inhalt der Rechtsordnung bildet, in relativ größter Übereinstimmung steht, das tritt hier – weil zum Inhalt einer *Rechts*norm erhoben – als *juristisches* Prinzip auf./ Dadurch, daß das *Faktische* zum Inhalt einer Norm wird, erfährt es einen ganz eigenartigen Bedeutungswandel, es wird sozusagen denaturiert, schlägt in sein Gegenteil um, wird selbst zum Normativen."

68   *Pitamic*: Nove smeri (Neue Richtungen, Fn. 38), S. 18. Siehe auch Kritische Bemerkungen, S. 351.

69   *Kelsen*: RR 1, S. 65 ff.

70   *Pitamic*: Čista pravna teorija in naravno pravo (Die Reine Rechtslehre und das Naturrecht), in: Razprave pravnega razreda Akademije znanosti in umetnosti v Ljubljani, 1 (1941), S. 180. Siehe auch die Buchbesprechung Kelsen: Reine Rechtslehre (Fn. 38), S. 414.

71   Darüber sprach *Pitamic* auch in einem umfangreichen Brief, den er am 16.8.1957 *Kelsen* sandte: siehe *Pavčnik*: Die Frage der rechtlichen Grundnorm (Pitamics Brief an Hans Kelsen, Fn. 61). Von Bedeutung ist z. B. diese Stelle: „Ich sage nicht, dass meine Ausführungen den Grund zu Ihrer Einstellung geboten haben, aber vielleicht haben sie Ihre Auffassung bestärkt. Freilich haben Sie mein seinerzeitiges ökonomisches Prinzip nicht als solches aufgenommen, sondern Sie haben die Wirksamkeit *in anderer Weise in Ihren Ideengang eingereiht* (hervorgehoben von M.P.). Wie ich von der *Mach*'schen wurden Sie, wie mir scheint, von der *Kant*'schen Philosophie beeinflusst, zwar nicht vom kategorischen Imperativ Kants, sondern von seiner Kategorienlehre. (…) Diese hypothetische Grundnorm spielt also für die Rechtswelt eine ähnliche Rolle, welche die Kategorien nach Kant überhaupt haben. Wie die Kategorien unserer Sinnenwelt, so ist ihre Grundnorm dem positiven Recht gegenüber transzendental, denn sie ist nicht im positiven Recht gesetzt, sondern vom Rechtsforscher vorausgesetzt, um das positive Recht als gesollt zu erkennen" (S. 91–92).

schen Ausführungen darüber aufgenommen hatte, wie man die Wirksamkeit des Rechts derart begründen könnte, dass sie annehmbar und mit der Reinen Rechtslehre vereinbar wäre. Ungeachtet der Intensität dieses Einflusses auf Kelsen[72] ist es eine Tatsache, dass ihn Kelsen nicht in jenem Punkt vertiefte, wo sich das Normative und das Faktische, das Faktische und das Normative überschneiden[73], sondern ihn in einem solchen Maße aufnahm und kanalisierte, dass die Ausgangspunkte der *Reinen* Rechtslehre unangetastet blieben.[74] In diesem Kontext stellte schon Behrend sehr bestimmt fest, dass durch „die Aufnahme des faktischen Effektivitätsmomentes in die Grundnormformulierung" das rein normlogische System der Reinen Rechtslehre nicht gesprengt wird, da die „Geltung und Wirksamkeit einer Rechtsordnung streng voneinander getrennt bleiben."[75]

5. Zurück zur Natur des Rechts

Im bereits erwähnten Brief, den er 1957 an Kelsen schrieb, kann man schön sehen, dass Pitamic die Bedeutung der Reinen Rechtslehre respektierte, obwohl er schon relativ bald begann, sich inhaltlich von ihr zu lösen. Er führte gern den Gedanken *„Hominum causa omne ius constitutum"* („Alles Recht ist um der Menschen willen geschaffen" – Hermogenianus, D. 1,5,2) an und war überzeugt, dass auch Rechtswissenschaft, die sich mit der Natur des Rechts befasst, ihn auf eine angemessene Weise berücksichtigen muss. In Slowenien ist besonders Pitamics Gedanke bekannt, mit dem er als der erste Dekan der Juristischen Fakultät der Universität in Ljubljana seine Antrittsvorlesung (1920) abschloss:

> „Wir werden das Recht weder schaffen noch austeilen und finden, wenn es
> in uns keine Gerechtigkeit gibt!"[76]

Pitamic hielt allmählich immer stärker an der Erkenntnis fest, dass das Recht nicht nur eine soziale *Technik*[77] ist und sein kann, weil seine Technik *sozial* sein muss, um rechtlich zu sein.[78] Er war nicht nur am Recht als einer ausgefeilten und fein ausgearbeiteten normativen Technik interessiert, sondern sah darin auch eine gesellschaft-

---

72   Vgl. *Pitamic*: Die Frage der rechtlichen Grundnorm (Fn. 37), S. 210. Siehe auch *Jürgen Behrend*: Untersuchungen zur Stufenbaulehre Adolfs Merkels und Hans Kelsens. Berlin 1977, S. 94: „Kelsens Aussage, dass die Grundnorm als hypothetischer Denkakt nur auf solche Rechtsordnungen bezogen wird, die von den Rechtsunterworfenen befolgt werden und damit im wesentlichen wirksam sind, entspricht dem von Pitamic herausgearbeiteten denkökonomischen Prinzip." Siehe auch S. 73 ff. Ebenso *Rudolf Thienel*: Kritischer Rationalismus und Jurisprudenz. Wien 1991, S. 117–118: „Und auch *Kelsen* hat – unter ausdrücklicher Berufung auf *Pitamic* – die Auswahl gerade der effektiven Ordnungen als *Recht*sordnungen damit begründet, dass dies dem *Grundsatz der Erkenntnisökonomie* entspreche, weil man damit jene Ordnungen erfasse, denen die Realität am nächsten komme."

73   Vgl. *Pitamic*: Die Buchbesprechung Kelsen: Das Problem der Souveränität (Fn. 60), S. 642.

74   Vgl. mit *Kelsens* Formulierungen der Grundnorm in seinen späteren Werken; siehe besonders General Theory of Law and State. Cambridge 1945 (im Folgenden abgekürzt als „GTLS"), S. 116–117, Reine Rechtslehre. 2. Aufl. Wien 1960. Nachdruck: Wien 2000 (nachfolgend „RR 2"), S. 209, und Allgemeine Theorie der Normen. Wien 1979 (nachfolgend „ATN"), S. 203 ff. Siehe auch Fn. 15.

75   *Behrend*: Untersuchungen zur Stufenbaulehre Adolfs Merkls und Hans Kelsens (Fn. 72), S. 94. Vgl. dazu auch *Robert Walter*: Wirksamkeit und Geltung, in: Österreichische Zeitschrift für öffentliches Recht, N.F. 11 (1961), S. 536 ff.

76   Pravo in revolucija (Recht und Revolution). Ljubljana 1920, S. 23.

77   Siehe *Kelsen*: RR 1, S. 28.

78   *Pitamic*: Čista pravna teorija in naravno pravo (Die Reine Rechtslehre und das Naturrecht, Fn. 70), S. 188.

lich wirksame Rechtsordnung, der die Qualität des Rechts zukommt, wenn sie das menschliche äußere Verhalten der Menschen überhaupt und insbesondere die Menschenrechte schützt (Menschlichkeit als Maßstab der Rechtlichkeit). Kennzeichnend ist z. B. der Gedanke,

> dass „Menschenrechte und Naturrecht … nichts von deren Wert als eine wichtige *Voraussetzung* (hervorgehoben von M. P.) für die Existenz des positiven Rechts eingebüßt haben. Denn nur jene Rechtsnormen, die wenigstens den wesentlichen und für das materielle und geistige Leben der Menschen notwendigen Erfordernissen entsprechen, werden sich dauernd halten können."[79]

Doch die „Voraussetzungen" des positiven Rechts befinden sich nicht nur außerhalb seiner selbst, zugleich sind sie auch ein *„anderes, heterogenes* (hervorgehoben von M. P.) System", das in das Rechtssystem reicht, ihm die Lebenskraft gibt und ihm als Stütze für die Auslegung der Rechtsnormen dient. Die Abhängigkeit von diesem „anderen, heterogenen System" ist am empfindlichsten und auch am offensichtlichsten bei der Auslegung der Verfassung, die an der Spitze der Pyramide des Staatsrechts steht.[80]

Von hier ist es nur noch ein Schritt zur endgültigen „Abrechnung" mit dem selbstzufriedenen „Rechtsdeduzieren".[81] „Rechtsdeduzieren" nimmt als seinen Ausgangspunkt die Rechtsnorm, die weder aufgestellt noch objektiv gültig, sondern vorausgesetzt ist. Ihre Fiktivität wird zwar gemildert, wenn sie sich auf eine wirksame Rechtsordnung bezieht; andererseits stimmt es wieder, dass auch „bei dieser Konstruktion ungeklärt bleibt, *warum* die menschliche Vernunft gerade eine solche wirksame Ordnung … als Rechtsordnung erkennen soll, warum sie gerade für sie und nicht für irgendwelche andere Ordnungen die Grundnorm entwerfen soll."[82] Wenn Pitamic so denkt, folgt er der Auslegung, dass sich die Quelle der Rechtsnormativität bereits im Gegenstand, den wir erkennen, und nicht nur in unserer Vernunft befindet:

> „So wie die Kausalität nicht nur eine Kategorie unserer Vernunft sein kann, sondern Objektives in den Gegenständen selbst sein muss, ist auch die Quelle der Rechtsnormativität nicht eine vom anschauenden Subjekt vorausgesetzte hypothetische Norm, sondern muss eine objektive, vom Rechtserkenner unabhängige Norm sein."[83]

---

79 *Pitamic*: Država (Der Staat, Fn. 19), S. 203.
80 *Pitamic*: Pravo in revolucija (Recht und Revolution, Fn. 76), S. 14. Siehe auch S. 18: „Das Verhältnis zwischen der Rechtsordnung und der Verwirklichung des Rechts, wenn man es konsequent durchzieht, … ähnelt dem Symbol, das von den alten Indern für Philosophie überhaupt gewählt wurde, nämlich einer Schlange, die in den eigenen Schwanz beißt."
81 *Pitamic*: Ustava in zakon (Verfassung und Gesetz, Fn. 17), S. 9.
82 *Pitamic*: O ideji prava (Von der Rechtsidee), in: Zbornik znanstvenih razprav, 19 (1943), S. 195.
83 *Pitamic*: Čista pravna teorija in naravno pravo (Die Reine Rechtslehre und das Naturrecht, Fn. 70), S. 184. Vgl. auch Die Frage der rechtlichen Grundnorm (Fn. 37), S. 211: „*Kant* selbst sagt an einer Stelle seiner ‚Kritik der reinen Vernunft', daß für uns der Gegenstand der Anschauung nur gegeben ist, wenn er das ‚Gemüth' auf gewisse Weise ‚affiziert'. Das ‚Affizieren' durch den Gegenstand ist doch auch eine Wirkung, deren Ursache im Gegenstand selbst liegt. Es ist also eine Kausalwirkung zugegeben, bevor noch die menschliche Kausalkategorie in Funktion treten kann, da letztere erst durch die *prä*kategoriale Kausalwirkung, nämlich das ebenerwähnte ‚Affizieren' ausgelöst wird." Ebenso schon in: Čista pravna teorija in naravno pravo (Die Reine Rechtslehre und das Naturrecht, Fn. 70), S. 183. Siehe auch die Stelle, auf die sich *Pitamic* bei *Kant* beruft: „… dass er (das ist der Gegenstand, bemerkt von L.P.) das Gemüt auf gewisse Weise affiziere" [*Kant*: Kritik der reinen Ver-

Die Rückkehr zum Gegenstand bedeutet für das Recht, dass seine objektive Gültigkeit von der niedrigsten bis zur höchsten Stufe nur in einer objektiv geltenden Norm begründet ist:

> „Es sollen solche Normen und solche Institutionen geschaffen werden, die im höchsten Maße ein friedliches Zusammenleben und einen friedlichen Verkehr zwischen den Staaten oder den darin gruppierten Menschen ermöglichen, und die tatsächliche Ausführung dieser Normen soll durch wirksame Garantien (auch durch Zwangsmaßnahmen) geschützt werden."[84]

Diese Grundnorm ist objektiv, weil sie ihren Inhalt aus dem Menschen als einem individuellen und gesellschaftlichen Wesen schöpft – aus dem Menschen als dem Endobjekt jedes Rechts.[85] Die Grundnorm ist nicht eine Rechtsnorm, sondern eine sozialethische Norm, die das Recht und seine Natur begründet.[86]

In der Natur des Rechtsobjekts liegt es, dass der Inhalt einer Norm nicht mehr rechtlich ist bzw. dass es sich nicht mehr um eine *Rechts*ordnung handelt, wenn die Norm das Objekt in seinem Wesen verfehlt:

> „Es gibt also Grundsätze, die der Natur des Menschen als eines gesellschaftlichen Wesens entstammen, die das Zusammenleben von Menschen betreffen und die für einzelne Menschen und für deren verschiedene Vereinigungen gelten. Diese Grundsätze sind Grundlagen oder Fundamente des Rechts. Der Inhalt der Grundsätze ist natürlich sehr allgemein und lässt verschiedene Weisen einer detaillierteren Bestimmung (einer Konkretisierung) zu. Doch muss diese Bestimmung innerhalb der Grenzen der Grundsätze bleiben und darf ihnen nicht prinzipiell widersprechen; sonst würde sie den Charakter des Rechts verlieren, obwohl sie sich diesen Namen beilegt."[87]

Diese Grundsätze wurden von Pitamic zunächst als Naturrecht, als „übergeordnete Rechtsquelle", bezeichnet[88], später spricht er von der „Gesamtheit des realen Rechts", die Naturrecht als die übergeordnete Rechtsquelle und in seinem Schutz geschaffenes positives und Gewohnheitsrecht umfasst,[89] bis sie schließlich die Natur des Rechts ausschöpft, die schon an sich Naturrecht einschließt.[90]

---

nunft. 1.–2. Aufl. hrsg. von *Wilhelm Weischedel*. WA III. Suhrkamp: Frankfurt am Main 1990, B. 33, 34].

84　*Pitamic*: Čista pravna teorija in naravno pravo (Die Reine Rechtslehre und das Naturrecht, Fn. 70), S. 185.

85　*Pitamic*: Čista pravna teorija in naravno pravo (Die Reine Rechtslehre und das Naturrecht, Fn. 70), S. 185–186.

86　*Pitamic*: Die Frage der rechtlichen Grundnorm (Fn. 37), S. 216.

87　*Pitamic*: O ideji prava (Von der Rechtsidee, Fn. 82), S. 198. Vgl. Čista pravna teorija in naravno pravo (Die Reine Rechtslehre und das Naturrecht, Fn. 70), S. 189.

88　*Pitamic*: Čista pravna teorija in naravno pravo (Die Reine Rechtslehre und das Naturrecht, Fn. 70), S. 189.

89　*Pitamic*: O ideji prava (Von der Rechtsidee, Fn. 82), S. 200.

90　*Pitamic*: Naturrecht und Natur des Rechtes, in: Österreichische Zeitschrift für öffentliches Recht, N.F. 7 (1956) 2 (Nachdruck in: *Pitamic*: An den Grenzen der RR), S. 206: „Wir haben uns begnügt, von einer, wie wir glauben, gemeinsamen Basis, nämlich dem Rechtsbegriff in seiner möglichsten Allgemeinheit ausgehend, seine beiden Grundelemente ‚Ordnung' und ‚menschliches Verhalten' zu beschreiben und gegenseitig zu wägen. Bevor man nach anderen Quellen sucht, muß man zuerst die nächste Quelle, das ist den Rechtsbegriff selbst, *ganz* ausschöpfen. Tut man dies gründlich, dann

Der Abstieg ins Recht und dessen Natur zeigt ihm, dass seine Hauptelemente Ordnung und menschliches Verhalten sind. Die *Ordnung* ist für Recht so

> „wesentlich, dass es aufhört Recht zu sein, wenn es nicht mehr ‚Ordnung‘ ist. Wenn die Normen einer Rechtsordnung nicht mehr dauernd ausgeführt werden, dienen sie nicht mehr der ‚Ordnung‘ in der Gemeinschaft, für die sie bestimmt sind; dann herrscht dort ‚Unordnung‘, ein rechtsloser Zustand, oder es ist eine andere Rechtsordnung wirksam geworden.“[91]

Doch ist die Ordnung, die von solcher Bedeutung für das Recht ist, keine inhaltlich entleerte Ordnung, sondern eine Ordnung, die das Verhalten und Handeln von *Menschen* regelt. Diese Regelung muss ihrem Gegenstand

> „zum mindesten insoweit Rechnung tragen, dass sie ihm nicht seinen Charakter nimmt. Um Recht zu bleiben, darf also das Recht nur äußeres menschliches Verhalten, nicht aber dessen Gegensatz, ‚unmenschliches Verhalten‘, anordnen oder zulassen, wenn es nicht die Rechtseigenschaft verlieren will.“[92]

Die Ordnung, die vom Recht gesichert wird, verliert die Natur des Rechts, wenn ihre Unmenschlichkeit das Maß übersteigt, wo noch die Existenz des Individuums und menschliches Zusammenleben möglich sind. Das ist der minimale Inhalt des Rechts, der am allgemeinsten bestimmt und für alle annehmbar ist, die Menschlichkeit als Wert annehmen:

> „Jede Ordnung, die durch Regelung des äußeren menschlichen Verhaltens das Leben der Menschen in Gemeinschaft *als Menschen* wirksam, auch mit Zwangsmaßnahmen, sichert, soll als Rechtsordnung gelten.“[93]

Darin besteht auch der gemeinsame Nenner, der ungeachtet der Weltanschauung annehmbar ist, die Grundlage, die man in einzelnen positiven Rechten noch detaillierter ausführen und konkretisieren soll. Es geht um einen gemeinsamen Nenner,

---

zeigt sich, dass das Wesen der fundamentalen, allgemeinen Rechtsgrundsätze, das sogenannte primäre Naturrecht (an dieser Stelle steht Fn. 20, in der er den Standpunkt von Verdross über den Inhalt des primären Naturrechts anführt, Bemerkung von M. P.), schon in der Natur des Rechtes enthalten ist und nicht in einem neben oder über dem positiven Recht schwebenden ‚Naturrecht‘ gesucht zu werden braucht.“

91 *Pitamic*: Naturrecht und Natur des Rechtes (Fn. 90), S. 192.

92 *Pitamic*: Naturrecht und Natur des Rechtes (Fn. 90), S. 194. Vgl. auch *Verdross*: Abendländische Rechtsphilosophie (Fn. 26), S. 296.

93 *Pitamic*: Die Frage der rechtlichen Grundnorm (Fn. 37), S. 216. Vgl. auch *Alfred Verdross*: Statisches und dynamisches Naturrecht. Freiburg 1971, S. 70. Im Kreis um Hans Kelsen war gerade Verdross dieser, der die ausführlichste naturrechtliche Theorie entwarf, deren Grundlagen im klassischen Naturrecht der Antike (insbesondere Aristoteles) liegen. Verdross’ Auffassung von Recht ist stufenartig (S. 92 ff.): zunächst ist hier das primäre Naturrecht – es umfasst anthropologische Konstanten wie Menschenwürde und Allgemeinwohl (S. 101 ff.), es folgt sekundäres Naturrecht – dieses ist dynamisch (veränderlich) und konkretisiert die Regeln des primären Naturrechts im Hinblick auf konkrete gesellschaftliche Verhältnisse (S. 110 ff., S. 116–117), und zuletzt kommt noch positives Recht, das eingehend die Rechte und Pflichten der Rechtssubjekte regelt. Das Naturrecht ist vorgegeben und „verlangt“, dass es zwischen ihm und dem positiven Recht ein angemessenes Zusammenwirken gibt. Die Grundaufgabe des positiven Rechts ist es, die Ziele des Naturrechts in konkreten Gemeinschaften zu verwirklichen (S. 115): *„So erweist sich das Naturrecht als das humane Gewissen des positiven Rechts.* Ohne Naturrecht würde es entweder erstarren oder mangels eines Kompasses sein Ziel verfehlen, in jeder geschichtlichen Lage das Zusammenleben der Menschen in geordneter Freiheit und unter Wahrung der Würde aller Menschen zu regeln“ (S. 114).

der über die Vielförmigkeit der naturrechtlichen Auffassungen hinausgehen und das Naturrecht dorthin zurückbringen soll, wohin es gehört – ins Recht und seine Natur.[94]

6. Methodologische Klarheit anstatt gegenständlicher Reinheit des Rechts

6.1. Freiheit der wissenschaftlichen Forschung und beliebiger Inhalt des Rechts

Die Wahl der Methode und die Art der Untersuchung des Gegenstands sind auch Sache der Freiheit der wissenschaftlichen Forschung. Es liegt in der Natur der Forschungsfreiheit, dass sie neue Gesichtspunkte und Nuancen sucht und eröffnet, die noch nicht eröffnet worden sind und die zur Erkenntnis des Rechts beitragen sollen. Kelsens reines normatives Verständnis des Rechts (reine Normativitätsthese) ist ein schöpferischer Fall eines derartigen wissenschaftlichen Suchens.[95] Das Suchen ist so lange schöpferisch, bis es in Einklang mit dem Recht und seiner Natur steht.

Kelsens Erkenntnis des Rechts ist in einem solchen Maß bereinigt, dass vom Recht als sozialer Wirklichkeit nur noch die formelle Struktur geblieben ist. Das Recht ist ein Bedeutungsschema von Normen, die als ein Netz in Pyramidenform die Menschen (die Gesellschaft) umschließen und ihnen zeigen, wo ihre Handlungsmöglichkeiten liegen. Kelsens Ansatz steht und fällt mit einer entsprechenden Stützung auf Tatsachen (Gesellschaftsverhältnissen) und Werte, die der Maßstab für das inhaltliche Gestalten und Verstehen von Rechtsnormen sind.

Im Verhältnis zu Tatsachen sucht Kelsen Zuflucht bei der Grundnorm, die als Annahme ein *grosso modo* wirksames Normensystem begründet. Die Begründung bezieht sich darauf, dass man Verfassungsnormen und ihnen untergeordnete Rechtsnormen als ein System von geltenden verbindlichen Normen akzeptiert (siehe Abschnitt 1). Dabei stellt sich die Frage, ob die folgende Feststellung tatsächlich stimmt: „Jeder beliebige Inhalt kann Recht sein, es gibt kein menschliches Verhalten, das als solches, kraft seines Gehalts, ausgeschlossen wäre, zum Inhalt einer Rechtsnorm zu werden."[96]

94　Über all das spricht *Pitamic* auch in dem bereits erwähnten Brief, den er am 16. 8. 1957 *Kelsen* schickte (siehe Fn. 61). In dem Brief erklärt er die Unterschiede zwischen *Kelsens* und seiner eigenen Sicht der Grundnorm; die Standpunkte, die er anführt, sind nicht neu, sondern es handelt sich um eine Zusammenfassung dessen, was er in slowenischen und deutschen Abhandlungen bereits gesagt hat. Diese Standpunkte sind an entsprechenden Stellen auch in diesem Beitrag angeführt. Die ganz persönliche Bemerkung, mit der *Pitamic* den Brief abschließt, sagt viel über seine Persönlichkeit aus: „Die Beschäftigung mit Ihrer Rechtsphilosophie und die vielfachen Diskussionen mit Ihnen haben in meinem Leben eine die wissenschaftliche Erkenntnis überragende Bedeutung gehabt. Ihr relativistischer Ideengang scheint mir die Kette der Folgerungen auch im Gebiete des Sollens ohne genügenden Grund mit einer hypothetischen Norm abzubrechen. Ohne diesen Bruch ginge die Stufenleiter weiter in infinitum, und dieser *regressus in infinitum* lässt sich nur durch ein *regressus* ad Infinitum vermeiden. Dieser Gedanke und alles, was an ihm hängt, war wohl einer der Faktoren – nicht der einzige – der die Wiederkehr zu meiner religiösen Einstellung förderte. Wenngleich dies von Ihnen nicht beabsichtigt war, so bin ich Ihnen doch für diese aberratio ictus sehr dankbar. Dieser Dank gilt auch für alles, wofür ich Ihnen in meinem wissenschaftlichen und überhaupt geistigen Leben schuldig bin."

95　Siehe die Erörterung von *Paulson*: Der Normativismus Hans Kelsens (Fn. 7), S. 529–536. Siehe insbesondere S. 534 ff.

96　*Kelsen*: RR 1, S. 63. Siehe auch RR 2, S. 201.

Der Einwand, dass Kelsen mit jedem Inhalt einverstanden ist, kehrt als Bumerang zurück.[97] Die richtige Frage ist nicht, ob der Gehalt eines *grosso modo* wirksamen Rechtssystems für die Reine Rechtslehre einen beliebigen Inhalt haben kann. Die richtige Frage ist, ob ein System von Normen mit jedem beliebigen Inhalt tatsächlich Recht sein kann. Ein System von Normen, die ausschließlich auf Gewalt beruhen und Menschenrechte mit den Füßen treten würden, kann nicht Recht sein. Die Bedingung, damit positives Recht überhaupt funktionieren kann, ist, dass es eine entsprechende inhaltliche Legitimität hat. In diese Richtung bewegt sich etwa Hart, der zugibt, dass positives Recht wenigstens einen minimalen naturrechtlichen Inhalt enthalten muss.[98]

6.2. Schöpferische Kraft des normativen Purismus

Pitamics These war es, dass die Methode, mit der man Recht erforscht, vom Gegenstand der Forschung nicht unabhängig ist. Der Gegenstand (d. h. die Natur dieses Gegenstands, also die Natur des Rechts) beeinflusst die Wahl der Methode(n), mit denen die Rechtswissenschaft das Recht erkennt. In der Abhandlung *O ideji prava* (*Von der Rechtsidee*) steht auch die folgende charakteristische Stelle:

> „Wie ein Modell großenteils gemäß dem Gegenstand, für den es als Modell bestimmt ist, gestaltet werden soll, muss auch das Recht als Form wenigstens größtenteils gemäß seinem Gegenstand gestaltet werden. Wenn der Modell so ist, dass es seinen Gegenstand merklich verdirbt, anstatt ihm angepasst zu sein, dann ist es nicht das richtige Modell für diesen Gegenstand."[99]

Pitamics Sprache ist symbolisch. Das Modell ist offensichtlich Kelsens Methode, die die gegenständliche Reinheit des Rechts schafft. Pitamics Einwand ist es, dass die methodologische Reinheit die inhaltliche Struktur des Rechts, die sich dem Forscher zur Untersuchung anbietet, übersieht. Der Einwand darf nicht bedeuten, dass ein partielles Erkennen des Rechts keine schöpferische Kraft hat. Die Stärke eines partiellen Ansatzes kann darin liegen, dass er klarer die Blickwinkel sieht, die etwa vom integrativen oder integralen (synthetischen) Verständnis des Rechts mit gleicher Kraft belichtet werden. Doch hier besteht andererseits auch die große Gefahr, dass der partielle Ansatz einen bestimmten Aspekt des Rechts übertrieben betont oder diesen Aspekt sogar so erkennt, dass er ihn im Vergleich mit anderen Aspekten verzerrt.

---

97   Siehe *Lothar Philipps*: Von Puppen aus Russland und einer Rechtslehre aus Wien. Der Rekursionsgedanke im Recht, in: Slovenian Law Review, 4 (2007) 1–2, S. 195–196: „Der Ausdruck ‚Stoppbedingung', den man anstelle von ‚Grundbedingung' verwenden kann, erinnert mich an etwas, das fast ein halbes Jahrhundert her ist. Ein Freund von mir und ich – wir waren Assistenten von Werner Maihofer – sind damals von Saarbrücken nach Mainz gefahren, um einen Vortrag von Hans Kelsen zu hören. An die Einzelheiten des Vortrags erinnere ich mich nicht mehr, wohl aber an eine Szene, die sich daran anschloss. Ein Student fragte Kelsen in deutlich kritischer Weise, ob der von ihm vertretene Positivismus wieder zu einer Diktatur wie der vergangenen führen könne. Kelsen antwortete: 'Ob eine solche Diktatur wieder eintritt, das hängt von keiner Rechtstheorie ab, sei sie nun positivistisch oder nicht. Das hängt nur davon ab, ob Menschen, jetzt die Menschen Ihrer Generation, rechtzeitig ‚Halt!' sagen.'"

98   *H.L.A. Hart*: The Concept of Law. 2. Aufl. Oxford 1994, S. 193 ff.

99   *Pitamic*: O ideji prava (Von der Rechtsidee, Fn. 82), S. 198.

Kelsens normativer Purismus wirkt schöpferisch überall dort, wo er ein Problemfeld, das gelöst werden soll, enthüllt. Kelsen eröffnet das Problem, es liegt jedoch nicht in der Kraft seiner Theorie, sich mit ihm inhaltlich zu befassen. Kelsens derartige *Enthüllungen* sind ausgeprägt, z. B. beim Vergleichen des Naturgesetzes mit dem Rechtsgesetz, beim Rechtssubjekt, bei Rechtslücken, bei der Auslegung der Rechtsakte (zusammen mit dem Stufenbau der Rechtsordnung), bei der Natur des Völkerrechts und noch an anderer Stelle.

Also der Reihe nach. Zunächst ist hier das *Rechtsgesetz*, das auf dem Grundsatz der Zurechnung beruht. Im Recht handelt es sich um keine Ursache-Folge-Verknüpfungen, sondern um seinsollende Verknüpfungen, dass bestimmte Tatbestände bestimmte Folgen haben. Die seinsollende Struktur der Rechtsnorm, die seinsollende Verknüpfung der Rechtsnormen und die seinsollende Hierarchie des Stufenbaus der Rechtsordnung sind typische normative Verknüpfungen, die sich im Mittelpunkt von Kelsens Aufmerksamkeit befinden. Das Seinsollen spricht auch über die menschlichen Schöpfungsfähigkeiten und über die Verantwortung des Menschen für sein Tun. Doch dieser Aspekt übersteigt die Reichweite von Kelsens Rechtslehre. Kelsen befasst sich mit dem Seinsollen als der Bedeutung des Willensaktes, doch er gibt sich mit den Willensakten selbst, die eine Frucht der schöpferischen Kraft des Menschen sind, nicht ab.

Weiter: Das *Rechtssubjekt* ist nicht mit dem natürlichen Subjekt identisch, es handelt sich immer um ein rechtlich geschaffenes Subjekt, sei es eine physische Person, der man eine Rechtssubjektivität zuschreibt, oder eine juristische Person, die nicht automatisch ein Rechtssubjekt ist. Hinter der juristischen Person stehen immer Individuen, deren Verhalten und Handeln der juristischen Person zugeschrieben werden. Eine noch so fürchterliche Gräueltat, die von einem Aggressorstaat begangen wird, ist eine Gräueltat von Menschen, die hinter dem Rechtsschleier des Staates stehen.[100]

Weiter: Eine *Rechtslücke* ist keine Lücke im Gesetz, sondern „eine typisch ideologische Formel"; wenn man es gut überdenkt, geht es nicht darum, dass im Falle einer sogenannten Lücke die Anwendung des gültigen Gesetzes unmöglich ist, sondern darum, dass für den Verteidiger der Lücke die Anwendung des Gesetzes „lediglich" ideologisch ungeeignet ist.[101] Kelsen ist da unerbittlich: „Jeder Rechtsstreit besteht darin, dass eine Partei gegen eine andere einen Anspruch erhebt; und die stattgebende oder abweisende Entscheidung hängt davon ab, ob das Gesetz, das heißt eine geltende, auf den konkreten Fall anzuwendende Norm die behauptete Rechtspflicht statuiert oder nicht."[102] Man befindet sich auf einem Gebiet, das gegenüber menschlicher Freiheit sehr empfindlich ist; man muss sich bewusst sein, die sogenannte Rechtslücke sei „somit nichts anderes als die Differenz zwischen dem positiven Recht und einer für besser, gerechter, richtiger gehaltenen Ordnung."[103]

Weiter: Die *Interpretation (Auslegung) des Gesetzes* ist ebenso wenig eine Tätigkeit, die sagen soll, welche Bedeutung eines Gesetzes seine richtige Bedeutung ist. Die Aufgabe der Wissenschaft ist es, alle möglichen Bedeutungen der Rechtsnormen, die in Rechtsakten enthalten sind, zu definieren; die Entscheidung des Anwenders ist

---

100　Siehe *Pitamic*: Kritični pogledi na juridično osebo (Kritische Betrachtungen über die juristische Person), in: Zbornik znanstevih razprav, 4 (1925), S. 241 f.
101　*Kelsen*: RR 1, S. 106. Siehe auch GTLS, S. 146 ff., und RR 2, S. 251 ff.
102　*Kelsen*: RR 1, S. 100.
103　*Kelsen*: RR 1, S.101–102. Siehe auch GTLS, S. 146 ff., und RR 2, S. 251 ff.

gesetzlich (rechtlich), wenn sie nur innerhalb des Bedeutungsrahmens der Norm bleibt, dem sie jede mögliche Bedeutung geben kann; welche Bedeutung der Rechtsnorm richtig ist, ist keine wissenschaftliche (rechtstheoretische), sondern ausschließlich eine rechtspolitische Frage, die nicht mehr Gegenstand der Reinen Rechtslehre ist. Wissenschaftlich kann man keine Methode entwickeln, „die ermöglicht, den festgestellten Rahmen richtig auszufüllen."[104]

Kelsen betont ausdrücklich, dass die Norm „nur einen Rahmen, innerhalb dessen mehrere Möglichkeiten der Vollziehung gegeben sind,"[105] darstellt. Wenn man diese Erkenntnisse noch mit der Theorie des Stufenbaus der Rechtsordnung verbindet, kann man gut sehen, dass die Auslegung und Anwendung von Rechtsakten (z. B. Gesetzen) sehr schöpferische Tätigkeiten sind; die Wissenschaft kann nicht die Frage beantworten, welche Richtung man einschlagen soll, sie kann jedoch die unkritische Ideologie entlarven, dass es sich lediglich um eine mechanische Gesetzesanwendung handelt.

Und nicht zuletzt: zu wohl begründeten und tiefdringenden Diskussionen gehört auch das genaue Untersuchen *des Staates und des Völkerrechts*. Kelsen befürwortet die Einheit des rechtlichen Weltbildes[106] und relativiert den Begriff des Staates; die Reine Rechtslehre schafft die erkenntnismäßige Einheit allen Rechts, „eine nicht unwesentliche Voraussetzung für die organisatorische Einheit einer zentralisierten Weltrechtsordnung".[107] Der Staat als Rechtsordnung, die eine bestimmte Stufe der Zentralisierung erreicht hat, beruht auf der Regelung des Völkerrechts. „Wenn die Etablierung einer normsetzenden Gewalt, deren Ordnung für einen bestimmten Bereich von dauernder Wirksamkeit ist, positivrechtlich die Entstehung einer rechtsetzenden Autorität darstellt, so darum", hebt Kelsen hervor, „weil ihr diese Qualität vom Völkerrecht verliehen (*zugerechnet* – zugefügt von M. P.) wird oder, was dasselbe bedeutet, weil dieses sie zur Rechtsetzung ermächtigt."[108] Wenn man metaphorisch spricht, ist der Staat ein Organ des Völkerrechts; der Staat ist der Ausdruck „für die einzelstaatliche Rechtsordnung, die mit der Völkerrechtsordnung und, durch diese vermittelt, mit allen anderen einzelstaatlichen Rechtsordnungen in jenem Delegationszusammenhang steht, dessen Struktur im Vorhergehenden geschildert wurde."[109] Kelsen spricht – um kein Missverständnis heraufzubeschwören – über die erkenntnismäßige und nicht über die organisatorische Einheit des Weltrechtssystems. Er schafft das Dogma der Staatssouveränität, das gegen das Völkerrecht gerichtet ist, ab. Die Reine Rechtslehre legt den Versuch offen, mit Hilfe von Souveränität die Kraft der Völkerrechtsordnung zu schwächen; das Argument der Souveränität ist kein unwiderlegbares logisches Argument, sondern ein politisches Argument, das jeden Augenblick „mit einem gleichartigen Gegenargument opponiert werden" kann.[110]

Die Produktivität, von der ich spreche, ist nur in jenem Umfang möglich, in dem das Recht als Form mit Recht als Inhalt übereinstimmt. Ein Beispiel der Divergenz zwischen Form und Inhalt ist etwa Kelsens Auffassung der Rechtsnorm. Der

104   *Kelsen*: RR 1, S. 95.
105   *Kelsen*: RR 1, S. 94 ff. Siehe auch RR 2, S. 347 ff.
106   Prim. *Alfred Verdross*: Die Einheit des rechtlichen Weltbildes auf Grundlage der Völkerrechtsverfassung. Tübingen 1923.
107   *Kelsen*: RR 1, S. 154.
108   *Kelsen*: RR 1, S. 148.
109   *Kelsen*: RR 1, S. 152–153.
110   *Kelsen*: RR 1, S. 154. Siehe auch GTLS, S. 388, und RR 2, S. 343–345.

gesellschaftlich-teleologische Sinn der Rechtsnormen ist es, das äußere Verhalten und Handeln der Rechtssubjekte zu festigen und zu lenken. Das primäre Ziel ist die Verwirklichung der Erlaubnisse, Gebote und Verbote, die Sanktion als das sekundäre Ziel tritt erst auf, wenn es zu einer Rechtsverletzung kommt. „Die Wirkungsweisen des Gesetzes," so bereits Modestinus, „sind diese: gebieten, verbieten, erlauben und strafen" (*Legis virtus haec est: imperare, vetare, permittere, punire*" – Modestinus, D. 1,3,7). Kelsen ist von dieser einfachen Wahrheit abgekommen. In der *Reinen Rechtslehre* behandelte er als primäre Rechtsnormen Sanktionsnormen, die für Strafrecht und überhaupt für Normen, die sich unmittelbar auf Rechtsverletzungen beziehen, besonders charakteristisch sind. Verhaltensnormen, die aussagen, was uns erlaubt, geboten und verboten ist, waren erst sekundäre Rechtsnormen. Diese Normen waren für Kelsen solche Normen, die aussagen, wie die Menschen sich verhalten sollen, damit „sie den angedrohten Zwangsakt vermeiden."[111] Im posthum erschienen Werk *Allgemeine Theorie der Normen* ergänzte er seine Ansicht und kehrte dorthin zurück, wo er hätte anfangen sollen. Die Hauptaufgaben der Rechtsnormen sind die Möglichkeiten, dass die Normen gebieten und verbieten, erlauben, ermächtigen – d. h. ermächtigen, dass die Normen gesetzt oder angewendet werden – sowie bereits gültige Normen aufheben (derogieren) und an ihrer Stelle neue einführen.[112] Diese Handlungsmöglichkeiten sind schließlich wieder der Inhalt der primären Normen, während jene Normen, die Sanktionen vorschreiben, als sekundäre Normen bezeichnet sind.[113]

6.3. Transformationen ins Recht und innerhalb des Rechts

Die Reine Rechtslehre hat mehrere Forschungsgebiete produktiv beeinflusst.[114] Eine der noch immer offenen Möglichkeiten könnte man wenigstens teilweise auch mit Pitamic und seinem methodologischen Beitrag zur Reinen Rechtslehre verbinden. Der Beitrag bestünde darin, Kelsens Verständnis des normativen Rechtsaufbaus und andere methodologische Ansätze, die diesen Aufbau inhaltlich auffüllen, in Verbindung zu bringen. Die Bedingung dazu wäre, dass es sich um einen reinen methodologischen Ansatz handelt, in dem alle der Natur des Rechts entsprechenden Methoden angewandt werden. Um einen reinen Ansatz handelt es sich, solange die Methoden scharf voneinander getrennt sind. In diesem Fall würden sich etwa die soziologische und die axiologische Methode (diese zwei Methoden finden in der Reinen Rechtslehre keine erkenntnistheoretische Resonanz) einerseits und die normative Methode andererseits „gegenseitig stützen" und es gäbe keine Gefahr, dass einzelne Dimensionen des Rechts überdeckt und „konfundiert" würden. Pitamics Gleichnis vom Berg (siehe Abschnitt 4.1.) ist ein gutes Beispiel des Rechtsverständnisses, das durch eine allseitige methodologische Ausleuchtung nur gewinnen würde.

111   *Kelsen:* RR 1, S. 30. Siehe auch die Kritik, die an Kelsen von *Peter Koller* gerichtet wird: Meilensteine des Rechtspositivismus im 20. Jahrhundert, in: Ota Weinberger / Werner Krawietz (Gesamtredaktion): Reine Rechtslehre im Spiegel ihrer Fortsetzer und Kritiker. Wien 1988, S. 136–147.

112   *Kelsen:* ATN, S. 76 ff.

113   *Kelsen:* ATN, S. 115.

114   Siehe z.B. *Robert Walter:* Vorrede zum zweiten Neudruck, in: *Kelsen:* RR 1, S. 5*–8*. Vgl. auch *Weinberger/Krawietz* (Gesamtredaktion): Reine Rechtslehre (Fn. 111); *Agostino Carrino / Günther Winkler* (Hrsg.): Rechtserfahrung und Reine Rechtslehre. Wien, New York 1995; *Paulson/Litschewski Paulson* (Hrsg.): Normativity and Norms (Fn. 7); *Horst Dreier:* Rezeption und Rolle der Reinen Rechtslehre. Wien 2001, und *Walter/Ogris/Olechowski* (Hrsg.): Hans Kelsen: Leben – Werk – Wirksamkeit (Fn. 7).

Es geht nicht nur darum, wie man den Berg besteigen und von ihm hinuntersteigen kann. Die Schlüsselfrage bezieht sich vor allem darauf, wie man die Wertbewegung zwischen dem Normativen und dem Faktischen, zwischen dem Faktischen und dem Normativen, also die Bewegung, die ein eigenartiges Herzstück und die treibende Kraft des Rechts ist, verstehen und begründen kann.[115] Pitamics Theorie nimmt besonders gut die Grenzen[116] (Seinstatsachen und Werte) wahr, auf denen der normative Aufbau beruht und innerhalb derer diese Bewegung stattfindet. Wenn man das praktisch betrachtet, sind das, so Pitamic, auch „die maßgebendsten Momente".[117] Alle diese „Momente" hat Kelsen vernachlässigt, weil seine Theorie alle Übergänge zwischen verschiedenen Systemen (z. B. zwischen Recht und Moral) ablehnt. Das wäre ein prinzipieller Rücktritt von der Reinheit des Rechts.[118]

6.4. Kelsen, Pitamic und Radbruch

Die Frage der normativen Begründung ist der rote Faden, durch den Kelsen und Pitamic verbunden waren, obwohl ihre Sichtweisen unterschiedlich waren. Um es kurz zu wiederholen, Kelsen vertrat den methodologisch reinen Ansatz, der einen reinen Gegenstand der Forschung schafft. Die methodologische Reinheit ist sogar so groß, dass der Gegenstand der Wissenschaft die Methode nicht mitbestimmt. Es gilt gerade das Umgekehrte: der Gegenstand, den die Wissenschaft erforscht, hängt von der Methode und ihrer Erkenntnisrichtung ab (siehe Abschnitte 4.1. und 4.2.). Pitamic ging schon ganz am Anfang einen anderen Weg: er war überzeugt, dass man das Recht nicht durch eine einzige Methode, der ein reiner Gegenstand der Forschung entspricht, verstehen und erkennen kann; er behauptete, es wäre nötig, neben der normativen Methode auch andere Methoden (vor allem die soziologische und die axiologische) anzuwenden, die man jedoch nicht miteinander konfundieren darf. Methodologischen Synkretismus kann man vermeiden, wenn man unter verschiedenen Aspekten des Rechts klar unterscheidet und wenn man zulässt, dass die Methoden einander stützen.

Diese Erkenntnisse führten bei Pitamic schrittweise dazu, dass er über die Natur des Rechts die positivrechtliche und die naturrechtliche Ansicht vereinte. Um es kurz zu wiederholen, für Pitamic sind die wesentlichen Elemente des Rechts Ordnung und menschliches Verhalten. Beide Elemente bedürfen einander. Die Ordnung ist mit Rechtsnormen, die das äußere menschliche Verhalten regeln, verbunden. Die Ordnung ist für das Recht so wesentlich, dass es sich nicht mehr um Recht handelt,

---

115 In diese Richtung geht auf seine eigene Weise *Alexander Peczenik*, der scharf zwischen Sprüngen ins Recht, Sprüngen innerhalb des Rechts und Argumenten, die diese Transformationen begründen, unterscheidet. Siehe z.B. Grundlagen der juristischen Argumentation. Wien/New York 1983, S. 5 ff., S. 55 ff.; On Law and Reason. Dordrecht u.a. 1989, S. 115 ff., 130–131, 295 ff., und Scientia Juris. Dordrecht 2005, S. 90 ff., S. 174 ff. Siehe auch *Aulis Aarnio / Robert Alexy / Alexander Peczenik*: Grundlagen der juristischen Argumentation, in: Metatheorie juristischer Argumentation (Schriften zur Rechtstheorie, Heft 108). Berlin 1983, S. 13 ff., S. 18 ff., S. 27 ff. und S. 36 ff. Vgl. *Pavčnik*: Juristisches Verstehen und Entscheiden. Wien, New York 1993, S. 77 ff., und *Stephan Kirste*: Recht als Transformation, in: Winfried Brugger / Ulfrid Neumann / Stephan Kirste (Hrsg.): Rechtsphilosophie im 21. Jahrhundert. Frankfurt/Main 2008, S. 134 ff.
116 Vgl. *Pavčnik*: An den Grenzen der Reinen Rechtslehre (Fn. 1), S. 170–173.
117 *Pitamic*: Kritische Bemerkungen, S. 548. Vgl. auch *Pitamic*: Naturrecht und Natur des Rechtes (Fn. 90), S. 206–207.
118 Siehe Fn. 16.

wenn die Normen eines Rechts nicht wenigstens *grosso modo* wirksam sind.[119] Ein Element des Rechts ist jedoch nicht irgendwelche Ordnung; die Bedingung ist eine Ordnung, die „nur äußeres menschliches Verhalten, nicht aber dessen Gegensatz, ‚unmenschliches Verhalten‘, anordnet oder zulässt, „wenn es nicht die Rechtseigenschaft verlieren will."[120]

Die Rechtsnorm „hört jedoch dann auf, Recht zu sein, wenn ihr Inhalt die Möglichkeit der Existenz und des Zusammenlebens der ihr unterworfenen Menschen ernstlich in Frage stellt."[121] Dafür genügt nicht irgendwelche Unmenschlichkeit des Inhalts der Rechtsnormen (z. B. hohe Steuern, die ungerecht sind), sondern es muss sich um „eine auffallende, offenkundige, schwere Unmenschlichkeit"[122] handeln (etwa massenhaftes Töten hilfloser Menschen). Es geht um die „grobe Störung" (etwa um Ausrottung von Menschen einer anderen Rasse), die so intensiv ins Recht eingreift, dass seine Natur negiert wird.[123]

Ulfrid Neumann stellt überzeugend fest, dass sich „Pitamic nicht auf ethische Maßstäbe jenseits des Rechts, sondern auf Elemente des Rechtsbegriffs selbst beruft."[124] Diese Art der Begründung stimmt im bestimmten Maße mit Radbruch und seiner Formel überein. Die Ähnlichkeiten zwischen Radbruch und Pitamic bestehen vorwiegend darin, dass es sich bei beiden um Begründung des Rechtsbegriffs handelt und dass beide auf eine ähnliche Weise die Grenze suchen, die ein Konflikt zwischen einzelnen Elementen des Rechts nicht überschreiten darf, wenn es sich noch um ein rechtliches Verhalten handeln soll. Der Rubikon ist überschritten, wenn die Ordnung „krass unmenschlich" ist. In diesem Fall geht es um eine offensichtliche Parallele mit Radbruchs „Unerträglichkeitsformel".[125]

Aus Pitamics Werken geht nicht hervor, dass er sich auf Radbruch gestützt hätte. Im bereits erwähnten Buch *An den Grenzen der Reinen Rechtslehre* erscheint Radbruchs Name nur einmal, und zwar in Verbindung mit heteronomen Verpflichtungen.[126] In Pitamics zentralem Buch *Država (Der Staat)* wird Radbruch nicht zitiert. Die Mehrzahl der Gründe ist darin zu suchen, dass Radbruch und Pitamic eine ähnliche Entwicklung erlebten, die schließlich zu einem ähnlichen Ergebnis führte. Radbruch als Neukantianer nahm den werttheoretischen Relativismus an und vertrat den Standpunkt, dass man Rechtswerte nicht „erkennen", sondern nur „bekennen" kann.[127] Der Umstand, dass man nicht erkennen kann, was der höchste inhaltliche Rechtswert ist, verlangt, dass auf Grund der Rechtssicherheit dieser Inhalt von der

119　*Pitamic*: Naturrecht und Natur des Rechtes (Fn. 90), S. 192–193.

120　*Pitamic*: Naturrecht und Natur des Rechtes (Fn. 90), S. 194.

121　*Pitamic*: Naturrecht und Natur des Rechtes (Fn. 90), S. 199.

122　*Pitamic*: Die Frage der rechtlichen Grundnorm (Fn. 37), S. 214.

123　*Pitamic*. Naturrecht und Natur des Rechtes (Fn. 90), S. 199. Siehe auch Die Frage der rechtlichen Grundnorm (Fn. 37), S. 215: „Es kann ja auch nach positivem Recht sogar eine rechtskräftige Entscheidung aus gewissen schwerwiegenden Gründen wegen krasser Verletzungen des positiven Rechtes angefochten und außer Kraft gesetzt werden."

124　*Ulfrid Neumann*: Leonid Pitamic, An den Grenzen der Reinen Rechtslehre. Herausgeber und Einführungsstudie: Marijan Pavčnik. Ljubljana 2009 (Erstausgabe 2005), in: ARSP, 97 (2011) 2, S. 281.

125　*Neumann*: Leonid Pitamic, An den Grenzen der Reinen Rechtslehre (Fn. 124), S. 281.

126　*Pitamic*: Eine „Juristische Grundlehre" (Fn. 5), S. 750.

127　*Gustav Radbruch*: Grundzüge der Rechtsphilosophie. Leipzig 1914. Zitiert nach dem Nachdruck in GRGA II. Heidelberg 1993, S. 22 und 162. Siehe auch *ders.*: Rechtsphilosophie, 3. Aufl., hrsg. von Erik Wolf und Hans-Peter Schneider, Stuttgart 1973, S. 96 (Nachdruck in GRGA II. Heidelberg 1993 und Rechtsphilosophie. Studienausgabe, hrsg. von Ralf Dreier und Stanley L. Paulson, Heidelberg 1999). Siehe auch *ders.*: Der Relativismus in der Rechtsphilosophie (1934), in: GRGA III, Heidelberg 1990, S. 17–22.

Staatsgewalt bestimmt wird.[128] Die Erfahrungen mit dem Nationalsozialismus verlangten, dass Radbruch seine Standpunkte vervollständigte und sie bezüglich des Verhältnisses der Rechtswerte nach dem Zweiten Weltkrieg auch etwas ergänzte. Die endgültige Ableitung ist es, dass man dann, wenn der Gegensatz zwischen dem positiven Gesetz und der Gerechtigkeit ein „unerträgliches Maß" erreicht, „das Gesetz als ‚unrichtiges Recht' der Gerechtigkeit zu weichen hat" (die Unerträglichkeitsformel). Neben dieser Formel gibt es noch die Verleugnungsformel; die ist dann gegeben, wenn das Gesetz bewusst die Gleichheit verleugnet. In diesem Fall ist das Gesetz „nicht nur ‚unrichtiges Recht', vielmehr entbehrt es überhaupt der Rechtsnatur."[129]

Pitamics Weg war ähnlich. In die Theorie und Philosophie des Rechts trat er als Kelsens Schüler ein und der normative Purismus begeisterte ihn als Form. Durch die scharfe Trennung zwischen Sein und Sollen wurde er nicht gänzlich geprägt, weil er das Recht auch soziologisch und axiologisch betrachtete. Die ganze Zeit störte ihn die Selbstgenügsamkeit des Rechts als eines seinsollenden Systems. Der Behauptung, dass Sollen nur aus Sollen entspringen kann, setzte er unter Berufung auf Aristoteles die These entgegen, dass der Mensch bereits gemäß seiner Natur in normative Beziehungen eingegliedert ist.[130] Die Erfahrungen mit den Barbareien des 20. Jahrhunderts übten sicher ihren Einfluss auf Pitamic aus, der so wie Radbruch das Recht auch wertmäßig verstand. Radbruch argumentierte mit Gerechtigkeit, zu der das Recht strebt, Pitamic sucht die Lösung im Begriff des Rechts, das auch menschlich sein muss. Die Radbruchsche Formel ist eingehender als Pitamics Rechtsbegriff aufgegliedert. Ungeachtet dessen kann man auch Pitamic so verstehen, dass bewusstes Verleugnen der Gleichheit unmenschlich ist, und dass Ungleichheit, die unerträglich unmenschlich ist, der Rechtsnatur entbehrt.

Ein eingehenderer Vergleich zwischen Radbruch und Pitamic ist nicht der Gegenstand dieses Beitrags. Ein Vergleich war trotzdem nötig, weil sich dadurch auch eine entsprechende Parallele mit Kelsens Normativitätsthese ziehen lässt. Kelsen hielt bis zu Ende an dieser These fest und war deshalb, vom Standpunkt seiner Theorie gesehen, indifferent zum Inhalt des positiven Rechts. Dieser war einfach kein Gegenstand seiner formell-seinsollenden Analyse des Rechts. Radbruch und Pitamic argumentierten auch inhaltlich und gliederten, jeder auf seine Weise, den inhaltlichen Maßstab in den Rechtsbegriff ein. Das ermöglichte ihnen, dass ihre Betrachtungsweisen des Rechts jenseits von Naturrecht und Rechtspositivismus einzuordnen sind. Noch genauer: ihre Betrachtungsweise von Recht ist, wenn ich mich auf Ro-

---

128 *Radbruch:* Rechtsphilosophie (1973, Fn. 127), S. 164–165.

129 *Radbruch:* Gesetzliches Unrecht und übergesetzliches Recht, in: Süddeutsche Juristenzeitung, 1 (1946), S. 105–108. Zitiert nach dem Nachdruck in Rechtsphilosophie (1973, Fn. 127), S. 345–346. Siehe auch *Radbruch:* Gesetzliches Unrecht und übergesetzliches Recht (1946). Mit einer Einführung von *Winfried Hassemer.* Baden-Baden 2002. – Über Radbruch und die Radbruchsche Formel siehe z.B. *Arthur Kaufmann:* Gustav Radbruch – Leben und Werk, in: GRGA I, Heidelberg 1987, S. 9–88; *Robert Alexy:* Begriff und Geltung des Rechts. München 1992, S. 52 ff.; *Frank Saliger:* Radbruchsche Formel und Rechtsstaat. Heidelberg 1995; *Gerhard Sprenger:* 50 Jahre Radbruchsche Formel oder: Von der Sprachnot der Juristen, in: Neue Justiz, 1 (1997), S. 3–7, und *Ralf Dreier, Stanley L. Paulson:* Einführung in die Rechtsphilosophie Radbruchs, in: Radbruch: Rechtsphilosophie. Studienausgabe (Fn. 127). Siehe auch *Ralf Dreier:* Gustav Radbruch, Hans Kelsen, Carl Schmitt, in: Staat und Recht. Festschrift für Günther Winkler, hrsg. von H. Haller et al., Wien/New York 1997, S. 193–215.

130 Siehe *Pitamic:* Die Frage der rechtlichen Grundnorm (Fn. 37), S. 212. Siehe auch *Pavčnik:* Die Frage der rechtlichen Grundnorm (Pitamics Brief an Hans Kelsen, Fn. 61), S. 93–94.

bert Alexy[131] stütze, dual. Das bedeutet, dass beide, wieder jeder auf seine Weise, in den Rechtsbegriff sowohl seine faktische als auch seine ideale Seite einbeziehen. Die faktische Seite umfasst die positive Rechtsordnung und die Wirksamkeit dieser Ordnung, die ideale Seite bezieht sich auf die inhaltliche (moralische) Richtigkeit des Rechts. Der gemeinsame Nenner beider ist, dass es sich um Recht handelt, solange sein Inhalt nicht extrem ungerecht beziehungsweise extrem unmenschlich ist.

Die Erkenntnis, dass die Natur des Rechts dual ist, ermöglicht einen Dialog – so auch Peter Koller – unter allen, die keine extremen Positivisten oder extremen Moralisten sind.[132] Extreme Positivisten akzeptieren einen beliebigen Inhalt des Rechts, extreme Moralisten rechtfertigen nur jenes Recht, das ihrem Moralideal entspricht. Die Reine Rechtslehre ist kein Beispiel eines extremen Positivismus; für sie ist der beliebige Inhalt nur Annahme, die eine inhaltlich gereinigte Analyse des Rechts ermöglicht. Kelsens Normativitätsthese ist für alle jene dialogisch, die am Inhalt der normativen Struktur des Rechts interessiert sind. Kelsens Theorie (insbesondere die Theorie des Stufenbaus der Rechtsordnung) enthüllt (und provoziert auf ihre eigene Weise) inhaltlichen Fragen des Rechts.[133]

Pitamic trug zum inhaltlichen Ausbau der Reinen Rechtslehre bei. Das Schlüsselargument ist die Natur des Rechts, der auch die Methode(n), mit denen das Recht erforscht und erkannt wird, entsprechen müssen. Das Erkennen der Natur des Rechts ist ein eigenartiges Vorverständnis, das den Forscher bei der Wahl der Methode(n), mit denen er sein Forschungsfeld betritt, lenkt. Wenn man so handelt und methodologisch klar argumentiert, gibt es auch Raum für Dialog und Gegenüberstellung von gegensätzlichen Standpunkten. „Dann,“ so Pitamic, „kann sich uns jenes Ziel nähern, das wir mit *allen* – wohlgemerkt mit *allen* – Mitteln anzustreben haben: *die Erkenntnis*.“[134]

---

131 *Robert Alexy*: 1. Hauptelemente einer Theorie der Doppelnatur des Rechts, in: ARSP, 95 (2009) 2, S. 151–166, und 2. The Dual Nature of Law, in: Rato Juris, 23 (2010) 2, S. 167–182. Siehe auch *Peter Koller*: 1. The Concept of Law and Its Conceptions, in: Ratio Juris, 19 (2006) 2, S. 180–196, und 2. Der Begriff des Rechts und seine Konzeptionen, in: Rechtsphilosophie im 21. Jahrhundert (Fn. 115), S. 157–180.
132 Siehe *Koller*: Der Begriff des Rechts und seine Konzeptionen (Fn. 131), S. 160 ff., S. 175 ff.
133 Siehe auch Abschnitt 6.2. dieses Beitrags.
134 *Pitamic*: Denkökonomische, S. 367.

Seana Valentine Shiffrin*

A Thinker-Based Approach To Freedom Of Speech

Introduction

Many contemporary autonomy theories of freedom of speech champion the perspective and freedom of just one side of the communicative relation – usually, the speaker or the listener(s). Such approaches seem to neglect or subordinate the autonomy interests of the other relevant parties. Other autonomy theories do not privilege one perspective on the communicative relation over another, but strangely treat the speakers' interests and the listeners' autonomy interests as rather discrete entities – disparate constituents both demanding our attention. Both strands gloss over a source of justification for free speech that both connects the two perspectives and recognizes the wider foundations that underpin their value (by contrast with the more narrow connections drawn between them by democracy theories). Specifically, both approaches celebrate one or more external manifestations of thought but do not focus on the source of speech and cognition – namely the *thinker* herself – and the conditions necessary for freedom of thought. I submit that a more plausible autonomy theory of freedom of speech arises from taking the free thinker as the central figure in a free speech theory and that we should understand freedom of speech as, centrally, protecting freedom of thought.

Hence, I propose to sketch a particular sort of autonomy theory of freedom of speech, namely a *thinker-based* foundation for freedom of speech. Although this account does not capture all of the values of freedom of speech or yield a comprehensive theory of freedom of speech, a thinker-based foundation can provide a stronger and more coherent foundation for the most important free speech protections than rival free speech theories, including the more common speaker-based or listener-based autonomy theories.[1]

*   Professor of Philosophy and Pete Kameron Professor of Law and Social Justice, UCLA. For enlightening criticism and commentary, I am grateful to Mark Greenberg, Jeffrey Helmreich, Barbara Herman, Heidi Kitrosser, Terry Stedman, participants in the Columbia Legal Theory Workshop, the Princeton Program in Ethics and Public Affairs and my free speech seminars at UCLA, and, of course, the members of the free speech discussion group from which this paper originates, especially Ed Baker and Steve Shiffrin. Terry Stedman also provided invaluable research assistance. This essay also appears in Constitutional Commentary (2011).

1   I have explored some aspects of a thinker-based approach in prior work. Vincent Blasi & Seana V. Shiffrin, *The Story of West Virginia Board of Education v. Barnette*, *in* Constitutional Law Stories 433 (Michael Dorf ed., 2d ed. 2009); Seana Valentine Shiffrin, *What is Really Wrong with Compelled Association?*, 99 Nw. U. L. Rev. 839 (2005). I do not mean to represent Vince as endorsing the general thinker-oriented approach I outline above, however. Some other authors have explored aspects of thinker-based approaches as well, although from different angles and with different emphases. *See, e.g.,* Charles Fried, *Modern Liberty* 95–123 (2007); Timothy Macklem, *Independence of Mind* 1–32 (2006); Susan Williams, *Truth, Autonomy, and Speech: Feminist Theory and the First Amendment* 130–229 (2004); Charles Fried, *The New First Amendment Jurisprudence: A Threat to Liberty*, 59 U. Chi. L. Rev. 225 (1992); Dana Remus Irwin, *Freedom of Thought: The First Amendment and the Scientific Method,* 2005 Wis. L. Rev. 1479; Neil M. Richards, *Intellectual Privacy*, 87 Tex. L. Rev. 387 (2008); Christina E. Wells, *Reinvigorating Autonomy: Freedom and Responsibility in the Supreme Court's First Amendment Jurisprudence*, 32 Harv. C.R.-C.L. L. Rev. 159 (1997). Although Ed Baker's writing often suggests a speaker-based ap-

In saying a thinker-based foundation undergirds the most important free speech protections, I mean 'most important' in a normative sense, and not in the sense that they are necessarily acknowledged as such, or at all, in contemporary free speech doctrine.[2] My paper aims to identify strong theoretical foundations for the protection of free speech but not to provide the best theoretical account of *our system* or *our current practices* of protecting (or failing to protect, as the case may be)[3] free speech. Articulating a theory of free speech along the former, more ideal lines, provides us with a framework to assess whether our current practices are justified or not, as well as which ones are outliers. An ideal theoretical approach also supplies both a measure for reform and some structural components to form the framework to assess new sorts of cases.

Which freedom of speech protections figure among the most important is, of course, contested. My position in that contest is that a decent regime of freedom of speech must provide a principled and strong form of protection for political speech and, in particular, for incendiary speech and other forms of dissent, for religious speech, for fiction, art – whether abstract or representational – and music, for diaries and other forms of discourse meant primarily for self-consumption, and for that private speech and discourse, e.g. personal conversations and letters, crucial to developing, pursuing, and maintaining personal relationships.[4]

Further, all of these forms of expression should enjoy foundational protection, by which I mean there should not be a lexical hierarchy of value between them, nor should the protections for some depend dominantly on their playing an instrumental role in securing the conditions for the flourishing practice of another. To put it more pointedly, an adequate free speech theory will avoid the convolutions associated with the more narrow democracy theories of freedom of speech and their efforts to explain why abstract art and music should gain free speech protection. Although a case *could* be made that the freedom to compose and to listen to Stravinsky is important to developing the sort of open personal and cultural character necessary for democracy to flourish or that it feeds the "sociological structure that is prerequisite for the formation of public opinion,"[5] that justification is strained and bizarrely indirect.[6] In

---

proach, in email correspondence about a draft of this paper he indicated that his true sympathies lay with a thinker-based approach. E-mail from Ed Baker to Seana Shiffrin (Feb. 13, 2009) (on file with author).

2   Seana Valentine Shiffrin, *Methodology in Free Speech Theory*, 97 Va. L. Rev. (forthcoming 2011) (defending a normative approach to free speech theory that does not take explanation of extant doctrine as foundational).

3   One free speech howler from the most recent term around which I would not care to tailor a free speech theory is Holder v. Humanitarian Law Project, 130 S. Ct. 2705, 2730–31 (2010) (upholding Congressional prohibition of assistance to designated terrorist organizations, including its application to mere speech that provides advice on how to petition the U.N. or how to use legal means to resolve conflicts peacefully).

4   These are, of course, theoretically informed, provisional starting points that strike me as highly intuitive, secure, illuminating, and important lodestars. Nonetheless, if a plausible theory cannot be found that supports and explains these judgments or if a more plausible theory would reject them for good reason, these judgments should be revised or discarded. That is, I regard their identification as just an early step in a process aimed at achieving reflective equilibrium and not as fixed or immutable 'results' that must be accommodated, no matter what the other theoretical costs. *See* John Rawls, *A Theory of Justice* 17–21, 46–53 (Original ed. 1971) (discussing reflective equilibrium). Further, the argument that follows does not, largely, use these starting points as premises. So, subscription to these starting points is not a precondition for the argument's success; it is merely that their accommodation and explanation seems to be desiderata of a satisfactory theory.

5   *See* Robert Post, *Participatory Democracy and Free Speech*, 97 Va. L. Rev. X, 10 (forthcoming 2011).

any case, the right of Stravinsky to compose and of audiences to listen (or to cringe in non-comprehension) should not depend upon whether *The Rite of Spring* breeds democrats or fascists, or whether it supports, detracts from, or is superfluous to a democratic culture.[7]

A good free speech theory should identify a non-contingent and direct foundation for its protection. On the other hand, protection for commercial and non-press, business corporate speech is a less central matter, one that reasonably may involve weaker protections and may reasonably rely heavily on more instrumental concerns. A good free speech theory should explain why commercial and business corporate speech may be different and why arguing for their protection may be a less straightforward matter.

Briefly put, I believe these desiderata are best satisfied by a thinker-based free speech theory that takes to be central the individual agent's interest in the protection of the free development and operation of her mind. Legal materials (by which I mean to encompass laws, regulations, court rulings, and resolutions) and government activity inconsistent with valuing this protection are inconsistent with a commitment to freedom of speech. In my view, legal materials or activity may be inconsistent with valuing this protection in three main ways: (1) the legal materials or the

---

6   Jim Weinstein offers a refreshingly candid admission of this difficulty. James Weinstein, *Participatory Democracy as the Central Value of American Free Speech Doctrine*, 97 Va. L. Rev. (forthcoming 2011). No more successful is the argument that democracy theories will protect the arts because to understand one another and to form a conception about what should be a public matter, we must have access to the forms of expression others engage in and deem important. *See, e.g.*, Robert Post, *Participatory Democracy and Free Speech*, 97 Va. L. Rev. (forthcoming 2011) ("So long as Brokeback Mountain, and indeed all forms of communication that sociologically we recognize as art, form part of the process by which society ponders what it believes and thinks, it is protected under a theory of the First Amendment that stresses democratic participation.") This justification is circuitous. It is parasitic upon others' developing the art form (which now we must have access to in order to understand them and their preferences) but either: does not provide foundational support for their freedom to develop it, or if it does, the argument lacks a fundamentally and specifically *democratic* form that is independent of and logically prior to an appeal to the interests of the autonomous thinker.

7   Joshua Cohen offers a far less narrow democratic account of free expression, one grounded in his deliberative democratic approach. His approach shows sensitivity to the interests of the citizen *qua* thinker and his approach provides a more plausible grounding for art, religious speech, erotic speech, and other forms of speech that are not explicitly or even indirectly political. Joshua Cohen, *Freedom of Expression*, 22 Phil. & Pub. Aff. 207 (1993), *reprinted in* Joshua Cohen, *Philosophy, Politics, Democracy* 98, 114–20 (2009); Joshua Cohen, *Democracy and Liberty*, *in* Deliberative Democracy 185 (Jon Elster ed., 1998), *reprinted in* Philosophy, Politics, Democracy, *supra* at 223, 248–54; Joshua Cohen, *Deliberation and Democratic Legitimacy*, *in* Deliberative Democracy 67 (James Bohman & William Rehg eds., 1997), *reprinted in* Philosophy, Politics, Democracy, *supra* at 16, 32–34 (2009).

     Although our approaches are fairly congenial, Cohen's case for rights of personal, non-political expression is usually voiced in terms of what the citizen "reasonably takes to be *compelling* considerations" or "substantial reasons" for expression (emphasis added). *See, e.g.*, Cohen, *Freedom of Expression*, *supra* at 115–17; Cohen, *Democracy and Liberty*, *supra* at 248–50. By contrast, I find unnecessary and over-demanding his stress upon agents' having *substantial, compelling* or *obligatory* reasons for their particular expression. Putting aside the peculiarly intense drive of the single-minded artist, many citizens' reasons for most of their speech, including a variety of images, melodies, artistic or quotidian thoughts, lack that charge. Nonetheless, in my view, they present no weaker of a case for protection. My aim is to develop an approach that does not rely on the idea that particular, personal expression is protected because its expression reasonably presents itself as akin to, or on a spectrum with, felt *obligations* of the speaker, interference of which would be unreasonable by the polity, but rather, an approach that is fully consistent with the admission that much personal and artistic speech is banal and unimportant in the grand scheme of things. A broader focus on the condition of the thinker, rather than on the (perceived) significance of the expression, seems better able to satisfy that desideratum.

government activity may, on their face, ban or attempt to ban the free development and operation of a person's mind or those activities or materials necessary for its free development and operation; (2) the effect of the legal materials, or of the activity, may objectionably interfere with the free development and operation of a person's mind; (3) the rationale for the materials, or the activity, may be inconsistent with valuing this protection.[8]

In developing this position I will proceed from the assumption that, for the most part, we are individual human agents with significant (though importantly imperfect) rational capacities, emotional capacities, perceptual capacities and capacities of sentience – all of which exert influence upon each other.[9] I will also assume that our possession and exercise of these capacities correctly constitute the core of what we value about ourselves.

I will not say much to defend these assumptions. I do not regard them as especially controversial. Indeed, many popular theories of freedom of speech only make sense if the individual mind and the autonomy of its operation (a notion I will say more about below) are valued and treated with respect. If we did not regard the autonomy of the individual mind as important, it is hard to see why we would value its expression or outputs in the way and to the degree that truth theories or democratic theories value speech. The same holds true of speaker-based and listener-based theories.[10] Still, each theory shares the presupposition that the autonomous thinker fundamentally matters, speaker, listener, and democracies theories start from an intermediate point and hone in on one activity of the thinker, rather than on the thinker herself. Reasoning from the standpoint of the thinker and her interests can yield a more comprehensive, unified foundation for much of the freedom of speech protection than is yielded by starting from a more partial intermediate point.

My aim in what follows is to show the supportive connection between valuing ourselves as so described and: (1) valuing speech; (2) valuing *freedom* of speech; (3) regarding speech as, in some politically and legally normative respects, special. With respect to this last item, contra Fred Schauer, I deny that an autonomy theory of free speech *must* show that speech is special or unique with respect to its relation to autonomy, in order to justify strong protections for freedom of speech. It may succeed at that justificatory project while articulating values that cast a broader net encompassing other forms of autonomous activity.[11] Indeed, I regard it as a general

---

8   *See also* Seana Valentine Shiffrin, *Speech, Death and Double Effect*, 78 N.Y.U. L. Rev. 1135, 1164–71 (2003).

9   In some of us, these capacities are fledgling, partial, or compromised. Nonetheless, agents with them have an interest in their development and operation. Although the degree of development and future potential may make some difference in some cases and contexts, I do not think that, at base, a free speech theory delivers fundamentally different results depending upon whether we are discussing children, the mentally disabled, those suffering dementia, or fully formed adults. The most salient context in which degree of development might be thought normatively to make a difference, the schoolroom, seems better explained by reference to time, place, and manner restrictions than to the developmental level of children. This, of course, is a normative claim and one that does not entirely square with doctrinal developments over the last twenty years. For discussions of children and the First Amendment see Blasi & Shiffrin, *supra* note 1; Colin M. Macleod, *A Liberal Theory of Freedom of Expression for Children*, 79 Chi.-Kent L. Rev. 55 (2004.) *See generally* Symposium, *Do Children Have the Same First Amendment Rights as Adults?*, 79 Chi.-Kent L. Rev. 3 (2004).

10 Some purely instrumental theories of freedom of speech that focus on the importance of controlling the excesses of state authority may differ on this point.

11 Frederick Schauer, *Must Speech Be Special?*, 78 Nw. U. L. Rev. 1284 (1984). Some of Post's criticisms of autonomy theories of freedom of speech appear to be versions of the complaint that such theo-

strength of autonomy theories that they explain the continuity between speech protections and rights of intimate association. But, although the plausibility of a theory of strong protections for freedom of speech does not depend upon its showing that speech is special, nonetheless, I do think speech occupies a special place in the life and politically germane needs of the autonomous thinker. It is worth showing how it is both special and, at the same time, how it connects to other autonomy interests.

Autonomous Agents And Freedom Of Speech

Having stated my aspirations, let me move on to the argument. I begin with an explicit, albeit perhaps partial, elaboration of the interests of autonomous thinkers.

If we do value ourselves as rational agents with the capacities previously described, then I submit we should recognize a more articulated (though sometimes overlapping) list of interests that emerge from our possession of these valuable capacities.

Namely, every individual, rational, *human* agent *qua* thinker has interests in:

a. A capacity for practical and theoretical thought.

Each agent has an interest in developing her mental capacities to be receptive of, appreciative of, and responsive to reasons and facts in practical and theoretical thought, i. e. to be aware of and appropriately responsive to the true, the false, and the unknown.

b. Apprehending the true.

Each agent has an interest in believing and understanding true things about herself, including the contents of her mind, and the features and forces of the environment from which she emerges and in which she interacts.

c. Exercising the imagination.

Rational agents also have interests in understanding and intellectually exploring non-existent possible and impossible environments. Such mental activities allow agents the ability to conceive of the future and what could be. Further, the ability to explore the non-existent and impossible provides an opportunity for the exercise of the philosophical capacities and the other parts of the imagination.[12]

d. Becoming a distinctive individual.

Each agent has an interest in developing a personality and engaging more broadly in a mental life that, while responsive to reasons and facts, is distinguished from others'

---

ries cannot explain why speech is special. *See* Post, *supra* note 5, at 3–4, 12.

12   *See* Jed Rubenfeld, *The Freedom of Imagination: Copyright's Constitutionality*, 112 Yale L.J. 1, 38–39 (2002).

personalities by individuating features, emotions, reactions, traits, thoughts, and experiences that contribute to a distinctive perspective that embodies and represents each individual's separateness as a person.

e. Moral agency.

Each agent has an interest in acquiring the relevant knowledge base and character traits as well as forming the relevant thoughts and intentions to comply with the requirements of morality. (This interest, of course, may already be contained in the previously articulated interests in developing the capacity for practical and theoretical thought, apprehending the true, and exercising the imagination (a–c)).

f. Responding authentically.

Each agent has an interest in pursuing (a–e) through processes that represent free and authentic forms of internal creation and recognition. By this, I mean roughly that rational agents have an interest in forming thoughts, beliefs, practical judgments, intentions and other mental contents on the basis of reasons, perceptions, and reactions through processes that, in the main and over the long term, are independent of distortive influences. So too they have an interest in revealing and sharing these mental contents at their discretion, i. e. at the time at which those contents seem to them correct, apt, or representative of themselves as well to those to whom (and at that time) such revelations and the relationship they forge seem appropriate or desirable. This is the intellectual aspect of being an autonomous agent. In saying these processes are independent of distortive influences, I mean they do not follow a trajectory fully or largely scripted by forces external to the person that are distinct from the reasons and other features of the world to which she is responding.

g. Living among others.

Each rational, human agent has an interest in living among other social, autonomous agents who have the opportunities to develop their capacities in like ways. Satisfaction of this interest does not merely serve natural desires for companionship but crucially enables other interests qua thinker to be achieved, including the development and recognition of a distinctive self and character, the acquisition and confirmation of knowledge, and the development and exercise of moral agency.

h. Appropriate recognition and treatment.

Each agent has an interst in being recognized by other agents for the person she is and having others treat her morally well.

This list may not be exhaustive, but I believe it identifies some of the more foundational and central interests that agents have, independent of their specific projects, interests, and desires, but just in virtue of their capacities for thought, broadly understood to include autonomous deliberation and reactions, practical judgment, and moral relations. Briefly summarized, these are interests in self-development, self-knowledge, knowledge of others, others' knowledge of and respect for oneself, knowledge of the environments in which they interact, opportunities for the exercise of one's intellectual capacities including the imagination, and the intellectual prerequisites of moral relations.[13]

Speech, and free speech in particular, are necessary conditions of the realization of these interests. First, given the opacity of our minds to one another, speech and expression are the only precise avenues by which one can be known *as the individual one is* by others. If what makes one a distinctive individual qua *person* is *largely* a matter of the contents of one's mind,[14] to be known by others requires the ability to transmit the contents of one's mind to others. Although some information about one's thoughts and beliefs may be gleaned from observation, such inferences are typically coarse-grained at best and cannot track the detail and nuance of the inner life of the observed. Communication of the contents of one's mind primarily through linguistic means, but also through pictorial, or even musical representation, uniquely furthers the interest in being known by others. It thereby also makes possible complex forms of social life.[15] Further, it helps to develop some of the capacities prerequisite to moral agency because successful communication demands having a sense of what others are in a position to know and understand. Practicing communication initiates the process of taking others' perspective to understand what others know and are in a position to grasp.

Being known by others as the distinct individual one is is important in itself. It is also essential for one to be fully respected by others. Further, having access to the contents of others' minds (at their discretion) is essential for being able to respect them, at least insofar as some forms of respect and other moral duties involve understanding and respecting individuals as separate persons and in light of features of their individuality, including their reasons, aims, and needs. Moreover, other forms of moral activity, as well as appreciation of the moral activity of others, require some recognition of agents' motives.

Furthermore, I suspect that one cannot fully develop a complex mental world, identify its contents, evaluate them, and distinguish between those that are merely

---

13   In other work, I have argued that it is a mandatory, central (and fully liberal) aim of law to accommodate and facilitate individuals' ability to engage in moral agency. *See* Seana Valentine Shiffrin, *Inducing Moral Deliberation: On the Occasional Virtues of Fog*, 123 Harv. L. Rev. 1214, 1222–29 (2010); Seana Valentine Shiffrin, *The Divergence of Contract and Promise*, 120 Harv. L. Rev. 708, 713–19 (2007). Although I have mainly focused on other legal contexts of moral accommodation and facilitation, free speech protections may represent the most important legal context for the legal support of agents' moral capacities. *See also* Seana Valentine Shiffrin, *Compelled Association, Morality, and Market Dynamics*, 41 Loy. L.A. L. Rev. 317, 324–26 (2007).

14   I do not mean what individuates one as a creature. In that respect, physical features including one's genetic composition and perhaps other physical, non-mental facts may be important.

15   This consideration figured large among the motivations behind Kant's views about truthfulness and lying. *See* Immanuel Kant, *Of Ethical Duties Towards Others, and Especially Truthfulness*, *in* Lectures on Ethics 200–209 (Peter Heath & J.B. Schneewind eds., trans. Peter Heath, 1997). Of course, individuals may not fully know themselves and, further, may be self-deceived. Hence, they may not be fully equipped to share all of the contents of their minds with others and to enable others fully to know themselves directly through testimony. This does not diminish my point. Even when people are self-deceived, what they take to be their beliefs, emotions and other mental contents is an important aspect of who they are; further, sharing these contents with others and confronting the reactions of others and their observations of one's contrary behavior is often crucial to resolving and eliminating self-ignorance and self-deception.

given and those one endorses, unless one has the ability to externalize bits of one's mind, formally distance those bits from one's mind, identify them as particulars, and then evaluate them to either endorse, reject, or modify them. For many people, some thoughts may only be fully identified and known to themselves if made linguistically or representationally explicit. Many find that difficult to do using merely mental language, especially with sufficiently complex ideas; one has to externalize what the thoughts are through verbal or written speech or through other forms of symbolic representation to identify them completely (and sometimes to form them at all), a prerequisite to evaluating their contents. Other thoughts and methods of tracking one's environment over time require some form of external representation because of the frailties of the human memory; to form the complex thought, one needs the device of external representation to keep track of portions of it over time.[16] The ability and opportunity to generate external representations may both make public what has already fully formed in the mind and may render possible the formation of new sorts of thoughts that cannot take full form in our limited mental space.[17]

Of course, it is not merely the development and identification of one's thoughts that requires the use of representation and external articulation. To pursue our interest in forming true beliefs about ourselves and our environment, we need the help of others' insights and beliefs, as well as their reactions and evaluative responses to our beliefs. Others can only have the basis for responding, and the means to respond with the sort of precision necessary to be helpful, if they are able to use speech.

My argument that rational human thinkers need access to other thinkers under conditions in which their mental contents may be known with some degree of precision, explicitly recognized as such, and reacted to, is partially but poignantly confirmed by the evidence of the disastrous effects of involuntary solitary confinement. Prisoners in solitary confinement deteriorate mentally and emotionally. They progressively lose their grip on reality, suffering hallucinations and paranoia, and many become psychotic.[18] "Human beings rely on social contact with others to test and validate their perceptions of the environment. Ultimately, a complete lack of social contact makes it difficult to distinguish what is real from what is not or what is external from what is internal."[19] Prisoners subject to solitary confinement suffer terrible depression, despair and anxiety; moreover, their emotional control and stability wanes and their abilities to interact with others atrophies.[20]

Of course, prisoners in solitary confinement endure more than just the lack of conversation and the absence of interlocutors; they lack fundamental forms of control over their lives, other sorts of interactions with persons, and other forms of per-

---

16   Tyler Burge, *Computer Proof, Apriori Knowledge, and Other Minds: The Sixth Philosophical Perspectives Lecture*, 32 Noûs Suppl. 12 1, 10–13, 19–22, 27–28 (1998); Tyler Burge, *Memory and Persons*, 112 Phil. Rev. 289, 300–03, 314–21 (2003).

17   *See also* Macklem, *supra* note 1, at 1–32.

18   *See, e.g.*, Bruce A. Arrigo & Jennifer Leslie Bullock, *The Psychological Effects of Solitary Confinement on Prisoners in Supermax Units: Reviewing What We Know and Recommending What Should Change*, 52 Int'l J. of Offender Therapy & Comp. Criminology 622, 627 (2008); Craig Haney, *Mental Health Issues in Long-Term Solitary and "Supermax" Confinement*, 49 Crime & Delinq. 124, 130–32 (2003).

19   Arrigo & Bullock, *supra* note 18, at 7 (citing the work of Haney, *supra* note 18). Similar evidence presents itself about the effects of uncorrected hearing loss. Stig Arlinger, *Negative Consequences of Uncorrected Hearing Loss: A Review*, 42 Int'l J. of Audiology 2S17, 2S17–20 (2003) (reporting the hearing loss may reduce intellectual and cultural stimulation, give rise to changes in the central nervous system, and may affect the development of dementia).

20   *See* Haney, *supra* note 18.

ceptual access to reality. But, most other prisoners lack this sort of control and lack broader forms of access to the world and yet do not suffer the degree of devastation to mental function that prisoners in solitary confinement do.[21] "Whether in Walpole or Beirut or Hanoi, all human beings experience *isolation* as torture."[22] What seems to push them over the edge is the absence of regular, bilateral, communication. My worry is that to forbid or substantially to restrict free expression is not tantamount to solitary incarceration but lies on a spectrum with it: it is to institute a sort of solitary confinement outside of prison but within one's mind.

So, in short, the view I am attracted to is that it is essential to the appropriate development and regulation of the self, and of one's relation to others, that one have wide-ranging access to the opportunity to externalize one's mental contents, to have the opportunity to make one's mental contents known to others in an unscripted and authentic way, and that one has protection from unchosen interference with one's mental contents from processes that would disrupt or disable the operation of these processes. That is to say, free speech is essential to the development and proper functioning of thinkers.

Further, because moral agency involves the ability to take the perspective of other people and to respond to their distinctive features as individuals, including some of their mental contents, then free speech also plays a foundational and necessary (though not sufficient) role in ensuring citizens develop the capacity for moral agency and have the opportunities and information necessary to discharge their moral duties. Politically, these arguments should resonate with us, yielding an argument for constitutional protection for freedom of speech, both from respect for the fundamental moral rights of the person and also because, as I have argued elsewhere, a well-functioning system of social cooperation and justice presupposes that the citizenry, by and large, have active, well-developed moral personalities.[23] The successful operation of a democratic polity, as well as its meaningfulness, would also seem to depend upon citizens' generally having strong and independent capacities for thought and judgment.

This view makes no important distinction, at the foundations, between communication about aesthetics, one's medical condition and treatment,[24] one's regard

---

21 *See id.* at 125.

22 Atul Gawande, *Hellhole*, The New Yorker, Mar. 30, 2009, at 36 (emphasis added).

23 Shiffrin, *Inducing Moral Deliberation: On the Occasional Virtues of Fog, supra* note 13, at 1231–32. *See also* John Stuart Mill, *Considerations on Representative Government* 24–25 (Currin Shields ed., 1958); Rawls *supra* note 4, at 395–587.

24 Respect for this right is far from a given. Prita Mulyasari was recently incarcerated in Indonesia for three weeks of pre-trial detention on charges of internet defamation after she sent an email to friends complaining about a wrongful diagnosis at a local hospital. After an international campaign in her defense, she was acquitted but the government is appealing her acquittal and seeking a 6 month prison sentence. *See* Norimitsu Onishi, *Trapped Inside a Broken Judicial System after Hitting Send*, N.Y. Times, Dec. 5, 2009, at A6; *Turning Critics Into Criminals: The Human Rights Consequences of Criminal Defamation Law in Indonesia*, Human Rights Watch, 5, 26–28 (May 2010) *available at* >http://www.hrw.org/node/90023< (discussing other criminal defamation cases for other consumer complaints).

Indonesia imposes criminal penalties for defamation, enhancing them if the communication is sent over the internet. Truth, on its own, is not a standard defense. Whether it is permitted at all seems to be a matter of the judge's discretion. Further, defendants seeking to use the truth defense in cases not involving public officials must bear the burden of proof and must show that the defamatory statement was offered from necessity or 'in the general interest.' Pursuing an unsuccessful truth defense may subject the defendant to an even harsher sentence of up to four years in prison. Human Rights Watch, *supra* at 16–17.

for another, one's sensory perceptions, the sense or lack thereof of the existence of a God, or one's political beliefs. All of these communications serve the fundamental function of allowing an agent to transmit (or attempt to transmit so far as possible) the contents of her mind to others and to externalize her mental contents in order to attempt to identify, evaluate, and endorse or react given contents as authentically one's own; further, they allow others to be granted access to the information necessary to appreciate the thinker, on voluntary terms, and to forge a full human relation with her. One's thoughts about political affairs are intrinsically and *ex ante* no more and no less central to the human self than thoughts about one's mortality or one's friends; in so far as a central function of free speech is to allow for the development, exercise, and recognition of the self, there is no reason to relegate the representation of thoughts about personal relations or self-reflection to a lesser or secondary category. Pictorial representations and music (and not merely discourse about them) should also gain foundational protection because they also represent the externalization of mental contents, contents that may not be accurately or well-captured through linguistic means; after all, not all thoughts are discursive or may be fully captured through discursive description.[25]

On the other hand, this approach can render sensible the notion that non-press, business corporate and commercial speech may be different and that their protection may assume a weaker form and may rest upon separate, more context-dependent and instrumental, foundations.[26] First, business corporate speech does not involve in any direct or straightforward fashion the revelation of individuals' mental contents.[27] Corporate-to-corporate as well as corporate-to-individual speech often bear only an indirect relation to the revelation and development of the thinker or the intellectual, emotional, or moral relations between thinkers. Of course, thinkers may have an interest in access to corporate speech because corporate and commercial speech may report information about one's given environment, but, in other circumstances, the point of corporate speech, as well as other commercial speech, is to *alter* the environment, e.g. to manufacture desire, not to report it.

To be sure, however, altering the environment is also the aim of advocacy speech by individuals as well. That aim in no way diminishes the protection that should be afforded to it. Advocacy speech represents a form of exercise of thinkers' interests in developing their moral agency and in treating one another well by attempting to discern and to persuade others of what each of us or what we together should think and do. By contrast, non-press, business corporate and commercial speech, by design, issue from an environment whose structure does not facilitate and, indeed, tends to discourage the authentic expression of individuals' judgment.

25   *See* Frank Jackson, *Epiphenomenal Qualia*, 32 Phil. Q. 127, 128–30, 133–36 (1982); Frank Jackson, *What Mary Didn't Know*, 83 The J. of Phil. 291 (1986).

26   For one example of its context-dependence on other features of the economic climate and our system of economic regulation, see Shiffrin, *Compelled Association, Morality, and Market Dynamics, supra* note 13, at 324, 327.

27   *See, e.g.,* Citizens United v. Fed. Election Comm'n, 130 S. Ct. 876, 971 (2010) (Stevens, J., dissenting) (discussing the differences between corporations and human beings and the distance between corporate speech and any individual points of view); C. Edwin Baker, *The First Amendment and Commercial Speech*, 84 Ind. L.J. 981, 987–89 (2009) (stressing that commercial corporations are limited forms of entities created for instrumental reasons and that the people who operate within them do not act fully autonomously); Steven H. Shiffrin, *The First Amendment and Economic Regulation: Away from a General Theory of the First Amendment*, 78 Nw. U. L. Rev. 1212, 1246 (1983) (discussing the structure of the corporation and the distance between its speech and the views of its shareholders).

As Ed Baker has argued, the competitive structure of the economic market and the narrowly defined aims of the corporate or commercial entity place substantial pressures on the content of corporate and commercial speech. So too may the internal structural design of the corporation.[28] In Baker's view, their content has a 'forced profit orientation,' and does not represent a 'manifestation of individual freedom or choice';[29] in my somewhat weaker terms, external environmental pressures render more tenuous any charitable presupposition that such speech is sincere, authentic, or the product of autonomous processes. As I have argued elsewhere, Baker's starkly-put position may involve a degree of over-generalization given market imperfections, market actors who are true believers, and market actors using the market and speech within it to further external and sincere moral goals.[30] Nonetheless, I concur with him that the market's structure tends "very strongly [to] determine [corporate and commercial] speech content."[31] These distortive influences render more precarious the claims that strong presumptions against speech regulation in this domain reliably serve the interests of the thinker-qua-speaker or the thinker-qua-listener as the recipient of such communications. Together, these considerations provide reason to treat non-press, business corporate and commercial speech as non-standard cases within a free speech domain and justifiably, depending on context and content, often to treat such speech as permissible targets of a more comprehensive scheme of economic regulation.[32]

Comparing A Thinker-Based Approach To Other Autonomy Approaches

This approach, one that showcases freedom of thought and the needs of thinkers as such as the central theme of a free speech perspective, is compatible with many of the traditional insights associated with speaker-based and listener-based theories (and with democracy and truth theories for that matter). All of these approaches, however, work from an overly narrow foundation or they start by valorizing one manifestation of free thought, while neglecting other manifestations that are no less important. Although the ability to externalize one's mental contents through speech is of prime importance on this account, it would make no sense to give it pride of place over ensuring that others could listen or take in these transmissions or over the protection of one's rational processes from interference or disruption.

Because this account derives the basic free speech protection from the foundational interests of the autonomous agent *qua* thinker, it therefore, rests on sparer assumptions than other autonomy accounts, such as Ed Baker's, that revolve around

---

28   *See* Shiffrin, *The First Amendment and Economic Regulation: Away from a General Theory of the First Amendment, supra* note 27.

29   *See* C. Edwin Baker, *Human Liberty and Freedom of Speech* 196, 204 (1989); C. Edwin Baker, *Paternalism, Politics, and Citizen Freedom: The Commercial Speech Quandary in Nike*, 54 Case W. Res. L. Rev. 1161, 1163 (2004); Baker, *The First Amendment and Commercial Speech, supra* note 27, at 985–987.

30   *See* Shiffrin, *Compelled Association, Morality, and Market Dynamics, supra* note 13, at 320.

31   *Id.*

32   *See also* Baker, *The First Amendment and Commercial Speech, supra* note 27, at 994. I have assumed throughout this part of the discussion that the government's motives in regulating commercial or business corporate speech would be permissible ones, that is to say that they were not driven by a rationale that is inconsistent with valuing the autonomous operation of the mind. The requirement that the government's rationale must be a permissible one, as I specify above, is not suspended in this domain (or any other).

the autonomous agent qua self-*governor*.[33] Whether in its substantive form (the agent as a person with the capacity "to pursue successfully the life she endorses") or its formal conception (the agent with "the authority to make decisions about her own meaningful actions [and resources]"), Baker's ideal invokes an attractive model towards which to aspire, but utilizes unnecessarily controversial assumptions.[34]

For instance, I do not believe that the autonomy case for protecting free speech hinges upon whether we have (or should have or should value) the full panoply of executive skills and control over our actions that the broader ideal of self-authorship and self-governance involves. We may have all the interests I identify (along with their capacities to pursue them) even if we lack the ability or authority to implement our decisions. Rightfully detained prisoners will lack both these features but, in my view (if not the Court's), enjoy the relevant moral right of freedom of speech.[35] Skepticism about the broader ideal therefore should not impugn the more narrowly tailored, thinker-centered case for free speech protections.[36] Further, a thinker-based approach is better positioned to undergird a more expansive free speech protection, or at least to do so in a more direct and obvious fashion, because our imagination and thoughts range more widely than our capacity for self-governance and self-authorship (at least if the latter is construed to involve self-regarding action and conduct). We are able to think and consider topics and subjects that have no specific and direct relation to ourselves and our pursuit of a life we endorse.

Explicitly making the *thinker* the central figure of free speech (as compared to focusing on the listener, the speaker, the self-governor or the functioning of the polity) may make a difference as far as what dangers and threats to free speech present themselves as salient. So, for example, although I find Tim Scanlon's emphasis on sovereignty of deliberation in the Millian principle at the center of his early listener-based theory highly congenial, its focus on the listener may distract us from equally significant forms of regulation that tamper with the sovereignty of deliberation but that are not directly targeted at interfering with a speaker-listener relation.[37]

---

33   *See* Edwin Baker, *Autonomy*, 27 Const. Comment. (forthcoming 2011). *See also* Baker, *Human Liberty and Freedom of Speech*, *supra* note 29, at 47–69; Baker, *The First Amendment and Commercial Speech*, *supra* note 27, at 990 (identifying autonomy in terms of embodying values in *action*).

34   See C. Edwin Baker, *Autonomy*, *supra* note 33.

35   Beard v. Banks, 548 U.S. 521, 530–33 (2006) (plurality opinion) (upholding ban on access to newspapers, magazines, and personal photographs by prisoners in the most restrictive level of incarceration); Turner v. Safley, 482 U.S. 78, 89 (1987) ("[W]hen a prison regulation impinges on inmates' constitutional rights, the regulation is valid if it is reasonably related to legitimate penological interests."); Bell v. Wolfish, 441 U.S. 520, 548–52 (1979) (upholding ban on pretrial detainees receiving hardback books by mail unless sent directly by the publisher or a bookstore); Jones v. N.C. Prisoners' Labor Union, Inc., 433 U.S. 119, 129–33 (1977) (upholding ban on bulk mailing and inmate-to-inmate solicitation to join prisoner's union); Pell v. Procunier, 417 U.S. 817, 822–28 (1974) (upholding ban on prisoners initiating interviews with the press). For critical commentary on the low protection afforded to prisoners' first amendment rights see James E. Robertson, *The Rehnquist Court and the "Turnerization" of Prisoners' Rights*, 10 N.Y. City L. Rev. 97 (2006); *The Supreme Court, 2005 Term – Leading Cases*, 120 Harv. L. Rev. 125, 263 (2006).

36   Further, arguing just from the foundational interests of the thinker as such does not elicit the same worries regarding why speech in particular merits special, strong protection.

37   *See* Thomas Scanlon, *A Theory of Freedom of Expression*, 1 Phil. & Pub. Aff. 204 (1972) *reprinted in* T.M. Scanlon, *The Difficulty of Tolerance* 6, 14–15 (2003). Scanlon subsequently criticized the Millian principle on other grounds than I explore here and embraced a modified, but broader, theory of freedom of speech that, inter alia, offers primary recognition to speaker and audience interests. T.M. Scanlon, Jr., *Freedom of Expression and Categories of Expression*, 40 U. Pitt. L. Rev. 519 (1979), *reprinted in* The Difficulty of Tolerance, *supra* at 84.

Scanlon's Millian principle states:

> [C]ertain harms which, although they would not occur but for certain acts
> of expression, nonetheless cannot be taken as part of a justification for le-
> gal restrictions . . . (a) harms to certain individuals which consist in their
> coming to have false beliefs as a result of those acts of expression; (b)
> harmful consequences of acts performed as a result of those acts of expres-
> sion, where the connection between [them] consists merely in the . . . ex-
> pression le[a]d[ing] the agents to believe . . . these acts to be worth per-
> forming.[38]

Although the insulation of the agent's opportunity to form beliefs and opinions of
her own is central to the thinker-based perspective, Scanlon's Millian principle – as
stated – has its limitations as a form of protection of the thinker. From a freedom of
thought perspective, such a principle is under-inclusive in an important respect.[39] It
is unclear why we should protect *only* autonomous or authentic processes from efforts to interfere with *belief and conclusion* formation. Should we not also ensure that
regulations are not propounded on the grounds that speech will yield emotional reactions of one sort or another or that speech will induce sensory reactions of one
sort or another? Aren't these processes also central to *human* thought at least?

Moreover, Scanlon's principle only reaches and condemns regulation aimed at
preventing the formation of false beliefs and practical judgments as *consequences* of
expression. It does not directly speak to the wrongfulness of regulations or government activity aimed at instilling beliefs, attitudes, or reasons through compulsion,
subliminal manipulation, or other efforts to circumvent rational deliberation.

Finally, it doesn't directly recognize the significance that assuming the role of
speaker may have to an agent's own rational development and cognition. Expanding
the theory to correct these forms of under-inclusion would not be, I take it, antithetical to the spirit of Scanlon's original approach.[40] Nonetheless, an *explicitly* thinker-
oriented approach more naturally yields a comprehensive explanation of what is
troubling about thought control, efforts at thought control, as well as other sorts of
efforts to disrupt the free operation of the mind, whether or not such efforts also
happen to operate through a mode of interfering interpersonal communication.

For example, as Vince Blasi and I argued at greater length elsewhere,[41] focusing
on freedom of thought as such may yield a more straightforward account of the pro-

---

38   Scanlon, *A Theory of Freedom of Expression, supra* note 37, at 213.
39   The Millian principle may be overinclusive in the following respect: the principle as stated does not
     provide a clear line to distinguish between false beliefs that result from fraud or intentional misrep-
     resentation and false beliefs that result from sincere communication (but poor judgment, under-
     standing or perception on the part of the speaker or the listener). The former may reasonably count
     as harms, I submit, on the grounds that a thinker-based view of freedom of speech provides no
     foundational protection for speech that aims to distort and control the thinker's rational processes
     of tracking and understanding her environment. Again, I doubt Scanlon would be hostile to this dis-
     tinction, as suggested by his apparent friendliness to at least some sorts of defamation actions, *id.* at
     12, and his later criticism in *Freedom of Expression and Categories of Expression* of the Millian principle
     for failing to allow laws on deceptive advertising. Scanlon, *A Theory of Freedom of Expression, supra*
     note 37, at 215. As originally stated, though, the Millian principle does not clearly make room for
     defamation liability.
40   *See, e.g.,* Thomas Scanlon, *Freedom of Expression and Categories of Expression, supra* note 37, at 91–2 (ob-
     serving the audience's interest "in having a good environment for the formation of one's beliefs and
     desires" and offering criticisms of subliminal speech).
41   *See* Blasi & Shiffrin, *supra* note 1.

tection in *West Virginia State Board of Education v. Barnette*.[42] It is not clear that the compelled pledge, so long as its origins are transparent, restricts listener opportunities, nor does its motivation violate strictures on respecting listeners and their deliberative capacities. Further, although it seems clear that the compelled pledge violates the free speech rights of the party who must speak the pledge, it is less clear that the standard themes that have occupied speaker-oriented theories are squarely engaged here. So long as it is clear the pledge is compelled and so long as the speaker may disavow the pledge, the speaker's ability to express herself faithfully is arguably not seriously abridged.[43] The speaker will not be misunderstood by reasonable observers. Although reciting others' speech may not be a part of one's project of self-creation, so long as others' uptake isn't disrupted and so long as the compelled speech is not especially time consuming, focusing on the speaker – as such – seems strained. A more straightforward explanation would not focus predominantly on either side of the speaker-audience relationship.

What seems most troubling about the compelled pledge is that the motive behind the regulation, and the possible effect, is to interfere with the autonomous thought processes of the compelled speaker. Significantly, the compelled speaker is also a compelled listener and is compelled to adopt postures that typically connote identification with her message. The aim, and I believe the potential effect, is to try to influence the speaker to associate herself with the message and implicitly to accept it, but through means that bypass the deliberative faculties of the agent. Compelled speech of this kind threatens (or at least aims) to interfere with free thinking processes of the speaker/listener and to influence mental content in ways and through methods that are illicit: nontransparent, via repetition, and through coercive manipulation of a character virtue, namely that of sincerity, that itself is closely connected to commitments of freedom of speech.

Another advantage of a thinker-centered approach is that it yields a distinctive approach to freedom of association that both explains its centrality and depicts the relation between 'intimate' and 'expressive' as continuous. Again, the approach is not antithetical to other theories of freedom of speech, e.g. speaker-based or listener-

---

42   319 U.S. 624 (1943).

43   Of course, the necessity of correcting a false impression conveyed to an audience that does not understand the significance of the speech being compelled may impinge upon the speaker's interest in remaining silent with respect to the pledge and the sentiments and commitments expressed therein; necessarily, the interests in self-expression must include the ability to gather one's thoughts and engage in self-creation at one's own pace. There is something to this point but I am not sure that it carries enough significance to bear the full weight of the *Barnette* protection. Correcting a misimpression only requires explaining the significance or fact of compulsion; it does not require the speaker to make up her mind or reveal anything substantive about the pledge. This point, however, may be less persuasive in contexts in which any sort of correction or explanation may implicitly reveal some reservations about the pledge and such revelations would be socially or politically dangerous. Still, I assume the *Barnette* protection holds even for compelled speech that is less fraught or that is compelled in less charged contexts. *See, e.g.*, Wooley v. Maynard, 430 U.S. 705 (1977).

In any case, it is unclear how much of the substance, whether the positive protection or the negative limits, of the First Amendment protection should revolve around how unreasonable people might interpret the significance of a speech performance. For example, the fact that unreasonable people might take my friend's speech to represent my own views and that their misunderstanding might prompt me to speak on a topic about which I'd prefer to remain silent does not begin to ground an argument that I have a right that my friend not speak in a way that may mislead the unreasonable interpreters. The republishing libel doctrine also wanders a little too close to my comfort to the view that the limits of the First Amendment may be dictated by the unreasonable reactions of readers. *See, e.g.*, Restatement (Second) of Torts § 578 (1977).

based theories. But, occupying a thinker-based perspective may orient one more immediately to the centrality of association than other theories which may lead one to value association through a more circuitous route. Even once one adopts a capacious view of the content covered by a free speech norm, speaker-oriented theories have tended to think of the point of associations as bundles of speakers who come together to amplify their speech – to render it louder or to garner more attention for their positions. The model has been to think of speakers as having a prior message that brings them together and that the associations facilitate more effective, clearer communication of these ideas, formed prior to association. The association is a conduit or a pass through: it enhances the effectiveness of the message but plays little formative role with respect to the actual speech.

A thinker-based view of the sort I have been sketching identifies, at least more immediately, the role of associations in a free speech theory. If, as a general matter, our intellectual development and, indeed, our basic sanity depends upon our communicative interaction with others, and, if we conceive of the function of speech as critical to this development, we are more likely to be attuned to the ways that associations serve as sites of idea formation and development, and to recognize the ways in which the development (and not merely the broadcasting) of content occurs through mutual collaboration and mutual influence in explicit and implicit ways. Such an approach would not focus predominantly on whether regulations affect the *message* of an association but on whether regulations interfere with the ability of associations to function as sites for mutual cognitive influence.[44]

What makes speech special?

I observed earlier that it seems to me to be a positive feature, rather than an embarrassment, of a speech theory that it can show the compatibility of and even the continuity between different core protections of individual autonomy. At the same time, it does seem as though speech is special in some way. An attractive free speech theory should draw some normative distinction between speech as an exercise of autonomy and at least some other behaviors that are exercises of autonomy; although some forms of autonomous action should perhaps gain the same high level of legal protection as free speech, not all autonomous action should. An attractive free speech theory will help to make some sense of the divide.

With respect to the first desideratum of making sense of the continuity, it strikes me as a strength of the thinker-based approach that it renders the penumbra theory of *Griswold*[45] and *Roe*[46] sensible. First, certain substantive due process protections provide the preconditions for a meaningful free speech protection. If we accept the First Amendment and its justifications and we accept that our form of rational agency requires social connections to develop and flourish, then we must provide for safe havens for thought, communication, and mutual influence: the relevant forms of safety come both in numbers (i. e. having associates with whom one may share thoughts and who may witness what happens to one) and in the ability to se-

---

44   I develop an argument of this kind in greater detail in Shiffrin, *What is Really Wrong with Compelled Association?*, *supra* note 1.
45   Griswold v. Connecticut, 381 U.S. 479 (1965).
46   Roe v. Wade, 410 U.S. 113 (1973).

lect with whom and in what ways one will share fundamental forms of intimacy. If the state could prevent intimate associations or if it could require them to occur (rendering the connection forced and inauthentic), it would obstruct individuals' ability to forge the sort of authentic social connections essential for the development and maintenance of the personality and the free intellect.

Second, the central substantive due process protections are extensions of the values protected by freedom of speech. Sexual intimacy, e. g., expresses and may reveal any of a variety of mental states towards another: in the good cases, feelings of love, affection or at least lusty attraction.

But although (free) sexual intimacy and speech are both exercises of autonomy, *both* are not standard forms of communication or transmission of mental content; hence my remark that many substantive due process protections are *extensions* of the values protected by a free speech principle, rather than instantiations of it. A kiss typically expresses a happy reaction, attraction, or a warm attitude, where here I mean to invoke the sense of 'express' that is not synonymous with 'communicate' but rather that means to display and to manifest, rather than just to transmit the fact of or to communicate.[47] Although the mental attitude may be inferred from it, the kiss is not typically deployed merely to convey the fact of its existence. It can be used that way but its communicative use is parasitic upon the connotations of its expressive function.

This, of course, is a fraught distinction[48] but it is one that I think has a point that connects to two of the reasons why speech is special. I have argued that speech facilitates some of the core interests of autonomous agents by rendering their mental contents available to others and vice versa, thereby enabling them to know one another, to cooperate with one another, to investigate the world, and to enhance one's understanding of our environment and our circumstances, and thereby enabling (though not ensuring) moral agency.

The external representation of mental content and its communication plays an especially foundational role in furthering these ends in large part because, in general,

---

47   Philosophers of language often use 'expressives' (and its cognate verb) to refer to speech acts that do more than convey content but also manifest it in a more active, direct way. *See, e.g.,* John R. Searle, *A Taxonomy of Illocutionary Acts, in* Language, Mind, and Knowledge 344 (Keith Gunderson ed., 1975), *reprinted in* John R. Searle, *Expression and Meaning: Studies in the Theories of Speech Acts* 1, 15 (1979); John R. Searle, *What is Language? Some Preliminary Remarks,* 11 Ethics & Pol. 173, 181 (2009). Other speech acts may do even more, as with commissives, performatives, and declarations. *See* J.L. Austin, *How to Do Things With Words* 32–33, 151–57 (1962); Kent Greenawalt, *Speech, Crime, and the Uses of Language* 57–63 (1989). By 'communicate' and its cognates, I mean to capture both the transmission of content as well as the transmission of one's (presumed and often implicit) agreement or belief in that content. Still, despite the familiarity of this use of 'express' in the philosophical literature, I couldn't be more aware that my use of 'express' is not a salutary term in a context in which 'freedom of expression' is right at hand and sometimes is used interchangeably with "freedom of speech." As the better term occurs, so will the substitution.

48   I will not go into detail here about the various fault-lines and strengths of different accounts of this distinction. Rubenfeld's general discussion of the distinction is basically sensible. *See* Rubenfeld, *supra* note 12 at 42–44. Articulating the distinction from the perspective of sorting regulations sensitive and insensitive to it, he asks whether the relevant harm that a regulation targets is caused by the communicative aspect of the expressive act or by some other element of it. I defended something like this approach in Seana Valentine Shiffrin, *Speech, Death, and Double Effect, supra* note 8. I disagree with him in thinking, however, that governmental intent to punish or restrict communication as such is a necessary condition of running afoul of First Amendment protections; we agree that it may be a sufficient condition. *See* Jed Rubenfeld, *The First Amendment's Purpose,* 53 Stan. L. Rev. 767, 775–78, 793–94 (2001).

it is so much more precise and informative than many of its non-essentially communicative, expressive counterparts. I mean something here as mundane as that an explanation of the reasons why one disapproves of another's conduct and a description of the emotional reactions that conduct gives rise to conveys more content than a wordless punch in the nose. Some content conveyed by communication cannot reliably and accurately be conveyed through other means. With respect to the interest in being recognized and known as the person one is and in providing an outlet from the isolation of each mind, curtailments on speech represent a severe incursion on this interest because speech provides unique modes of access to the contents of other minds. I do not mean to include only discursive communication here: a melody or painting of the image in my mind – a external representation of my internal visual imagery – may convey more of my mental contents – including but not limited to my mood – than approving or disapproving behavior; it necessarily conveys more about my private mental contents than silence and its visual analog.

As a general matter, regulations on the non-essentially communicative expression, manifestation or implementation of mental contents *as such* do not preclude the communication or transmission of the mental contents they express. Restrictions on my ability to express my anger through violence do not preclude my transmitting my anger through communicative means: saying I'm angry, detailing my complaints, and depicting my emotional maelstrom through words, images, or sounds. A restriction on the emotion's non-essentially communicative expression does not threaten to isolate me in my mind; a restriction on communication does.

I hasten to add that this general point is perfectly compatible with the recognition that some forms of expression convey more than words, images, or sounds could on certain occasions. It may well be that, on some occasions, the depth of my anger can only be conveyed through violent aggression. I am neither arguing that agents have absolute rights to ensure that (any and all) others fully understand their mental contents on all occasions nor that externalized representations of thoughts always convey more than behavior that acts upon those thoughts in ways different than merely externalizing a representation. But, by and large, speech is special because it is a uniquely specific mechanism for the transmission of mental contents and their discussion, evaluation, development and refinement, independent from and prior to their implementation.

Of course, I do not deny that the transmission of mental contents sometimes immediately effects or implements them: directed at the relevant person, the desire to insult or, in certain contexts, to humiliate or to subordinate can be implemented merely by being communicated. But as a general matter, communicative methods of transmitting mental contents generate the possibility of an intermediate workshop-like space in which one may experiment with, advance tentatively, or try on, revise or reject a potential aspect or element of the self or of one's potential history before directly affirming it through endorsement or implementation.[49] One cannot preface one's thrown punch with 'maybe' or 'consider the possibility' and thereby, make the assault less of a punch in the way that prefatory remarks will qualify a proposition subsequently articulated so that it becomes less than a full-blown assertion. We find both intelligible and significant our abilities effectively to revise, clarify, or even re-

---

49 Nevertheless, on occasion, even purely exploratory communication of thoughts and ideas may have moral significance and may be inappropriate to convey to some people, however explicitly inchoate they are in form.

tract what one has begun to say just using further words.[50] Whereas, I cannot *revise* or *retract* my intentional punch by following it immediately with more violence, cringing, or even with regretful words. A further stream of punches may *clarify* my assault was intentional but beyond that rudimentary clarification, further light – why I threw the punch – will typically require words.

The capacity of speech to be tentative and exploratory – to allow us in a noncommittal way to try on an idea, whether to formulate it at all or to assess its plausibility or fit with oneself – is closely related to and helps to underpin a more familiar idea about the specialness of speech, namely that we must protect the ability to discuss and conceive of even those actions we may reasonably outlaw, because protecting our speech and conception of them permits us to revisit and justify our regulation; thereby, we may retain the ability to assess the aptness and legitimacy of our regulation and to preserve the ability to change course if we are mistaken.

Not all speech stops short of action and I am not arguing there is an especially clear speech/action divide, but there are some special features that hold generally of speech that render it distinct from other forms of autonomous action that go beyond revelation of mental content. These distinctive features, I submit, play some role in explaining why speech is special and why autonomy accounts, especially those focused on the freedom of thought, may reasonably place a particular premium on preserving and protecting speech.

---

50   Although sometimes the further speech will have to follow on immediately to be effective as a retraction as opposed to a later rethinking, our linguistic practice allows us to use speech to formulate and even generate our thoughts without the first stab at articulation rigidly gelling immediately into a final draft: we can try on an idea by articulating it without it immediately sticking to us or representing us. Such tentativeness is less possible with most actions (putting aside the special case of speech acts).

Tercio Sampaio Ferraz Junior

Erosion of Subjective Rights by Reason of Technical Development (Patent, Copyright)

> *Every thing has become so intricate that for its mastery an exceptional degree of understanding is required. For it is not enough any longer to be able to play the game well; but the question is again and again: what sort of game is to be played now anyway?*

> Wittgenstein: Vermischte Bemerkungen[1]

The reflection that I propose in this presentation has the subjective right that refers to the so-called *immaterial property* as its core. Without sticking to dogmatic distinctions between copyright, industrial property rights, and between the normative protections afforded to distinctively different objects such as trademarks and patents, industrial designs, trade names and artworks, what particularly interests me is the authorship phenomenon and the set of legal institutes, which in western tradition, have come to qualify the *auctor* as someone who holds the rights of his/her intellectual, or also called *immaterial* production[2].

The characterization of *copyright* (*Urheberrecht*) constitutes, for the purpose of this reflection, a rich source of doctrinal debate. New cases and the diversity of uses or forms of exploring intellectual products require constant interpretation of the rules that apply to them from doctrines and jurisprudence. More than that, given the quality of innovations as to the exploration regimes and the new forms of distribution via new media technologies, they demand reflection even regarding its *nature*. It is noticed that in doctrinal disputes in favor of one or another regulatory solution for a hypothetical case, the panelists start from contradictory answers about key issues such as: *what is copyright? which product is protected? what is the intellectual work? what is the purpose of its protection?*

The classic structure of copyright defines it as property rights, especially with regard to its economic exploitation.[3] It is property in the broad sense that the phrase acquires in the constitutional text (any property right, or product susceptible to economic valuation). In the words of Portuguese civilist José de Oliveira Ascensão, *"(…) there is a specific constitutional sense of ownership; and this sense does not coincide with the meaning of property in the sense of a right in a thing (real right – dingliches Recht), as prototypically regulated by the Law of Things (Sachenrecht)"*.[4] The property, for example, referred in the Brazilian Constitution (1988), is not confined to real rights (dingliche Rechte); it also

---

1   Ludwig Wittgenstein: Culture and Value/Vermischte Bemerkungen, ed. by Von Wright, Blackwell, 2006, MS 118 20r: 27.8.1937.
2   See K. Larenz: Allgemeiner Teil des Deutschen bürgerlichen Rechts, Beck, München, 1967, p. 299.
3   See Bittar, Carlos Alberto. *Direito de Autor*. 3. ed. Rio de Janeiro: Forense, 2000, p. 10–11.
4   Ascensão, José de Oliveira. *Princípios constitucionais do direito de autor*. Revista Brasileira de Direito Constitucional, n. 5, jan./jun. 2005, p. 434.

covers rights relating to intangible things. And, given that incorporeity, it is understood as *movable thing* (bewegliche Sache).

In this regard, it is worth noting that Brazilian Copyright Law (Law No. 9.610/1998) provides that *"copyrights are reckoned, for legal purposes, as movable things"* (art. 3).

It is known that the increasing use of computing and the consolidation of the world wide web, profoundly changed the possibilities of communication between individuals and private and public corporations, with consequences for the subjective right of property of the author. In fact, these changes in social relationships bring about the perception that the liberty of creating intellectual products go on to depend on possibilities of access to and control of these new technologies and the information disclosed therein.

From this perception, two topics have become essential in the so-called *information networks societies*: on the one hand, with respect to the disclosed information, the individual freedom before the control information and the need for the universalization of access to new information and, on the other hand, with respect to the vehicle information, how to disseminate technological knowledge and promote: both topics, relating to information policy, are closely related to the law, either as a cause for changes in the legal system, and as a result of such changes. The theme of freedom in the virtual space of the communications network[5] deserves therefore a reflection, which causes immediate repercussions on the notion of subjective rights (copyright as subjective right of an author). Anyway, the definition of the opening or enclosure of computer literacy is still done through the definition of subjective rights concerning this knowledge or the product of this knowledge, resulting, however, in significant practical problems.

In fact, as a consequence of these rapid changes in the structure of society and society's very perceptions of these changes, the understanding of the legal order that regulates it is also altered. That is, even without changing the legal order, social changes of this magnitude cause, necessarily, a reinterpretation of the existing valid order. This reinterpretation may be local, regarding a specific rule, as, for instance, the problem of determining whether a contract signed through the Internet should be considered a contract *between absent parties* or *between present parties*; or it may be global regarding the *topoi* that organize the legal system, such as the conceptualization of the notion of freedom within an environment of computer information.

From this perception, the topics, relating to IT policy, are closely related to disputes within the scope of legal dogmatics.

Take, for example, the intense debate over what should be the model or form of the preponderant subjective right, adopted for the use of *software*. The criticisms are mainly based on those who wish to break the proprietary model, which accentuates the patrimonial aspect of subjective rights.

In summary, the controversy boils down to the following. As creation, *softwares* are embedded in the traditional regime of intellectual property and copyright, which grants the author broad powers over his/her creation, including the power to exclude others. However, in this creation, there is a form of knowledge, which becomes inaccessible or too costly to access, when the source code is closed. This dual

---

5   Ferraz Jr., Tercio Sampaio. *A liberdade como autonomia recíproca de acesso à informação*, in: Greco, Marco Aurélio & Martins, Ives Gandra da Silva (org.). Direito e Internet: relações jurídicas na sociedade informatizada. São Paulo, 2001, S. 241–248.

nature, of *creation* or *intellectual product* with a well-defined practical use on one hand and *knowledge* on the other hand, underlies the controversy.

The controversy faces the dogmatic use of language, which is typically legal. We are faced here with the ancient legal concept of the "nature of things". The difficulty lies in attributing the nature of *res* to *softwares*, as the legal common sense does. Treating it as *knowledge* or as a *product* means to grant it features that it would have as a substrate. However, when compared to literary works by law (Law 9609/98, art. 2º), the idea of substrate proves inappropriate.

Therefore, as the literary work does not exist without a deed (or a memorized speech), but is not limited to it, it is also difficult to treat *software* as *res*.

Reflection on immateriality.

The difficulty in treating *software* as *res* or even as an *intangible thing* or yet as an *immaterial object* allows for a quick semantics incursion. The Latin word *materia* results from the attempt of the Romans to translate the Greek *hylé*, which originally meant *wood* (timber, lumber, Holz, Bauholz)[6]. The Spanish word *madera* (in Portuguese: *madeira*) is reminiscent of that use the Latin word (*materia*). In reality, it referred to the wood stored in the workshops of carpenters. In that sense, something *amorphous* (from *morphé*), waiting for the form that it would be given by the carpenter. The *form-matter* dualism, therefore, remits to the term *stuff*, from the verb *to stuff*, as a world ("*stuffed*" *world*) that only comes to be when it becomes the filling (*stuffing*) of something. Hence, the material world as something that fills forms (*stuffing*). The corresponding word in French is *farce* (in German *Füllsel*, *Füllung*, in English *farcing*), whence the possibility of understanding the material world (*stoffliche Welt*) as *Farce* (*farce*)[7].

It is not my intention to enter the well-known philosophical controversies on the subject. Although, in a dangerous synthesis, it can be said that this was the original sense of the form/matter dualism that was lost with the advent of modern experimental science (experiment as the controlled observation of sensory matter: *res*). It is this same dualism, however, that seems to return under the impact of information technology.

I will explain.

If the known tangible universe (houses, furniture, chairs, tables, cigarettes, books, pictures, etc.) was until now the environment of our existence (*Dasein*), orienting oneself in the world meant to move between *things*, separating them, i. e. classifying them into different *forms* (tangible/intangible, movable/immovable, sensitive/intellective, material/immaterial, etc), projecting them in regulated spaces: mine, yours, ours, theirs.

It is precisely this environment that has been changed by this *non-thing* (*Unding*) we now call *information*. For the electronic images on the television screen, data stored on your computer, holograms and programs are so *impalpable* that they seem to entirely escape the possibility of being grasped (*capere*) with our hands even upon understanding/conceiving/grasp (*conceptum*/concept/Begriff). *Information* in terms of

---

6   See Heidegger: *Zollikoner Seminare: Protokolle – Zwiegespräche – Briefe*, Klostermann, Frankfurt am Main, 1987 (II – 3. März. 1966).

7   Vilém Flusser, *Dinge und Undinge: phänomenologische Skizzen*, München/Wien, Carl Hanser Verlag, 1993.

computers has to do with technical equipment that allow the screens to present algorithms (mathematical formulas) *in the form of* images, color images, moving images, even texts, text-files (e-books) that have no matter to be put in a form (*in-formed*, shaped). On the contrary, it has to do with *forms* (numeric codes) that allow other worlds of *forms* to appear. This turns the criteria for distinguishing the *false* from the *true* and, consequently, the *correct* (righteous, *gerecht*) from the *incorrect* (unrichtig, Unrecht), the object of an entirely new task. This happens because, unlike the traditional world in which the *immaterial* (*form*) allowed the *matter* to appear and its adequate condition (*adaequatio*) was taken, commonly, as a record of fact, now we deal only with *virtual* worlds.

> To understand this transformation, the Anthropological strength of *grabbing with your hands* deserves to be underlined. Thus, if the first "industrial revolution" of humanity came about with the invention of the tool as an extension of the hand (the chipped stone, the wooden staff, the arrowhead), the *tool* world was a device dependent (function) on humans for thousands of years. The man-tool makes himself into what he is: the Carpenter does not make tables only, but due to his activity, he becomes a carpenter. Hence, the need for *ars* and *techné*. And, for the sake of stability of the human activity in these conditions, came the need for fences around properties, for territorial boundaries around the city, for laws to govern behavior. In politics, the citizen has a "privilege" (in the social sense, not in the legal sense): he is the subject of *jus civile* and as such participates in the government. There is no need, per se, for an opposition between "rights". The connection of humans to their instrument (tool) is *direct*: disputes between private citizens do not have an original "right" as a foundation, but an *injuria* (in a sacred sense: impurity).

> The Roman *vindicatio*, for example, therefore is not a claiming of a thing (*rei-vindicatio*) in the sense of modern ownership, but a procedural *status* act (*actio*), in other words, an issue on relevance to the community of citizens (*civitas*) by reason of possession of land, (*fundus* approximately meaning, member of the community or *communal*, to which the Greek correspondent is *kleros*)[8].

With the second industrial revolution (a little over two hundred years ago), which came about with the invention of the machine, the world is changed by changing the man/extension relationship, giving rise to the factories. The world of factories is the world of the man-machine. Its existence depends on the machine as a kind of tool designed and built from a scientific theory and that gives meaning to the existence (*Dasein*): the man is no longer, what he does, but he does what the machine determines. To that extent, he is replaceable, works in shifts and to be what he is, he leaves home and goes towards a device (the factory) that dominates him. The relationship is reversed: *Man* becomes a function of the machine. Legally, what is mine and yours, theirs and ours are organized according to captured spaces, abstractly conceived under the title of property: *property right.* Namely, in the eyes of *homo faber*, the work force is only a means to produce an object for use or an object for exchange. In this society, a society dominated by the idea of exchange, the right is re-

---

8   Weber, *Wirtschaft und Gesellschaft*, Tübigen, 1976, II. Halbband, VII, § 2°.

garded as a good that is produced (it is *manufactured*). It is the identification of *jus* with *lex*. The good that is produced through the issue of standards is therefore an object of use, something that is owned, a space that is protected, acquired, which can be assigned. In short, something that has exchange value. Hence its own *space:* the *subjective right* as *a realm, within the man rules independent of any others will.*[9]

But the third, the current industrial revolution, is the one that involves the substitution of machinery for electronics, increasingly miniaturized into units of technological convergence. With this, the topology of the world environment is changed since the spaces of manufacture cease to be important. In its place appears a new relationship between man and world, i. e. the relationship between human being-electronic device, in which, on the one hand, the dependence relationship is reversible: man carries his device (computer, phone) wherever he goes; on the other hand, he acts only as per the capacity of its appliance. In this reversibility, its activity depends on the activity of the other in a different way: neither mechanical nor organic, but in a *network*. In this new way of being, the *device*-man (*Apparatmensch*) seems to *live together* in classical terms, not in the factory as the place of *negotium* (*nec otium, aschole*), but to exist in a kind of *school* (*schole, otium*) to acquire information. *Homo faber* is replaced by a *homo ludens*. He does not deal with things (*res*) any longer or acts with his hands (to *handle*). The existence (*Dasein*) is no longer a *drama* (*actio*) and becomes a spectacle (*show*).

In this new world, the computer memory is a *non-thing* (*Unding*). Not quite *immaterial*, because it is not really *consumable*. Although it exists in enclosed things (silicon chips, *lasers*), is not an object of use[10].

It is not at hand's reach (*at hand, vorhanden*), although it is available (*on hand, zuhanden*). What still needs to be "done", that is, what has to be *apprehended and produced*, is performed automatically by non-things (Unding), by programs.

In these terms, a technically *sui generis* relationship is inaugurated. Although the software written in natural language (source code) and software translated into machine language (object code) are equivalent in terms of computer processing to which they are addressed, they are not equivalent with regard to the information content expressed by them.[11] While the program in *object code* does not express any justification of the functions that the commands perform in the program, the program in natural language (source code) grants access to justification (*metaprogram*) insofar as it enables the understanding of each instruction and its function in the program. This, in turn, allows the programmer to understand the function of the program as a whole (*metametaprogram*).

As the access to source code allows an individual to control the reasons that make the program effective[12], an opportunity arises for the program to be developed as to adapt to new situations or seek a solution to new problems. This feature is relevant in view of the „defeasible" nature of the justification, in other words, new data

9   Savigny, Friedrich Carl von. *System des heutigen römischen Rechts*, I. 1840, S. 7 (*ein Gebiet, in welchem der Mensch unabhängig von jedem fremden Willen zu herrschen hat*).

10   Flusser, Vilém. *Dinge und Undinge: phänomenologische Skizzen*. München; Wien, 1993.

11   Sartor, Giovanni. "Proprietà e comunione del sapere informatico". In M. Bertani (ed.) *Open Source*, Milano, Giuffré, 126–153. References are from the manuscript available at >http://www.cirsfid. unibo.it/~sartor/ GSCirsfidOnlineMaterials/GSPublications.pdf<.

12   There is also reverse engineering that constitutes an inductive method of reconstruction of the program in natural language from the machine language.

or new practical requirements can make information content not justified.[13] A certain effective knowledge may prove inept to explain phenomena or to produce successful results in different application contexts, so that knowledge is not a static set of information but a dynamic process of revision and improvement of such content. In other words, *industrial production* is converted into a complex *network* that makes use of information from (improperly speaking) several *auctores*.

Thus, there is a qualitative distinction between accessing the program only in object code and the access that includes its source code. In the first case, access to *software* is a simple *computing solution*, where the information content is accessed simply as the program's rules. In the second case, access to the *software* is a "*metaprogram*" (*computer knowledge*).

In this new condition, the human being is under discussion not as a *persona* of concrete actions, but as a performer (*Spieler*), which does not *act*, but *types*. What is left of his hands are just the fingers (fingertips). Instead of capturing (*fassen*) and conceiving (*auffassen*), seeing (*schauen*) and playing (*schauspielern*).

Therefore, in short, let's point out the elements of the computing condition:

a) a new vehicle: computing environment (electronic device);
b) a new way of playing: digitalization;
c) a system for instantaneous and global communication;
d) a "device" human being (*Apparatmensch*).

Hence the following "*un-thingnification*" (*Verundinglichung*) of intellectual/immaterial creations in computer terms: *bit* as intangible support (according to Brazilian art. 7 of Law 9610/98).

Indeed, the notion of *intangibility* is inadequate, since it is built from the nuclear physical perception of reality. Properly, the *bit* is not the denial of the tangible (*tangere* as *touching with your fingers*). Therefore, a non-thing (*Unding*) is mentioned. The popularized term to express this new state or form of being is *virtual*. The *virtual*, in this new sense, is not tangible or intangible; nor does it bear reference to the mere physical possibility by some skill; *virtual* not as a product of *virtus*/virtue, but as *ludic*, according to a *code*.

Hence the problem of protecting the contents: not only intellectual creations, but also the database.

Take, for instance, the concept of reproduction. Before it was the setting in a tangible medium (print), now it is the electronic access: storage in digital form as an equivalent to reproduction.

This puts in check the storage as a temporary fix, transitory or incidental in nature. This applies, for example, to reproduction for teaching purposes. Another example is remote access as a copy (electronic processing and computer use).

Note, then, the convergence of three technical elements: digitalization, compression, virtual transmission means. Faced with the virtual world, even when using artificial storage mechanisms, comes the question of criteria for selection of information to be processed: operations are carried out in groups of human and artificial elements, whose outcome cannot be attributed to a single *auctor*.

---

13   Concerning "defeasibility" of knowledge and justification before new circumstances see Lewis, David. "Elusive Knowledge", *Australasian Journal of Philosophy* 74, 4 (1996), pp. 549–67. See also "Widerlegung" in science as pointed by Karl Popper (*Conjecturas e Refutações*, Coimbra, 2003).

Hence the problem faced today by the theory of the law (*Rechtslehre*): how to deal with the *subjective right of the author* (copyright) in the computer world?

Profile of copyright on *software*

I start with the *software*, which use can be subject to rules, that, allowing or preventing access to the source code, may define its cognitive or merely functional character. This way, the legal regime adopted defines the nature of the use of *software* and user interface with this intellectual/intangible product.

Initially, I use legal profile assigned by the Brazilian legislation on the rights to *software* and the profile defined in the *Trade Related Aspects of Intellectual Property Rights-TRIP/GATT 47 to the right to software*. In Brazil, as in the *Berne Convention*, this right is treated as copyright, being the *software* equivalent to literary works (Access to Information Act, Law 9609/98, art. 2). Such qualification, as copyright (the Brazilian Law of Copyright, Law 9610/98) and not of Industrial Intellectual Property (Brazilian Law 9279/96), brings an important legal consequence: what it protects is not the *res*, which specifies the creation, but creation itself, expressed in a certain way (artistic). It is this aesthetic sense of the work and its originality, which justify the protection of copyright through the assignment of rights concerning the work.[14] These rights over works (and not the works themselves) are considered personal property (Law 9610/98, art. 3).

As an expression of the intellect, the work reflects and has an intimate connection with the author's personality, hence the moral dimension of such right, protected by warranties such as: claiming authorship of the work, having the author's name announced, keeping it unpublished, opposing to changes or acts that may harm the author's reputation, withdraw the work from circulation or suspending any form of use previously permitted (Law No. 9610/98, art. 24/also Berne Convention). According to the Brazilian Law of Copyright, such rights are *inalienable* because they are related to the very personality of the creator (the law refers to inalienability and impossibility to renounce, art. 27). With regard to *software*, Law 9610/98 partially waives the author's moral rights, remaining only the right to demand the paternity of the work and that of opposing to the reproductions that offend its honor or reputation (art. 2, § 1).

On the other hand, there is the protection of property interests that the author may have with respect to his creation. That is the order of the rules that grant the author the exclusive right of use, fruition and disposal (Law 9610/98 art. 28).[15] Under the legal system, authors are granted full powers to exploit their works and dispose of their exclusive rights of use, which is incorporated by the legislation on *software*.

As regards such patrimonial rights, the holder of a copyright is the subject of distinct levels of rules: (i) *primarily* (rules of conduct) the holder of copyright holds, with exclusivity, the right to use the program, i. e., run it in a machine, copy, distribute and modify it (permission of use); (ii) *secondarily* (competence rules) the holder of

---

14   Bittar, Carlos Alberto. *Direito de Autor*, Forense, São Paulo, 3a ed. 2001, pp. 30–31.
15   For the German Law: Larenz, p. 299.

copyright holds the power to alter the rules that define its system of use, granting these rights to third parties in the whole or in part.[16]

By legal definition adopted in Brazil (Law 9609/98, art. 1)[17], such rights concern both the source code and object code and are independent of the registration of the work (art. 2, § 3).

If the copyright is exclusive to the source code and the program in natural language is the key to the justification of the program, would there be, here, an exclusive right to knowledge or the idea behind the *software*?

At this point, it should be noted that rights (exclusive use, copy, modification, etc.) fall back on the intellectual creation, i. e. the form of expression, not on the underlying knowledge. So that, in the field of scientific works, "... *the protection will fall on literary or artistic form, not covering their scientific or technical content ...*" (Law 9610/98, art. 7 § 3). There is no property rights for the knowledge involved in creating the *software*, once the idea is not subject to protection as copyright law (Law No. 9610/98, art. 8º, inc. I)[18]. Thus, although it is perfectly possible to implement the rule of protection to the form of expression for literary works and at the same time, allow the propagation of knowledge or culture, as a non-appropriable product, in the case of *softwares*, in which the language is coded for execution through a machine, copyright for the source code closes an apparent contradiction.

For example, a *software* can successfully solve the problem of making a robot find the exit of a room by using more than one sensor for receiving information about presence/absence of obstacles. Without access to the source code, however, knowledge can remain private to the programmer as could a particular idea of paraconsistent logic (which efficiently processes contradictory information) used as the underlying system of the programming. This knowledge, under Copyright Law, may not be appropriated (there is no ownership), but the *Software* Law allows it to become inaccessible to others.

The apparent conflict would be resolved when one observes that knowledge can be contained in the *software* itself, in the sense that only the owner has access to the justification of the program, but does not own it, i. e. you cannot market it or legally prevent it from being used by others. But the difference, therefore, is *de facto* not *legal*. If the knowledge contained in literary works is immediately disclosed and becomes common with its economic exploitation, in the case of *software,* that knowledge can continue to be the copyright owner's even if its use is licensed to third parties (where the license only allows for the execution of the program in object code).

Thus, any extension of rights conferred by the author on his program to a third party is relevant in determining *their function (right)* as a propagator of knowledge or as a simple computing solution. This power of the author to modify the legal use of

16 For a discussion of the distinction between standards of conduct and competence in subjective rights, see Alf Ross. *Sobre el Derecho y la Justicia*, Eudeba, Buenos Aires, 1994, p. 164 et seq. For a conceptualization of primary and secondary rules to explain the regulatory system, see Hart, The Concept of Law, Oxford, 1997, p. 79 et seq.

17 Law 9609/98, art. 1: Computer program is the expression of an organized set of instructions in *natural* or *codified* language, contained in physical support of any kind, of necessary use in automatic information processing machines, devices, instruments or peripheral equipment, based on digital analog technique, to make it function in the manner and for specific ends of 11 (not in the original underlined).

18 According to the Berne Convention, the "*idea*" is not subject to protection as "*copyright*".

software is exercised through the license agreement (Law 9609/98, art.9), by which *software* rights are granted to third parties (action standards, as permission of use, distribution, modification, etc).

Note that in the license agreement, the owner retains the power to change the legal status of the work, that is, unlike what happens with the intellectual property, in which the *res* (as if it were *res*: thing, *Ding*), once transferred, will integrate the assets of the purchaser and *the licensed work continues under the purview of the author.*[19] However, there is the possibility of total or partial assignment of property rights, in which case the purchaser becomes the owner of copyright (one may use, change the rules of use and oppose to use by others), incorporating its prerogatives, except for moral rights (Law9610/98, art. 49).

Legal regimes for use of the software

The existing rules on copyright laws and *Software* rights do not pre-determine the usage regime of the computer program, whether proprietary or free, granting, rather, the copyright holder broad disposing powers over the work. Such powers are compatible with both regimes. I thus examine some license arrangements relevant to this presentation.

Permission to use the *software* can only cover the execution of the program in object code, in which case the licensee does not develop any cognitive activity and only „consumes" a certain computing solution.

It may also cover the use of source code and the right to study the architecture of the program and adapt it to the needs of the licensee. In this case, the licensee acquires and is interested not only in the use of a specific solution but also in certain computing knowledge. This is the so-called *open source software: free software*. Remember that the subjective right rests with the object of creation, expressed in natural language, and access to knowledge is a factual result of exercising that right.

The legal regime for the assumption that free *software* is not limited to *open source*, including, besides the right to run the program and study its source code, the right to reproduce, modify and redistribute the software. These permissions to third parties, which consist of primary standards, are added to the so-called *copyleft*, in other words, the requirement that any derivations developed by third parties be licensed with the same rights, or what is the same thing, the prohibition of altering, in the derivations, the open use regime of the original work. Therefore, *copyleft* is the revocation of third party competence regarding the disposition of the derivative work.[20] This prohibition (or revocation) acts at the secondary normative level.

This possibility of revoking the powers and rights of exclusive use of the author of the derivative work on the derivation does not imply violation of the prerogatives of the authorized author? Although, admittedly, the author of the derivative work is the holder of the rights to derivation, the derivation itself depends, according to Law 9610/98, art. 29, inc. III, on prior written permission of the original work. By the argument *a majore ad minus*, if the originating author may prohibit the derivation, he

---

19   Bittar, op. cit. p. 5.
20   It is, for example, the regime adopted by the GNU GPL (GNU General Public License), considered by the Free Software Foundation (FSF) as a prototype for the definition of free software. For this paper, we will consider as free the licensing that meets the FSF's definition (according to: >http://www.gnu.org/philosophy/free-sw.html<).

may condition the use of the authorized derivation. Copyright, therefore, still maintains the original author's rights on the derivation.

Specifically for *software*, bearing in mind that the moral right to revoke uses of previously authorized uses did not survive, the conditions for the use of derivative work must be present at the time of the authorization. *Software* Law is even clearer about the possibility of conditioning, stating that "*the rights of the authorized derivations by the holder of the rights of the computer program, including its economic exploitation, will be owned by the authorized person who does so, except in contractual stipulation stating otherwise*" (Law 9609/98, art. 5). Thus, the contract may "revoke" the property rights and jurisdiction of the derivative author to determine the usage regime of the derivation by agreement between original author and author of the derivation. Obviously, the author of the derivative work still maintains moral rights to claim authorship and to oppose the offensive uses of his derivation.

With *copyleft*, established as a condition for permission of use, the derivations eventually produced, become effectively communitarian, in the sense that everyone is allowed to use in all its forms and no one is given the power to amend such classification rules. The hypothesis of free *software* is significant because it thus creates an effective chain of creation and production of computer knowledge. In fact, in this chain, only the originating producer holds the power to modify the free regime of the derivations. The derivations produced by the original author himself may be appropriated, since, obviously, he does not celebrate the license and is not subject to *copyleft*. Therefore, it is possible to create junctions in the communitarian production chain so that the same *software* can be developed in the free regime and have one of its derivations appropriated by the original author, which is then distributed in the closed regime.[21]

This form of exercising the competence of modifying the *software*, which makes its use *free* turns to the dissemination of the program and the knowledge that underlies it, in terms of developing a communitarian and mutual cognitive activity. The original computing solution is thus subjected to a dynamic of adaptations and derivations, so that the underlying knowledge is constantly improved and these improvements are not owned by any user, but remain shared by the community of programmers (rather than *negotium: nec otium*, knowledge/school: *scholé, otium*).

Non exclusive Exercise of the subjective right of the author

Thus, an important issue to address consists in the character of resignation or not the exclusive rights of copyright, through licensing of the software under a free regime. For the integrated cognitive activity triggered by the opening of the original software can be seen as an alternative mode of production to the model of property and market. As Yochai Benkler shows, in this alternative model, which he calls "*commons-based peer-production*", rather than production meaning cost to be paid by the exclusive appropriation of the benefits, the costs of hiring programmers and pro-

---

21   See Boyle, James. "*The Second Enclosure Movement and the Construction of the Public Domain*", available at >http://www.law.duke.edu/journals/66LCPBoyle<; Rifkin, J. *The age of Access: How the shift from ownership to access is transforming modern life*, London, Penguin, 2000; Lessig, L. *Free Culture: How Big Media Uses Technology and the Law to Lock Down Culture and Control Creativity*. New York, Penguin, 2004; Benkler, Y. "Coase's Penguin, or Linux and the nature of the firm", *The Yale Law Journal*, 2002. Available at: >http://www.benkler.org/CoasesPenguin.PDF<.

gram testing are reduced to zero, and there is still sufficient motivation (given the large number of participants) for agents to develop the productive activity.[22]

This affects the perception of the work as a manifestation of the personality of the creator *versus* new technologies. Especially when the creative act is not performed by a *subject/persona,* but by a program (*software*) capable of producing another.

If the 19th Century understood the creative process as marked by the personality of the author, today, the creations require updates and upgrades, or by virtue of the interactive process (internet), or creation of derivative works (*multimedia* technology: text + image + drawings + sounds + photos + programs/*software*).

Moreover, not only man but also *the machine itself „creates" works of aesthetic nature, where there is copyright without the author:* who is the author? the creator of the program?

Thus, arose in place of personalization, the functional character of the work and, consequently, the depersonalization: what determines the work is not the personal authorship, but the function it exerts.

Hence, for example, the need for an effort to identify global identification systems for protected content, such as the so-called *tattoo* (type of mark or sign) for the opportunity to download a file.

Thus, the cultural object is not independent of the creator or those who have access to it. It *is* in terms of communication. Hence, its understanding as a necessarily social object. Not *social* in terms of individual interaction (nuclear individuals), but access communication system that only has a social purpose in order to promote *virtual* access to culture: as a social product, it *is* only in the dimension of *access (to access).*

This questions the concept of originality, an apparent questioning in the case of multimedia. It is not about the quality of a substance – the work – either, but a functional reference of the work, itself perceived as a function of the triad *author/work/public.* Hence the uniqueness of the setting, with reference to central decision of disclosing intellectual creation or not, in other words, to make it a *work* or not. By law, only the creator is given to start the triad, i. e., the right *"to conserve the unpublished work"* (mentioned in Brazilian Law, art. 24, III). Strictly speaking, however, in the functional sense, it is the creation that is unpublished. The work exists only in the relationship with the public.

This affects the notion of *exclusivity:* right to exclusive use *versus* virtual availability.

Here, the introduced communicative relationship is also regulated so as to safeguard the author against public acts, such as the right to oppose any act that may affect the integrity of the work so as to affect him in his honor or reputation (art. 24, IV). In fact, the functionalization of *exclusivity* makes us realize that an important rule for this communicative relationship is ensuring the later manifestations of the author, through the work, as the right to *"modify the work, before or after use"* (art. 24, V). However, in this relationship, the public is safeguarded as well. Thus the author's right to interrupt the communicative relationship, denying public access by *"withdrawing the work from circulation or suspending any form of previously authorized use"* is subject to a justification grounded in the right to honor. Or the interruption of the relationship, by the author, who has a privileged position to set forth his will univocally, in

---

22   Benkler, Yochai, Coase's Penguin, or Linux and the nature of the firm. *Yale Law Journal.* Available at: >http://www.benkler.org/CoasesPenguin.PDF<.

regard to the group of undefined individuals comprising the "public", will be admitted only *"when circulation or use imply offense to his reputation and image"* (art. 24,VI).

This last rule is clearly directed towards the protection of the *right* to public *access* to the work. This, in turn, is affected, problematically, by the concept of private use in case of *downloading*.

This has to do with access as a faculty to be controlled. Take, for instance, the relationship of the provider in the balance between property rights and right to public use.

With this, we notice the presence of a new key concept: *access*, where there is a new sense of freedom. And, consequently, a significant change in the legal perception of *subjective rights*.

Subjective right: conclusion

The classic notion of subjective rights was typically built on three factors: (i) a privilege or exclusive advantage to the holder that is opposed by a duty of another or of all others; (ii) the jurisdiction or power to change this legal situation; (iii) the power to start procedures upon infringement of these rights by others.[23]

These typical traits of subjective rights are based on the notion of freedom as conceived by economic liberalism founded on free enterprise and free market and where the State played only a protective role for those freedoms. It is a common knowledge that freedom in this concept has a double meaning: of no impediment and autonomy. In a negative sense, of no impediment, freedom has a connotation of resistance, being free is to ensure a space for action that resists the free action of others. But freedom also appears in a positive sense of autonomy, of being able to determined for something and through the will use that determination valid for others.

The result of this freedom, built in the modern era, is the opening to opportunities for the individual to employ his products in the market without external constraints. In fact, this freedom is exercised through the property and rights to such property, hence the notion of privilege or advantage (i). Hence, also, the State's protection against violations of these privileges, through the initiation of certain procedures (ii). Autonomy is institutionalized in the figure of the contract, which is reflected in the construction of the subjective right as the power of disposition of the rights (iii).

This still usual dogmatic construction of subjective rights is guided by rules that assign duties and competences to individuals. But we must bear in mind that this constitutes a construction, and it instrumentalizes these rules. It is not easy in the current context, to argue that the subjective right constitutes an entity or substrate distinct from the rules, or that it contains the essence that would comprise those three hallmarks.

Thus, the typical notion of subjective right meets a certain conception of freedom, which obviously endured and continues to endure mutations. With these mutations, the legal order or the interpretation of the legal order changes, which allows for a reinterpretation of the very notion of subjective right with the underlying con-

---

23   This is a simplification according to the dominant legal theory. See Larenz, op. cit. p. 216.

ception of freedom as a common place (topos) that guides this interpretation.[24] Thus, there is hardly a substantial unity of subjective rights, but legal situations in which the set of applicable rules allows for talk about subjective rights with their typical or atypical features, with respect to its construction in the modern era.[25]

In the scope of the information society, the classic notion of freedom as a space for action not restricted by the freedom of others, which manifests itself on products whose use excludes the use of others, tends to suffer revision. As a matter of fact, it throws us onto a limit of abstraction, whose concept seems to go beyond an atypical alternative use. In the computing field, in the absence of physical limitation, we deal with property (information and knowledge), whose use by one does not exclude use by others. In fact, it comes to be conceptually impossible to define that "one". Not even as a "collective subject". That is, the space of action may continue to be free regardless of the action of others. More than that, in this sphere, the action space for the subject is relevant in that it allows for *communication* with others. Cyberspace[26], for example, is only built as each space of action for each subject is designed to communicate with the others, without which the environment itself becomes meaningless.

It is not quite "space" as *res materialis* or even *immaterialis*. Although it does not remove us from the space in which we live, culturally it overcomes it (*aufhebt*).

We experience, of course, several uses for the word *space*: geographical or territorial, space in the sense of physics, space as social, religious environment, regulating space (e. g.: *domicile* as opposed to *residence, jurisdiction*), political space (nationality). In common usage, these uses interact, which allows us to deal with the spaces through categories. The so-called cyberspace, in this context, seems to release us from the territorial bonds, of regulatory jurisdictions or policies (*rechtsfreier Raum*), the finiteness of a *place*, when casting us in the virtual ubiquity, which affects time in terms of simultaneity/speed. This causes legal negotiations (*Rechtsgeschäfte*) to be made without simultaneous physical presence and yet with simultaneous confirmatory wills: *speedier and speedier webs the spider its spider web around the world*[27].

From this perception of change in the conception of freedom in the computing field, whose exercise takes place in a relationship of reciprocity, Wolfgang Hoffmann-Riem argues that *"the right to informational self-determination is, therefore, not a privatistic defense right of the individual who opposes part of society, but aims to allow each one to participate in communication processes. Others [human beings] are the social context in which the limits of each one's personality expands: autonomy, rather than anomie, of the individual is the directing image of the Constitution. Autonomy should be possible in vital spaces that are socially connected, where freedom of communication – or better: common freedom cannot be oriented to a limiting concept of protection to egocentric expansion, but should be understood as the exercise of freedom in reciprocity. This freedom is not to be free of others, but freedom through others."*[28]

---

24   For an analysis of the historical evolution of the concept of freedom and subjective right, see Ferraz Junior, Tercio Sampaio. Direito e Liberdade, in *Estudos de Filosofia do Direito*, Atlas, 2nd ed. 2003, pp. 75 to 132.

25   According to Alf Ross, op. cit. p. 172 et seq.

26   This expression appeared by the first time in a science fiction book by William Gibson.

27   *Immer schneller webt die Spinne ihr Netz um die Welt. Süddeutsche Zeitung (18.07.1995)*, cited by Flechsig, Norbert *in* Rechtsprobleme internationaler Datennetze, Becker, Jürgen (org.), Nomos, Baden-Baden, 1996, p. 57.

28   Wolfgang Hoffmann-Riem. Rechtliche Rahmenbedingungen in *Der neue Datenschutz*, Helmut Bäumler (org.), Neuwied/Kriftel, Luchterhand, 1998, p. 13.

In fact, one can go further, because this way, it changes the ancient principle that human dignity is focused on individual freedom and one's freedom ends where another's freedom begins. Indeed, the environment where communication and reciprocity are means for individual achievement, dignity focuses on living in open communication with each other. And here we speak of "means" not as a "*tool*" but as "*environment*". Thus, freedom in the information society could be well captured by the phrase "one's freedom begins where the freedom of others begins."[29] Based on this freedom, the lawful subject (Rechtssubjekt) is thought not as an agent that dominates the computing products, but as an agent that communicates *in the midst* of such property. While the exploration of the manufactured property (the machine world) is exercised with the exclusion of others, the retribution due to the recognition of the value of digital authorship is not exercised with the exclusion of the public, but begins with it and assumes it.

For example: take a form, any linkable numerical algorithm; introduce this form, through a computer, in a *plotter*, fill this form as much as possible with particles, and observe: "worlds" will emerge.

But with one important difference.

In the digital world, the intellectual or cultural or immaterial product, whatever it may be called, ceases to be the result of a process in which what is given (*Gegebenes*) is converted into something that is made (*Gemachtes*). In this process, human activity diverts (*entwendet*) something (*Gegebenes*) from its natural course, to convert it (*umwenden*) into something manufactured (*Gemachtes*), to give it applicability (*anwenden*) in a market of exchanges (object of exchange) and use it (*verwenden*) as its own (object of use). In the digital process, it is just a *spin* (*wenden*) of one (pro)*gram* into another (pro)*gram*.

Observe again, for example, the so-called "free" exploration of the software. In the relationship established by the free *software* license, all licensees, *patients* of the exercise of their right to exploit the work, are also *agents* in the sense that they consume the computing solution and at the same time, at least potentially, produce it and make it circulate. Moreover, to any member of the chain of licenses it is possible to seek judicial protection against violations of those rights, in other words, for the protection of this reciprocal freedom. The violation occurs precisely in the attempt to appropriate, i. e. the exclusion of agents members of this free activity. These rules give the subjective right a distinct configuration from the classic: the author does not lose the advantage of using the product, but this advantage is no longer a privilege that excludes the other, to include it.[30]

The third revolution, the digital revolution, thus seems to be destroying the old public space. Ortega y Gasset[31] has been overcome: In the current revolution of the

---

29   Ferraz Junior, Tercio Sampaio, A liberdade como autonomia recíproca de acesso à informação, in *Direito e Internet*, RT, São Paulo, 2001, pp. 241–247.

30   Although there is the possibility of privatistic (exclusive) exploration, this is not the only way to benefit from intellectual creation. The benefit may be granted by the very interaction of an undetermined number of programmers who can enhance the creation, testing the work and developing it to solve new problems and adapt the original program to new requirements. In turn, this communication and the spread of use of software to create conditions for that computing knowledge to be standardized, which could mean a gain for the creator as it dominates the standardized technology.

31   La rebelión de las masas, in Obras Completas, II vol., Madrid, 1947, p. 19 (*yo soy yo y mis circunstancias*).

masses – which occurs now – the circumstance becomes *ego* and the *ego* becomes circumstance.

With the substitution of writing by digits, the world of images replaces the world of concepts; the public space of the right becomes the space of appearance in a new sense: *show*, spectacle. Indeed, instead of *reading*, *roaming*.[32]

In conclusion: for Helmut Coing, in the early 60's (1962), the concept of subjective right, even if not for everything, seemed essential for a scientific understanding (Erfassung) of private law. Accordingly, it still seemed to be essential to determine to whom the utility (Nutzung) and the power to dispose (Verfügungsgewalt) of a specific legal position (Rechtsposition) would be transferred (übertragen) to define who is a legitimate part (*wem das Recht zusteht*), in other words, to whom the right (wem das Recht zusteht) belongs to, above all to serve to maintain each one's freedom (*Freiheit des einzelnen*) in society[33].

Subjective rights are emerged and developed in a *structural* conception of law as a concatenated system of concepts, In the computer world where the sense of communitarian relations is inherent, its concept seems to slightly slip into the sense of *subjective legal situation* (Duguit)[34] and from there to precarious positions that *homo ludens* occupies in the *network*, more in the direction of a *functional* conception (Bobbio)[35]. This happens, however, in a truly disturbing manner. For, in a world where the amount of information is highly complex, the capacity of an individual memory overcomes the subjective situation, hence the problem of selecting information and the necessary actions in groups composed of human and artificial elements.

That is, the cultural revolution brought by the digital world makes us realize that, slowly, old and firm notions, such as *subjective rights*, in addition to no longer being "the central concept of private law" (der zentrale Begriff *des Privatsrechts* – von Tuhr: 1910 – *apud* Coing), is no longer able to handle this disintegration into pieces (*bits*) of the complete structure of things. For the cultural and, to that extent, the legal revolution, which enables us to build alternative and parallel universes to the supposedly *given* world (*Gegebenes*), converts the *sub-jecti* – single individuals – in *pro-jecti* of several worlds.

---

32 Take, for example, the preservation of the activity of informing, representing and negotiating, which in good faith, justifies in a democracy, the existence of certain limits (rights) for full immediacy of the transparency of diplomatic activity, as shown by Celso Lafer in his paper Vazamentos, sigilo, diplomacia: a propósito do significado do WikiLeaks, in *Política Externa*, vol. 19, n° 4, mar/abr/ maio, São Paulo, 2011, p. 12: *"The great sea of information leaked by WikiLeaks has been revealing more or less questionable conduct. (...) The scandal, in addition to being a part of the political battle may also provide entertainment and trivialization of what is discussed in public spaces, generating, in the words of Mario Vargas Llosa, an 'informative exhibitionism' that, besides questioning the dominance of the private, hinders the good functioning of democratic institutions. I would therefore say, in conclusion, that the WikiLeaks phenomenon is primarily a precedent that, facilitated by the Digital Revolution, manufactured a type of risk that undermines the fullness of the activity of informing, negotiating and representing the diplomatic function. I believe that not even human beings, in their unique individuality, or the institutionalized diplomatic activity can support, with ease, the daily immediacy of the lights of full transparency".*

33 Zur Geschichte des Privatrechtssytems, Frankfurt am Main, 1962, p. 54.

34 Traité de Droit Constitutionel, 3rd ed., tome I, p. 307 et seq.

35 Dalla struttura alla funzione, Milano, Edizone di Comunità, 1977.

Carl Wellman

The Internationalization of the IVR

The founders of the IVR believed that progress in the philosophy of law and social philosophy required the cooperation of scholars from many nations. Hence in 1907 they created an international journal to be a central organ for the consideration of scientific investigation of the entire civilized world concerning those disciplines. And two years later they established an international association for the care and furthering of philosophy of law and social philosophy in all civilized countries. Although all three of the original presidents were German, indeed all Berliners, the membership list of 1909 features a committee of fifteen representatives of countries outside of Germany, including the United States, Argentina, Brazil and India. Clearly their intention was to create a world-wide scholarly organization.

However, the process of building a global association began slowly and is still unfinished. The IVR held its first congress in Berlin in May of 1910. The academic program consisted of fewer than a dozen presentations followed by discussions from the floor. Of the 76 participants, only thirteen were from outside Germany and none from outside Europe.

The first IVR World Congress was held in October 1957 in Saarbrücken. Its size and format were essentially the same as the previous congresses. The academic program consisted of a small number of presentations followed by discussion, and there were about 100 participants in all.

The 1975 Saint Louis World Congress, organized by Gray Dorsey, introduced a radically new kind of international congress. In addition to a somewhat larger number of lectures followed by discussions in plenary sessions, it included working groups in which a rapporteur summarized a set of papers on a general theme to set the stage for more extensive discussion. Thus, more than 120 papers were presented and subsequently published. There were more than 275 participants representing at least 48 countries. The Saint Louis congress served as a pattern for the world congresses that followed in a way that has greatly increased the internationalization of the IVR. About 550 members participated in the 2003 Lund World Congress and over 600 in the 2005 Granada World Congress. And about 900 members have registered for this Frankfurt World Congress. With this increase in numbers of participants came a greater diversity of nations with a voice in IVR congresses.

Although during the first half-century of its existence several groups of German members of the IVR became sub-ordinate sections of the International Association, there was no provision for the formation of national sections until the Constitution of 1959. Almost immediately national sections were founded in Finland and Germany. By 1964, there were national sections in Australia, Austria, Brazil, Finland, Germany, Mexico, The Netherlands, Spain, Turkey and the United States. These sections contributed to the internationalization of the IVR in two important ways. First, they distributed the activities of the IVR more widely in the world by organizing their own conferences and publishing collections of papers presented. Second, they recruited members from a variety of nations into the International Association. Thus, by 1978 the number of national sections had doubled to twenty and the membership of the IVR had grown to more than 700. Although the majority of these members were European, the Japanese section had 78 members and the North American section 150. Today the number of national sections has more than doubled again so that there are now over forty, including 16 outside Europe. Thus, the IVR has national sections on every continent except Antarctica.

Some of these national sections have introduced a new dimension of internationalization by organizing regional conferences. For example, members of the Danish, Finnish, Norwegian and Swedish sections have met together to hold Nordic conferences. For several years the Austrian and Hungarian sections held joint meetings and published the papers presented and discussed. And in 2000 the Chinese national section hosted members of the Japanese and Korean sections in the Third Asian Symposium in Jurisprudence.

The internationalization of the IVR has been reflected in its organizational structure. Before the introduction of national sections, the administration of the IVR was carried out by its three presidents. Although there was an advisory committee that would normally represent a number of nations, it had no control over the administrative actions of the Presidents. The constitution of 1959 introduced a new administrative body, an Executive Committee consisting of a President, two Vice-Presidents and six additional members. It specified that the membership of this Committee must be international, and in practice this has meant that only under special circumstances could more than one of its members be from the same country. The constitution of 1979 recognized the increased number of national sections by enlarging the Executive Committee to include the President, four Vice-Presidents and fifteen additional members. But because its membership remained relatively fixed, an increasing number of national sections felt excluded from any significant voice in the administration of the International Association. Therefore, the constitution of 1987 introduced a Nomination Committee consisting of the members of the outgoing Executive Committee, a member from each national section that has no member on the Executive Committee and one member to represent the members of the IVR who do not belong to any national section. Thus, although not all national sections can have a member on the Executive Committee, they can all take part in selecting those who will serve in this capacity.

Creating and maintaining an effective international association requires solutions to a number of serious practical problems. One problem that has confronted the IVR is the limited competence of its members and administrators in foreign languages. For over three decades, almost all of the articles published in its journal were written in German. Only in volume 38 were articles in French and English as well as German regularly accepted for publication. Although these are the only constitutionally established languages, articles in Spanish have been published since 1991. Obviously, this excludes the native languages of a great many members, but it has proven impractical to increase the number of languages beyond these four.

The problem of limited competence in foreign languages is much more serious in conducting congresses. Reading a paper in a foreign language is one thing; listening to a lecture in a foreign language another. One can read at one's own pace, perhaps consulting a dictionary from time to time, but the flow of spoken words moves forward irresistibly, often too rapidly to be comprehended by many members of the audience. Participating in the give and take of discussion requires an even higher level of linguistic competence. At least by the 1971 Brussels World Congress, there was simultaneous translation of the main lectures into the three official languages of the IVR – German, French and English. Occasionally there was also translation into the language of the host country, for example Japanese in the 1987 Kobe World Congress. However, simultaneous translation has never been available in the many working group discussions where it is most needed. More recently organizers of world congresses have found themselves unable to raise funds sufficient to pay the very high cost of professional translators and the necessary equipment. Therefore, world congresses are now conducted almost entirely in English. Fortunately, English is increasingly becoming something like a global language.

When he was President of the IVR, Chaim Perelman decided that the business of the Executive Committee should be conducted entirely in English. I have always been grateful that this decision was made before the administration of the IVR moved to the United States, for the only languages in which I am competent are English and American. However, this is the only practical policy, for English is the only language which all the members of an international group, like the Executive Committee, can speak and understand easily.

A second practical problem that arose in the internationalization of the IVR is maintaining effective communications. It is obviously essential to keep the members of any international association informed of its activities. From the first, future congresses were announced in the *Archiv* and members invited to attend. Soon other information for members was added, especially reports on past congresses, reports on the election of officers of the IVR and occasionally membership lists. Subsequently announcements of forthcoming conferences organized by sections of the IVR and reports of their past conferences and other activities were published in this journal. However, this method of communication was not very effective. Not many members of the IVR subscribed to its journal and because it was very expensive only a minority of academic libraries did either. Moreover, there was a considerable time-lag between the preparation of copy for publication and the arrival of the journal in any library. Hence, published information was often out-of-date by the time members of the IVR had access to it.

Therefore, the IVR introduced a Newsletter in 1976. Originally it was printed by the Secretary General four times each year, mailed in batches to the national sections and sent by them to its members. The general policy was that official documents and information that ought to be on record would be published in the *Archiv* and information of more immediate but perhaps less lasting interest would be circulated more rapidly in the Newsletter. Although this improved communication with the members of the IVR, international postal service was not always prompt and some national sections failed to forward copies of the Newsletter to their members. Today Newsletters are posted on the official IVR website so that they are immediately available to all members who own or have access to computers.

Unfortunately, this does not completely solve the problem of communication within the IVR. Editors of the *Archiv* and the Newsletter can publish only as much information as they receive. Some national sections never send information about their officers and activities to either publication, and others do so infrequently. Even the Secretary General sometimes neglects to forward important information about the IVR to the editors of its journal or its Newsletter.

One especially important sort of information concerns invitations to future world congresses. This includes the location and dates of the congress, the topics for submitted papers, when and how to register for participation, and information about available accommodation. Originally, members of the IVR had to ask the organizing committee about these matters by mail or, more often, telephone. Today each organizing committee establishes its own website, linked to the official IVR website, that contains this information and often enables members to register for the congress and reserve accommodation on-line. Although this is a vast improvement in communication, it, together with the posting of Newsletters on the IVR website, does pose the problem of finding persons with the technical competence to create and update websites.

A central part of the problem of communication within the IVR is that of maintaining effective interchange between the International Association, in practice its Executive Committee, and its national sections. Originally this took place primarily by international mail and, if speed mattered, by telephone. The new technologies of e-mail and the world-wide web have transformed international communication for the better. However, any medium of communication is only as effective as those who employ it. Twice in the history of the IVR communication almost completely broke down because of the lack of an active and responsible Secretary General. And even the most conscientious Secretary General cannot keep in touch with national sections that do not have either a President or Secretary who sends and responds to communications. Here and elsewhere the administration of any international association depends upon finding and enlisting able administrators.

A third practical problem created by the internationalization of the IVR is the increasing complexity of its administration. According to the constitution of 1909, its three Presidents together governed all of its activities. This arrangement seems to have worked well, for it was retained in the two following constitutions. However, the constitution of 1959 introduced a new administrative body, an Executive Committee. It authorized the Executive Committee to appoint a Secretary General to manage the affairs of the IVR. Because the Executive Committee meets only once a year, in practice it is the President and Secretary General who carry most of the administrative burden. From 1975-1979 when I was Secretary General, I sent and received almost all the correspondence, wrote official documents such as reports on the meetings of the Executive Committee and General Assembly, requested and received the dues, paid the bills, and wrote, printed and mailed the newsletters. Subsequent experience demonstrated that the IVR could not rely upon a single Secretary General to perform all of these administrative functions. Therefore, Aulis Aarnio created an administrative team consisting of a Secretary General, a Treasurer and the Editor of the Newsletter. This is a much more satisfactory arrangement provided that the President can find persons willing and able to serve efficiently in each of these capacities.

Probably the most arduous task in the administration of the IVR is organizing its congresses. In the early days when these were relatively small, this was easily managed. The organizer or organizers needed only to select a few main speakers and find places to carry out the academic program together with a few receptions. These were typically readily available at some host university, and accommodation for the participants was near at hand. Participants could register upon arrival and local logistics were minimal. But after the 1975 Saint Louis World Congress introduced a new paradigm for congresses, the demands upon the organizing committee, especially its chairperson, became much more pressing. An auditorium to hold plenary sessions attended by hundreds of people and a considerable number of smaller rooms for discussions of working group and workshop papers were usually to be had only in some large hotel or conference center. Also the organizers had to negotiate special rates with hotels in several price ranges to accommodate the various needs of the participants. Arrangements had to be made to receive and circulate hundreds of papers. And, of course, there was the invitation of and providing for the needs of the main speakers. Today it is necessary to set up and frequently update a website to convey information about the forthcoming congress to prospective participants and to enable them to register in advance, know when and how to submit their papers, and to enable them to reserve accommodation. All of this must be done in co-ordination with the IVR Executive Committee.

A fourth and eminently practical problem arising from the internationalization of the IVR is the rapidly increasing costs of carrying out its activities. When the IVR was a small association with the majority of its members in or near Germany, its expenses were modest. Normally the university or universities with which its president or presidents were affiliated could be expected to provide postal and telephone service and occasional secretarial assistance for correspondence. The first few congresses of the IVR had only a few main speakers and relatively few participants. Facilities for the academic program and any receptions were available on the campus of the host institution and provided at little or no expense. And since most of the participants were European, they could afford to pay their own train or other travel fares.

After the 1975 Saint Louis World Congress, the costs imposed upon the organizing committees have grown exponentially. Much larger and more complex facilities, usually with sound systems and other technical equipment, are required for plenary sessions with an audience of several hundred and a large number of conference rooms for working groups and, more recently, workshops. The organizing committee is expected to pay the travel expenses, often from distant lands, and provide accommodation for the main speakers and to provide for the accommodation of the members of the Executive Committee as well. It must set up and frequently update a congress web-site. It must deal with a mass of correspondence through its web-site, by e-mail and even snail-mail. And, of course, the social program including receptions for hundreds of participants and accompanying persons are not inexpensive. Over the years the task of raising the funds necessary to host an IVR world congress has become formidable indeed.

The IVR Executive Committee meets even in years when there is no world congress. Since 1978, it has been customary for one of the national sections to host these business meetings in conjunction with an associated academic conference. Although the expenses incurred in this way are much less than those of organizing a world congress, they are not negligible. Accommodation and most of the meals for any invited speakers and the members of the Executive Committee must be provided. And facilities for the meetings of the EC and for the sessions of the conference may be costly. Fortunately, the national section hosting these interim meetings of the Executive Committee are not expected to pay the travel expenses of the participants.

However, the expenses of travel from one's home university to events sponsored by the IVR have increased dramatically with the internationalization of the International Association. When the majority of the members of the IVR were German and most of the others European, its members were able to travel very short distances at very little cost to participate in its activities. But as its membership grew in countries far from Europe, it became much more costly for non-European members to travel to world congresses or other conferences held on the Continent. Conversely, after world congresses became common on other continents, it was much more expensive for European members to take part in them. Many members of the IVR, especially its younger members, now find they cannot afford to participate in its activities.

Is internationalization worth so much expense and effort? There have long been those who have challenged the wisdom of pursuing this goal. In 1976, the German national section urged the Executive Committee to cancel the Australian World Congress, but it refused. In 1977, the Swiss organizing committee presented its plans for the 1979 World Congress. It rejected the Saint Louis model and insisted on holding a much smaller congress with only a few plenary lectures. At this point, the Executive Committee withdrew authorization from the original Swiss committee and Professor Trappe organized the 1979 Basel World Congress with many more invited lectures and a large number of working groups. Although the Executive Committee thus persisted in the further internationalization of the IVR, not all of its members thought this wise. Professors Cotta and Raphael, in particular, argued that this was a mistake.

What reasons might one have for resisting the ideal of a truly global IVR? One is that this is incompatible with maintaining the quality of its intellectual intercourse and its publications. Some argued that membership in the IVR and participation in its congresses ought to be limited to those with demonstrated competence in philosophy of law or social philosophy. Even more insisted that only genuinely important papers ought to be published under its auspices. Although I favored open membership in the IVR and the policy that any paper submitted by a member for discussion in a working group would be accepted, I did side with those who wished to publish only the best papers. To my mind the flood of mediocre publications was distracting serious thinkers from the relatively few original and important books and journal articles. However, Professor Klenner disagreed with me. He argued that there are no truly objective standards of philosophical quality so that in practice selective publication would reflect the philosophical prejudices of the most influential members of the Executive Committee and thus be incompatible with the constitutional principle that in the IVR no philosophical orientation is excluded. As usual, Hermann was wiser than I. I find that I learn very little when I read the publications by or discuss philosophical issues with those whose opinions are similar to mine. It is those with whom I disagree, often radically, that force me to rethink my theses and reexamine my arguments and who suggest new and more illuminating approaches to the philosophical problems with which I am struggling. The principle that no philosophical orientation is excluded from the IVR proved very valuable during the cold war when members from both sides of the iron curtain could meet in world congresses and discuss their very different philosophies of law and social philosophies frankly and in a spirit of collegiality.

No doubt openness to diverse philosophical and cultural perspectives is of value, but there are limits to our mutual understanding. A second reason for resisting the ideal of a global IVR is the diminishing philosophical utility of expanding one's intellectual horizons. Some members of the Executive Committee argued that any full understanding of a lecture or worthwhile discussion with a colleague required a familiarity with his or her presuppositions and a sympathy with the approach taken that are lacking when the participants have radically different philosophical orientations, especially when these reflect deep cultural differences. Therefore, they favored restricting the IVR to a Euro-centric association with a few colonies in countries such as the United States or Argentina with close cultural ties to Europe.

I feel the force of this objection to the internationalization of the IVR also. I often find myself frustrated when I attempt to discuss theoretical problems with members whose perspectives are radically different from any of those with which I am familiar. It is not that we disagree and are unable to reach agreement. It is that I cannot understand their reasoning or why they would accept assumptions that seem wildly implausible to me. In fact, I sometimes wonder if we are both talking about the same subject. Nevertheless, I persist in attempting to comprehend diverse perspectives because I find success, even when partial, well worth the effort.

But does this really imply that the internationalization of the IVR is valuable to us as philosophers of law and social philosophers? If so, how? For one thing, our goal is to develop and defend theories of law and other social institutions. This requires generalization. To explain any social phenomenon, one must subsume it under some general principle; and to evaluate any law, legal system or other institution, one must apply general norms. However, generalization on the basis of a limited sample of one's subject matter is unreliable at best and often highly misleading. This is not to say that one ought to try to obtain an unlimited number of instances. Much more important is the diversity of examples, for increasing the number of very similar instances seldom disconfirms a mistaken generalization. And finding a wide variety of kinds of social institutions, legal or non-legal, is best achieved by learning about societies with very different cultures and that have developed institutions appropriate to very different conditions on the six inhabited continents. Unless one has the time and energy to devote many years to field work throughout the world, the easiest way to accomplish this is to learn from colleagues from many countries. The internationalization of the IVR enables each of us to meet with and learn from those who are willing and able to provide information about diverse legal and social institutions with which we are unfamiliar.

Secondly, philosophy is, or at least ought to be, a critical enterprise. Although we need not emulate Socrates by drinking hemlock, we are committing philosophical suicide if we do not question the beliefs commonly accepted in our societies. And as philosophers of law and social philosophers, we should challenge the presuppositions of the relevant sciences, such as sociology, anthropology, political science and legal theory. Above all, we need to question our own assumptions and methodologies. This is especially difficult for our presuppositions tend to be shared by most of our colleagues. Only by frank and incisive discussion with philosophers with radically different systems of beliefs and ways of thinking, typically from distant lands, will we be forced to rethink our own views. The world congresses of the IVR enable us to do this by its internationalization and its principle that no philosophical orientation is excluded.

A third reason we need the internationalization of the IVR is that our subject matter is itself increasingly internationalized. We are engaged in applied philosophy, philosophy of legal and other social institutions. Centuries ago the legal systems, economies, family structures and other social institutions of each nation were largely independent of those in other countries, but that is a bygone era. Today international treaties greatly modify our national legal systems, our economies depend upon importing and exporting goods and services, and many persons not only travel to distant lands but reside in more than one country. International corporations deeply influence our lives as do other international organizations such as NATO or the World Bank. The United Nations and its many agencies today have a global reach. It is one thing to read about these international institutions, but much more is required to understand their influences globally and in various nation states and to evaluate them. If we are to develop philosophies of law and social philosophies that realistically reflect our subject matter, we need colleagues from around the world to inform us of how these institutions interpenetrate our diverse social systems and to correct the biases of the media in our own countries. If my reasoning is valid, we ought to welcome and move forward with the internationalization of the IVR.

But before we congratulate ourselves for being members of an international, almost a global, association, let us ask an awkward question. Why should anyone pay us for doing what we love? What value, if any, do our disciplines, philosophy of law and social philosophy, have for our respective societies and for our world? Far too often none at all, for typically we choose to think and write about esoteric subjects with no discernible practical relevance and of interest only to a few colleagues in our narrow specializations. Nevertheless our disciplines do have the potential to improve the lives of our fellow citizens and even all humanity. As philosophers seeking to generalize about diverse legal systems and social institutions, we should be able to suggest alternative legal or social institutions that might be more beneficial than the existing ones. As critical thinkers who question the generally accepted norms and propose new normative legal and social theories, we are in a position to evaluate social institutions, both national and international, more adequately than politicians answerable to their constituents.

I do not believe, as Plato did, that philosophers are necessarily best qualified to rule. But I am suggesting that as philosophers of law and social philosophers, we have a responsibility to address the practical problems that the rulers of our nation states and the officials in the international organizations that influence our lives must solve. In our time these include the collapse of our interdependent financial institutions with resulting massive unemployment, international terrorism and the military intervention it engenders, the protection of international human rights and preventing the destruction of our global environment. To address such issues in our increasingly global world, we need the assistance of colleagues in a fully international IVR. So let us be grateful that the internationalization of the IVR could enable us to fulfill its constitutional purpose, the cultivation and promotion of legal and social philosophy on a national and international level, in a way that is of value to others and not merely profitable to ourselves.

Authors

Prof. Dr. Dr. h.c. mult. Robert Alexy
Christian-Albrechts-Universität zu Kiel / Germany

Prof. Dr. Samantha Besson
University of Fribourg / Switzerland

Prof. Dr. Olivier Jouanjan
University of Strasbourg / France

Prof. Dr. Hiroshi Kamemoto
Kyoto University, Kyoto / Japan

Dr. Adrian Künzler LL.M.
Yale Law School / USA

Prof. Dr. Marijan Pavčnik
University of Ljubljana / Slovenia

Prof. Dr. Dr. h.c. mult. Stanley L. Paulson
ehedem DFG-Mercator Professor und
seitdem Gastprofessor an der Christian-Albrechts-Universität zu Kiel / Germany

Prof. Dr. Tercio Sampaio Ferraz Junior
University of São Paulo / Brasil

Prof. Dr. Seana Valentine Shiffrin
Professor of Philosophy and Pete Kameron Professor of Law and Social Justice
UCLA / USA

Prof. Dr. Carl Wellman
Washington University in St. Louis / USA

ARCHIV FÜR RECHTS- UND SOZIALPHILOSOPHIE – BEIHEFTE

Herausgeben von der Internationalen Vereinigung für Rechts- und Sozialphilosophie (IVR).
Die Bände 1–4 sind im Luchterhand-Fachverlag erschienen.

Franz Steiner Verlag   ISSN 0341–079X

103. Carsten Bäcker / Stefan Baufeld (Hg.)
Objektivität und Flexibilität
im Recht
Tagungen des Jungen Forums Rechtsphilosophie in der Internationalen Vereinigung für Rechts- und Sozialphilosophie im
September 2004 in Kiel und im April 2005
in Hagen
2005. 213 S., kt.
ISBN 978-3-515-08743-8

104. Robert Alexy (Hg.)
Juristische Grundlagenforschung
Tagung der Deutschen Sektion der Inter-
nationalen Vereinigung für Rechts- und
Sozialphilosophie vom 23.–25. September
2004 in Kiel
2005. 251 S., kt.
ISBN 978-3-515-08640-0

105. Philippe Mastronardi / Denis Taubert (Hg.)
Staats- und Verfassungstheorie
im Spannungsfeld der Disziplinen
Tagung der Schweizerischen Vereinigung
für Rechts- und Sozialphilosophie vom
12.–13. November 2004 an der Universität
St. Gallen
2006. 255 S., kt.
ISBN 978-3-515-08851-0

106. José Juan Moreso (Hg.)
Legal Theory / Teoría del derecho
Legal Positivism and Conceptual Analysis /
Positivismo juridico y análisis conceptual.
Proceedings of the 22nd World Congress
of the International Association for
Philosophy of Law and Social Philosophy
in Granada, 2005
Volume 1
2007. 263 S., kt.
ISBN 978-3-515-08910-4

107. José Rubio Carrecedo (Hg.)
Political Philosophy /
Filosofía política
New Proposals for New Questions / Nuevas
propuestas para nuevas cuestiones. Proceedings of the 22nd World Congress of the
International Association for Philosophy
of Law and Social Philosophy in Granada,
2005

Volume 2
2007. 239 S., kt.
ISBN 978-3-515-08911-1

108. Andrés Ollero (Hg.)
Human Rights and Ethics /
Derechos humanos y Ética
Proceedings of the 22nd World Congress
of the International Association for
Philosophy of Law and Social Philosophy
in Granada, 2005
Volume 3
2007. 323 S., kt.
ISBN 978-3-515-08912-8

109. Nicolás López Calera (Hg.)
Globalization, Law and Economy /
Globalización, Derecho y Economía
Proceedings of the 22nd World Congress
of the International Association for
Philosophy of Law and Social Philosophy
in Granada, 2005
Volume 4
2007. 321 S., kt
ISBN 978-3-515-08913-5

110. Josep Aguiló-Regla (Hg.)
Logic, Argumentation and
Interpretation / Lógica,
Argumentación e Interpretación
Proceedings of the 22nd World Congress
of the International Association for
Philosophy of Law and Social Philosophy
in Granada, 2005
Volume 5
2007. 206 S., kt.
ISBN 978-3-515-08914-2

111. Marcel Senn / Dániel Puskás (Hg.)
Gehirnforschung und
rechtliche Verantwortung
Fachtagung der Scheizerischen Vereinigung
für Rechts- und Sozialphilosophie vom
19.–20. Mai 2006 an der Universität Bern
2006. 171 S., kt.
ISBN 978-3-515-08963-0

112. Annette Brockmöller (Hg.)
Hundert Jahre Archiv für Rechts-
und Sozialphilosophie (1907–2007)
Auswahl 14 bedeutender Aufsätze
von Kelsen, Radbruch, Luhmann u. a.

2007. 330 S., kt.
ISBN 978-3-515-09100-8

113. Horst Dreier / Eric Hilgendorf (Hg.)
Kulturelle Identität als Grund und Grenze des Rechts
Akten der Tagung der Internationalen Vereinigung für Rechts- und Sozialphilosophie vom 28.–30. September 2006 in Würzburg
2008. 374 S., geb.
ISBN 978-3-515-09101-5

114. Jochen Bung / Brian Valerius / Sascha Ziemann (Hg.)
Normativität und Rechtskritik
Tagungen des Jungen Forums Rechtsphilosophie in der Internationalen Vereinigung für Rechts- und Sozialphilosophie im September 2006 in Würzburg und im März 2007 in Frankfurt am Main
2007. 269 S., kt.
ISBN 978-3-515-09130-5

115. Marcel Senn / Dániel Puskás (Hg.)
Rechtswissenschaft als Kulturwissenschaft?
Kongress der Schweizerischen Vereinigung für Rechts- und Sozialphilosophie vom 15.–16. Juni 2007 an der Universität Zürich
2007. 220 S., kt.
ISBN 978-3-515-09149-7

116. Annette Brockmöller / Eric Hilgendorf (Hg.)
Rechtsphilosophie im 20. Jahrhundert
100 Jahre Archiv für Rechts- und Sozialphilosophie
2009. 207 S., kt.
ISBN 978-3-515-09285-2

117. Marcel Senn / Barbara Fritschi (Hg.)
Rechtswissenschaft und Hermeneutik
Kongress der Schweizerischen Vereinigung für Rechts- und Sozialphilosophie vom 16.–17. Mai 2008 an der Universität Zürich
2009. 258 S., kt.
ISBN 978-3-515-09155-8

118. Bart C. Labuschagne / Ari M. Solon (Hg.)
Religion and State
From separation to cooperation?
Proceedings of the Special Workshop "Legal-philosophical reflections for a de-secularized world" held at the 23rd World Congress of the International Association for Philosophy of Law and Social Philosophy in Kraków, 2007
2009. 209 S., kt.
ISBN 978-3-515-09368-2

119. Martin Borowski (Hg.)
On the Nature of Legal Principles
Proceedings of the Special Workshop "The Principles Theory" held at the 23rd World Congress of the International Association for Philosophy of Law and Social Philosophy in Kraków, 2007
2010. 182 S., kt.
ISBN 978-3-515-09608-9

120. Friedrich Toepel (Hg.)
Free Will in Criminal Law and Procedure
Proceedings of the 23rd and 24th World Congress of the International Association for Philosophy of Law and Social Philosophy in Kraków, 2007, and in Beijing, 2009
2010. 122 S., kt.
ISBN 978-3-515-09320-0

121. Marcel Senn / Bénédict Winiger / Barbara Fritschi / Philippe Avramov (Hg.)
Recht und Globalisierung / Droit et Mondialisation
Kongress der Schweizerischen Vereinigung für Rechts- und Sozialphilosophie, 15.–16. Mai 2009, Universität Genf / Congrès de l'Association Suisse de Philosophie du Droit et de Philosophie Sociale, 15–16 mai 2009, Université de Genève
2010. 196 S., kt.
ISBN 978-3-515-09673-7

122. Imer B. Flores / Uygur Gülriz (Hg.)
Alternative Methods in the Education of Philosophy of Law and the Importance of Legal Philosophy in the Legal Education
Proceedings of the 23rd World Congress of the International Associaction for Philosophy of Law and Social Philosophy "Law and Legal Cultures in the 21st Century: Diversity and Unity" in Kraków, 2007
2010. 114 S., kt.
ISBN 978-3-515-09695-9

123. Sascha Ziemann
Archiv für Rechts- und Sozialphilosophie: Bibliographie und Dokumentation (1907–2009)
2010. 434 S., kt.
ISBN 978-3-515-09719-2

124. Jan-Reinard Sieckmann (Hg.)
Legal Reasoning: The Methods of Balancing
Proceedings of the Special Workshop "Legal Reasoning: The Methods of Balancing" held at the 24th World Congress of the International Association for

Philosophy of Law and Social Philosophy (IVR), Beijing, 2009
2010. 205 S., kt.
ISBN 978-3-515-09723-9

125. Edward Schramm / Wibke Frey / Lorenz Kähler / Sabine Müller-Mall / Friederike Wapler (Hg.)
Konflikte im Recht – Recht der Konflikte
Tagungen des Jungen Forums Rechtsphilosophie in der Internationalen Vereinigung für Rechts- und Sozialphilosophie in Tübingen und Göttingen
2010. 308 S., kt.
ISBN 978-3-515-09729-1

126. Kristian Kühl (Hg.)
Zur Kompetenz der Rechtsphilosophie in Rechtsfragen
Tagung der Deutschen Sektion der Internationalen Vereinigung für Rechts- und Sozialphilosophie vom 24.–26. September 2008 in Tübingen
2011. 140 S., kt.
ISBN 978-3-515-09816-8

127. Stephan Kirste / Anne van Aaken / Michael Anderheiden / Pasquale Policastro (Hg.)
Interdisciplinary Research in Jurisprudence and Constitutionalism
2012. 267 S. mit 2 Abb. und 2 Tab., kt.
ISBN 978-3-515-09941-7

128. Stephan Ast / Julia Hänni / Klaus Mathis / Benno Zabel (Hg.)
Gleichheit und Universalität
Tagungen des Jungen Forums Rechtsphilosophie (JFR) in der Internationalen Vereinigung für Rechts- und Sozialphilosophie (IVR) im September 2010 in Halle (Saale) und im Februar 2011 in Luzern
2012. 315 S., kt.
ISBN 978-3-515-10067-0

129. Bénédict Winiger / Matthias Mahlmann / Philippe Avramov / Peter Gailhofer (Hg.)
Recht und Verantwortung / Droit et responsabilité
Kongress der Schweizerischen Vereinigung für Rechts- und Sozialphilosophie, 11.–12. Juni 2010, Universität Zürich / Congrès de l'Association Suisse de Philosophie du Droit et de Philosophie Sociale, 11–12 juin 2010, Université de Zurich
2012. 206 S. mit 6 Abb., kt.
ISBN 978-3-515-10066-3

130. Thomas Bustamante / Oche Onazi (Hg.)
Global Harmony and the Rule of Law
Proceedings of the 24th World Congress of the International Association for Philosophy of Law and Social Philosophy, Beijing, 2009. Vol. 1
2012. 133 S., kt.
ISBN 978-3-515-10081-6

131. Thomas Bustamante / Oche Onazi (Hg.)
Human Rights, Language and Law
Proceedings of the 24th World Congress of the International Association for Philosophy of Law and Social Philosophy, Beijing, 2009. Vol. 2
2012. 192 S., kt.
ISBN 978-3-515-10082-3

132. Yasutomo Morigiwa / Hirohide Takikawa (Hg.)
Judicial Minimalism – For and Against
Proceedings of the 9th Kobe Lectures. Tokyo, Nagoya, and Kyoto, June 2008
2012. 99 S., kt.
ISBN 978-3-515-10136-3

133. Thomas Bustamante / Carlos Bernal Pulido (Hg.)
On the Philosophy of Precedent
Proceedings of the 24th World Congress of the International Association for Philosophy of Law and Social Philosophy, Beijing, 2009
Volume 3
2012. 144 S., kt.
ISBN 978-3-515-10150-9

134. Matthias Kaufmann / Joachim Renzikowski (Hg.)
Zurechnung und Verantwortung
Tagung der Deutschen Sektion der Internationalen Vereinigung für Rechts- und Sozialphilosophie vom 22.–24. September 2010 in Halle (Saale)
2012. 184 S., kt.
ISBN 978-3-515-10180-6

135. Carsten Bäcker / Sascha Ziemann (Hg.)
Junge Rechtsphilosophie
2012. 214 S., kt.
ISBN 978-3-515-10268-1

136. Ulfrid Neumann / Klaus Günther / Lorenz Schulz (Hg.)
Law, Science, Technology
Plenary lectures presented at the 25th World Congress of the International Association for Philosophy of Law and Social Philosophy, Frankfurt am Main, 2011
2012. 173 S., kt.
ISBN 978-3-515-10328-2